THE ESSENTIALS OF
PERFORMANCE ANALYSIS

What is performance analysis and how does its use benefit sports performance?

How can you use performance analysis in your sport?

The Essentials of Performance Analysis answers your questions, providing a complete guide to the foundational elements of match and performance analysis for new students and beginners.

As well as a basic introduction to the sport science and theory that underlies performance analysis, the book contains many practical examples to show performance analysis in its applied context. It includes discussion of:

- approaches to analysing sport performance
- the use of feedback technologies
- the use of video and biomechanical analysis
- interpreting data
- coaching with notational analysis

The Essentials of Performance Analysis is a straightforward, concise and authoritative guide for students of sport science and sports coaching, as well as for coaches and athletes looking to develop their insight into sports performance analysis.

Mike Hughes is Professor and Head of the Centre for Performance Analysis and Course Director of the Masters in Performance Analysis at the University of Wales Institute, Cardiff.

Ian M. Franks is Professor and Director of the Motor Control and Learning Laboratory, University of British Columbia, Vancouver.

THE ESSENTIALS OF PERFORMANCE ANALYSIS

An introduction

EDITED BY MIKE HUGHES AND IAN M. FRANKS

Routledge
Taylor & Francis Group

LONDON AND NEW YORK

First published 2008
by Routledge
2 Park Square, Milton Park, Abingdon, Oxon OX14 4RN

Simultaneously published in the USA and Canada
by Routledge
270 Madison Ave, New York, NY 10016

Routledge is an imprint of the Taylor & Francis Group, an informa business

© 2008 selection and editorial matter Mike Hughes and Ian M. Franks; individual chapters, the contributors

Typeset in Zapf Humanist and Eras by
RefineCatch Limited, Bungay, Suffolk
Printed and bound in Great Britain
by Antony Rowe Ltd, Chippenham, Wiltshire

British Library Cataloguing in Publication Data
A catalogue record for this book is available from the British Library

Library of Congress Cataloging-in-Publication Data
Hughes, Mike (Michael G.)
The essentials of performance analysis: an introduction/Mike Hughes and Ian M. Franks.
p.c.
Includes biographical references
 1. Sports sciences. 2. Physical education and training. 3. Performance. I. Franks, Ian M. II. Title.
GV558.H84 2007–07–17 613.7'1—dc22
2007024801

ISBN10: 0–415–42379–1 (hbk)
ISBN10: 0–415–42380–5 (pbk)
ISBN10: 0–203–93806–2 (ebk)

ISBN13: 978–0–415–42379–3 (hbk)
ISBN13: 978–0–415–42380–9 (pbk)
ISBN13: 978–0–203–93806–5 (ebk)

CONTENTS

Notes on contributors   xiii
Preface   xxi
Introduction   xxii
Acknowledgements   xxxii

1 THE NEED FOR FEEDBACK   1

Dana Maslovat and Ian M. Franks

1.1   Introduction: feedback   1
1.2   The coaching process and its problems   3
1.3   The need for objective information   4

2 WHAT IS PERFORMANCE ANALYSIS?   8

Mike Hughes and Roger Bartlett

2.1   Introduction   8
2.2   Notational analysis   9
       2.2.1   Introduction   9
       2.2.2   The applications of notation   11
                2.2.2.1   Tactical evaluation   11
                2.2.2.2   Technical evaluation   12
                2.2.2.3   Movement analysis   13
                2.2.2.4   Development of a database and modelling   14
                2.2.2.5   Educational applications   15
2.3   Biomechanics – what is the biomechanical view of
       performance analysis?   15

Nicola J. Hodges and Ian M. Franks

3.1	Introduction	21
3.2	Augmented feedback	23
	3.2.1 Positive effects	23
	3.2.2 Negative effects	24
	3.2.3 Additional factors to consider when providing feedback	27
3.3	Demonstrations and instructions	28
	3.3.1 Positive effects	28
	3.3.1.1 Providing a reference-of-correctness	28
	3.3.1.2 Effective demonstrations	29
	3.3.1.3 Conveying a strategy	30
	3.3.1.4 Comparing pre-practice methods	30
	3.3.2 Negative effects	31
	3.3.2.1 Movement strategies	31
	3.3.2.2 Searching for the critical information	32
	3.3.2.3 Attentional focus	34
	3.3.2.4 Implicit learning/re-investment	35
	3.3.3 Overview of instructions and demonstrations	37
3.4	Conclusions	37

Dario G. Liebermann and Ian M. Franks

4.1	Introduction	40
4.2	Extrinsic and intrinsic feedback in sports	41
4.3	Visual feedback, video and motor learning	42
4.4	Qualitative feedback and quantification of performance using video-based technologies	44
4.5	Quantitative feedback derived from complex simulations	46
4.6	Watching versus performing movements in three-dimensions: virtual and real environments	47
4.7	Video technology and temporal feedback	48
4.8	Immediacy as a pre-requisite for the effective use of feedback during skill acquisition	49

5 AN OVERVIEW OF THE DEVELOPMENT OF NOTATIONAL ANALYSIS — 51

Mike Hughes

5.1	Introduction	51
5.2	The development of sport-specific notation systems (hand notation)	53
5.3	Introduction to computerized notational analysis	58
5.4	Some research using computer systems	60
5.5	Modelling	65
	5.5.1 Empirical models	66
	5.5.2 Dynamic systems	67
	5.5.2.1 Critical incident technique	68
	5.5.3 Statistical techniques	71
	5.5.4 Artificial Intelligence	74
5.6	Current areas of research and support	74
5.7	Research into the methodology and theory of notational analysis	79
5.8	The future of notational analysis	81

6 SPORTS ANALYSIS — 85

Mike Hughes

6.1	Introduction	85
6.2	Creating flowcharts	86
6.3	Levels of analysis – the team, subsidiary units and individuals	92

7 HOW DO WE DESIGN SIMPLE SYSTEMS? HOW TO DEVELOP A NOTATION SYSTEM — 98

Mike Hughes

7.1	Introduction	98
7.2	Data collection systems	98
	7.2.1 Scatter diagrams	98
	7.2.2 Frequency tables	101
	7.2.3 Sequential data systems	103
7.3	Data collection systems in general	108

Mike Hughes

8.1	Introduction	111
8.2	Individual sports	111
	8.2.1 A notation system for tennis	111
	8.2.1.1 Description of point	113
	8.2.1.2 Results	116
	8.2.1.3 Summary of results	117
	8.2.1.4 Discussion and conclusions	117
	8.2.2 A notation system for boxing	117
	8.2.2.1 Collated data and results	121
	8.2.2.2 Conclusions	123
8.3	Team sports	124
	8.3.1 A notation system for basketball	124
	8.3.1.1 Conclusion and discussion	126
	8.3.2 A notation system for soccer	127
	8.3.2.1 Method	127
	8.3.2.2 Results	128
	8.3.2.3 Analysis	128
	8.3.2.4 Discussion	132
	8.3.2.5 Adjustments to the system	133
	8.3.3 A notation system for netball	134
	8.3.3.1 Method	135
	8.3.3.2 Notation symbols	135
	8.3.3.3 The record sheet	137
	8.3.3.4 Recording a sequence	137
	8.3.3.5 Results	137
	8.3.4 A motion analysis of work-rate in different positional roles in field hockey	140
	8.3.4.1 Aim	140
	8.3.4.2 Hypothesis	140
	8.3.4.3 Devising the method	140
	8.3.4.4 Pilot study	141
	8.3.4.5 Finalized method	141
	8.3.4.6 Limitations	143
	8.3.4.7 Operational definitions	143
	8.3.4.8 Reliability	143

8.3.4.9	*Results*	145
8.3.4.10	*Application*	149
8.3.4.11	*Conclusion*	149
8.3.4.12	*Recommendations for further research*	149

9 ANALYSIS OF NOTATION DATA: RELIABILITY 150

Mike Hughes

9.1	Introduction	150
9.2	The nature of the data; the depth of analysis	151
9.2.1	Sample data	151
9.2.2	The sequential nature of data	152
9.3	Consistency of percentage difference calculations	153
9.4	Processing data	154
9.5	Visual interpretation of the data (a modified Bland and Altman plot)	156
9.5.1	Sample data	157

10 QUALITATIVE BIOMECHANICAL ANALYSIS OF TECHNIQUE 162

Adrian Lees

10.1	Introduction	162
10.2	The phase analysis model and movement principles	164
10.2.1	The phase analysis model	164
10.2.2	Movement principles	166
10.2.2.1	*Speed (S) principles*	167
10.2.2.2	*Force (F) principles*	168
10.2.2.3	*Coordination (C) principles*	170
10.2.2.4	*Specific performance (P) principles*	172
10.3	An application of the phase analysis model and movement principles	172
10.4	The performance outcome model	176
10.5	An application of the Hay and Reid performance outcome model	177

11 TIME–MOTION ANALYSIS 180

Peter G. O'Donoghue

11.1   Introduction   180
11.2   Time–motion analysis of running events   182
11.3   Time–motion analysis of racket sports   185
11.4   Team games   191
11.5   The Bloomfield movement classification   201

12 PROBABILITY ANALYSIS OF NOTATED EVENTS IN SPORT CONTESTS: SKILL AND CHANCE 206

Tim McGarry

12.1   Introduction   206
       12.1.1   Sports contests   206
       12.1.2   Skill and chance   207
       12.1.3   Probability: stationarity and independence 207
       12.1.4   Taking a random walk in a field of probabilities 208
12.2   Taking a random walk in sports contests: investigation of
       scoring structure   210
12.3   Taking a random walk in sports contests: investigation of
       behaviours (shots) and outcomes in squash contests 213
       12.3.1   Stochastic processes, shot selections and outcomes in
                squash contests   213
       12.3.2   Computer simulation   220
       12.3.3   Identification of optimal decision-making strategies 220
       12.3.4   Interactions between the winner–error profiles 221
       12.3.5   Interactions between shot–response profiles 223

13 RULE CHANGES IN SPORT AND THE ROLE OF NOTATION 226

Jason Williams

13.1   Introduction   226
13.2   Safety   228
13.3   Natural development and progression   231
13.4   Entertainment, commercialization and the media   234

13.5   The role of notational analysis in tracking the effect of
rules changes   238
13.6   Conclusion   241

14 PERFORMANCE ANALYSIS IN THE MEDIA   243

Nic James

14.1   Introduction   243
14.2   Classifying games   244
14.3   Invasion games   245
    14.3.1   Soccer   245
    14.3.2   Rugby union   249
    14.3.3   Basketball   250
14.4   Net and wall games   253
14.5   Striking and fielding games   256
    14.5.1   Golf   257
    14.5.2   Cricket   259

15 NOTATIONAL ANALYSIS OF COACHING BEHAVIOUR   264

Kenny More

15.1   Introduction: the coaching process   264
15.2   Notational analysis of coaching behaviour   265
    15.2.1   Effective coaching   265
    15.2.2   Teaching and coaching behaviour – a historical
          perspective   266
    15.2.3   Systematic observation   267
    15.2.4   Systematic observation instruments   267
15.3   Effective coaching behaviours   270
    15.3.1   Understanding the data   270
    15.3.2   Should comments be skill- or non-skill related?   271
    15.3.3   The focus of skill-related comments   272
    15.3.4   The timing of skill-related comments   273
    15.3.5   The delivery of skill-related comments   273
    15.3.6   The emphasis of skill-related comments   274
    15.3.7   The case for non-skill-related comments   274
15.4   Modification of coaching behaviour   274

Bibliography   277
Glossary of terms   300
Index   302

NOTES ON CONTRIBUTORS

Roger Bartlett is a Professor in the School of Physical Education, University of Otago, NZ.

Before moving to New Zealand in July, 2004, Roger was Professor of Sport Science at Manchester Metropolitan University until 1998; Professor of Sport and Exercise Science and Associate Dean of the School of Health at Staffordshire University; and, latterly, Professor of Sports Biomechanics and Director of the Centre for Sport and Exercise Science at Sheffield Hallam University since 1999. He has also been a Visiting Professor at the Universities of Salzburg and Innsbruck. He is an Honorary Fellow of the British Association of Sport and Exercise Sciences, of which he was Chairman from 1991 to 1994, and a member of the New Zealand Society of Sports Sciences. Roger is currently editor of *Sports Biomechanics* and a member of the editorial boards of the *International Journal of Sports Science and Coaching, International Journal of Performance Analysis in Sport* and *Journal of Neuro-engineering and Rehabilitation*; he was editor-in-chief of the *Journal of Sports Sciences* from 1996 to 2001. Until his move to New Zealand, he was the Chair of the Performance Analysis Steering Group of the British Olympic Association and a member of their Olympic Performance Planning Group; he was a World Class Advisor to Sport England and UK Sport and the Innovation and Technology advisor to the UK Sport Institute. He is author of *An Introduction to Sports Biomechanics* (1997), the second edition of which was published in August 2007, and *Sports Biomechanics: Reducing Injury and Improving Performance* (1999). He is co-editor of the *Encyclopaedia of International Sports Studies*, published in 2006, and the *Routledge Handbook of Biomechanics and Human Movement Science*, and *Biomechanical Evaluation of Movement in Sport and Exercise*, both scheduled for publication late in 2007. In 2005, he presented the Geoffrey Dyson Memorial

Lecture to the Beijing Congress of the ISBS, the highest honour bestowed by the Society.

Research interests

Roger's research interests include the biomechanics of javelin throwing, and the biomechanics of injury in cricket fast bowlers. His current research interests are centred around the coordination of, and variability in, sports movements, important themes that emerged from his empirical research and mathematical modelling in throwing skills. His current interests have led to strong inter-disciplinary programmes with motor skills specialists, exploring the functional significance of movement variability and the best ways to quantify coordination and variability, in activities as disparate as running and throwing. Research into the application of non-linear measures and artificial neural networks in studying coordination and variability are emerging thrusts of Roger's research at the University of Otago.

Ian M. Franks is at the School of Human Kinetics, University of British Columbia, Vancouver.

Ian attended: St Luke's College, Exeter where he achieved a Cert. Ed. in 1968; McGill University, a BEd Physical Education in 1975; University of Alberta, an MSc Motor Learning and Control in 1977; and University of Alberta, PhD Motor Learning and Control in 1980. He specializes in exercise science – human motor control, motor skill acquisition, analysis of coaching behaviour and sport analysis.

Research interests

Ian's research is concerned with the control and acquisition of human motor skills. Two programmes of research are presently underway to address specific questions in the area of motor learning and control. First, the program of research funded by NSERC is intended to investigate the processes responsible for the preparation, initiation and execution of voluntary actions. Second, the programme of research funded by SSHRC is intended to uncover the precise nature of the effects of instruction and demonstration on the acquisition of motor skills. His current projects are 'Effective instruction in coaching and teaching' (SSHRC) and 'The development of effective movement control strategies' (NSERC).

Nicola J. Hodges is at the School of Human Kinetics, University of British Columbia, Vancouver.

Nicola has a BSc (Hons) in Psychology, University of Hertfordshire (UK); an MSc in Human Biodynamics, McMaster University; and a PhD in Human Kinetics, University of British Columbia. She specializes in human motor control and learning across the life-span; motor expertise; learning and coordination; instructions, feedback and observational learning.

The motor skills laboratory

The motor skills research laboratory is a large space which permits the study of a variety of whole-body motor skills. It is equipped with a 3D 'Phoenix technologies' motion analysis system enabling the remote capture of movement within and among individuals. Although the laboratory is operational, multi-media developments are underway which will enable the manipulation of real-time and off-line visual feedback.

Research interests

Nicola's research is broadly divided into two: the NSERC funded research 'Perceptual and motor constraints in learning coordination skills' involves examination of the role of vision in the acquisition of complex motor skills. As well as looking at whole-body movement skills, a coordination paradigm has been adopted to examine the learning process and the types of constraints which limit and encourage acquisition and performance across individuals of varying levels of ability. In addition to the role of vision during action, an additional area of interest is in the nature of information extracted and used from demonstrations when children and adults observe with the intention to acquire and refine movement skills. The SSHRC funded research 'Effective instruction for learning and performance of motor skills' involves examination of the mechanisms underlying effective instruction, both the content of the information and the timing of provision. The expertise paradigm is also used to further understand the processes underlying successful performance, particularly with reference to deliberate practice theory and the development and maintenance of expert levels of motor performance, as well as the nature of the control strategies which define performance at high levels of motor skill.

Mike Hughes is at the Centre for Performance Analysis, University of Wales Institute, Cardiff.

Mike is Head of the Centre for Performance Analysis and Course Director –

Masters in Performance Analysis. Mike has an extensive sporting profile, which includes: Rugby: 1968–9 Captain and Coach – Manchester University; 1969, English UAU. Squash: 1979–86 County Player; 1980 SRA Part II Coach; 1981 County Coach; 1982–93 Professional Coach – New Brighton Squash Club 1; 1992 SRA Part III (Level IV – Professional Coach); 1993 National Squad Coach – England under-19 Boys Squad; 1995 – Director of the Academy of Squash, University of Wales Institute, Cardiff (UWIC); 1995–7 Welsh National Squad Coach – under-19 Girls Squad; 1996–2002 British Universities Coach – Won Team 2 Gold Medals, 3 Silver and 3 Bronze at different World Student Squash Championships.

Research interests
His research interests include: analysis of sports performance; the effect of fluid dynamics in sport; analysis of coaching behaviour; developing methodologies in notational analysis; and modelling of sports performance. He is a member of many professional institutions and societies, most notably: the British Olympic Association; Sport England; Computer in Sports Science Society and currently is President of the International Society of Performance Analysis. As a Level IV squash coach (Professional), Mike has coached with the English and Welsh national squads and is currently, Director of the UWIC Academy of Squash, and also coach to the GB University squash squad.

Nic James is at the Centre for Performance Analysis, University of Wales Institute, Cardiff.

Nic is a Senior Lecturer in Performance Analysis. He has a BA, PGCE (PE), PhD and Level IV Coach (Squash). Nic's sporting profile includes: Squash – County Player 1997–9; Welsh over-35 Player 1993–2001; Professional coach – Swansea Tennis and Squash Club 1995–2001; West Wales development squad coach 1995–8; Welsh U13 Boys coach 1998–2000; Welsh U19 Girls coach.

Research interests
Nic's research interests include: analysis of sports performance; statistical methods; visual perception and search strategies related to motor performance; expertise; decision-making, anticipation and situation awareness.

Adrian Lees is in the Research Institute for Sport and Exercise Sciences, Liverpool; John Moores University Henry Cotton Campus, Webster Street, Liverpool.

Adrian is Professor of Biomechanics and Deputy Director of the Research

Institute for Sport and Exercise Sciences at Liverpool John Moores University. He has taught and researched in sport and exercise biomechanics for over 20 years. He has contributed to many national and international conferences and has published widely on a variety of topics in Sport and Exercise Biomechanics. These topics include biomechanical analysis of sports skills, biomechanical techniques, biomechanics of injury and the biomechanics of muscle performance and training. He has been involved with providing biomechanical support for elite field event athletes for several years which has complemented his interest in the analysis of sports technique and strength development.

Research interests
Adrian's research interests include: biomechanical analysis of sports skills; biomechanical techniques; biomechanics of injury; biomechanics of muscle performance and training. He is currently working on: biomechanics of long jump performance; influence of the upper limbs in jumping; science and racket sports; and the influence of exercise on balance ability of the young and elderly.

Dario G. Liebermann is in the Department of Physical Therapy at Stanley Steyer School of Health Professions, Sackler Faculty of Medicine, University of Tel Aviv, Israel.

Dario was educated at Zinman College, Wingate Institute, where he achieved a Teaching Certificate (Adapted Physical Education) in 1983; Zinman College, BEd 1986; Simon Fraser University, MSc Motor Control, 1988; Weizmann Institute of Science, PhD Applied Mathematics (Computational Motor Control & Robotics), 1998. He is a Senior Lecturer working with the Sacker Faculty of Medicine, University of Tel Aviv. He assumed the faculty appointment in 2000, after completing two years of post-doctoral research in the Faculty of Medicine (Clinical Neurosciences) and in the Faculty of Kinesiology (Sport Technology Research) at the University of Calgary. He specializes in motor control, skill acquisition, clinical applications of motor control, robot-based technologies in motor rehabilitation, applied biomechanics.

Research interests
Dario headed the Movement Science Unit of the Ribstein Centre for Research and Sport Medicine Sciences at the Wingate Institute in Israel from 1989 until 1997. During that period, he focused on research and applications of sport biomechanics for the assessment and enhancement of performance of young-gifted and elite adult athletes at the National, International and Olympic levels in

diverse sports areas (e.g. judo, tennis, basketball, soccer and the jumps in athletics). Most recently (1999–today), he has carried out research on elite speed-skating performances (long- and short-track). Today he is particularly interested in the motion patterns of elite athletes as models of optimal control.

Dana Maslovat is at the School of Human Kinetics, University of British Columbia, Vancouver.

Dana has an MSc (HKIN), University of British Columbia (2000–2); Contextual Interference in Motor Skill Learning; BSc (Kinesiology), Simon Fraser University (1988–96); National Coaching Certification Program Course Conductor; Theory (Level 1, 2 & 3) and Basketball Technical (Level 1, 2 & 3). He specializes in exercise science – human motor control, motor skill acquisition and learning and coaching and sport analysis.

Research interests
Dana is currently pursuing his PhD degree under Dr Ian M. Franks at the University of British Columbia. His research involves motor skill acquisition and examines neurological changes that occur with learning as well as how programming changes with practice. Dana is employed as a faculty member in the Human Kinetics Department at Langara College in Vancouver and has been a sessional instructor at the University of British Columbia. He has played competitive basketball for many years, including a National Collegiate Championship as both a player (1997–8) and coach (1998–9) and is training to compete in his first Ironman Triathlon in Penticton, Canada.

Tim McGarry is in the Faculty of Kinesiology, University of New Brunswick, Fredericton.

Tim has a BSc Sports Science (Liverpool); MSc (Bradford); MPE (UBC); PhD (UBC) Motor control. Following his PhD, he assumed a research post at San Francisco State University for one year, before accepting a faculty appointment at the University of New Brunswick.

Research interests
Tim's research interests include: motor control: brain, behaviour, muscle, excitatory-inhibitory control on-line control, reaction time, kinematics, electro-myogram sports performance: system analysis, dynamics, pattern detection, decision-making, strategies and tactics.

Kenny More is with Elite Sports Analysis Ltd, Scotland.

Kenny has a BEd degree from the Scottish School of Physical Education, and an MA, completed at UBC in Vancouver with Ian Franks, conducting research into the analysis of coaching behaviour. He is a Director of Elite Sports Analysis, working as a Performance Analysis Consultant in a wide range of Olympic, Commonwealth, and Professional Sports. Kenny works extensively for the Scottish and United Kingdom Institutes of Sport, and has BASES 'High Performance Accreditation' as a Sport and Exercise Scientist.

Peter G. O'Donoghue is at the Centre for Performance Analysis, University of Wales Institute, Cardiff.

Peter obtained his BSc (Hons) Computer Science from the Ulster Polytechnic in 1984; MSc Information Technology in 1985 from University of Ulster and PhD in Computer Science from the University of Ulster in 1993. He was a lecturer of Computer Studies at Robert Gordon Institute of Technology in Aberdeen between 1985 and 1987, before returning to University of Ulster to work as a research officer from 1987 to 1990 and a lecturer of Computer Science from 1990 to 1999. After completing an MSc in Sport, Exercise and Leisure in 1999, Peter became a lecturer of Sport, Exercise and Leisure in 1999 before moving to University of Wales Institute, Cardiff in 2003, where he is now a Reader. Peter is the Chair of the International Society of Performance Analysis of Sport, a level 6 accredited performance analyst and is the performance analyst for the Welsh Netball Association. He has represented Northern Ireland in the marathon.

Research interests
Peter's interests include: time–motion analysis; effectiveness of motivational and instructional feedback; tennis performance; performance prediction.

Jason Williams is at the Centre for Performance Analysis, University of Wales Institute, Cardiff.

Jason joined UWIC in 1996 as a research assistant in the School of Sport after completing his degree at the University of Glamorgan and his PGCE at the University of Wales College Newport. He then spent some time managing the training department within NTL online before deciding to return to academia. Jason's initial role within UWIC was as a research assistant for the International Rugby Board and involved analysing rugby union matches using statistics. There he developed and maintained the software for the project, undertook numerous research projects and liaised and worked with a number of international and rugby club sides. He also taught a number of Sport Science and Computing courses. In 2003, he began lecturing full time in Computing. He specializes in teaching programming, databases and Human Computer Interaction.

Research interests

Jason's research interests are in notational analysis and the use of computers within sport.

PREFACE

The main function of this book is to act as an introductory manual for the sports scientist, coach, athlete or any interested reader. It is probably impossible to write sections of a book such as this, that would be readable and appealing to all this cross-section of intended clientele. Consequently, the various chapters in the book should be regarded as the different sections of a manual – many can be used as stand alone units without reference to others, some, on the other hand, have recommended prior reading. Notational analysis is a developing subject area, attractive to many sports scientists and coaches because of the applied nature of any material developed or data gathered. For anyone who wishes to understand their own sport, and thereby the structure and tactics of most other sports, there is no better way of understanding the real logic behind the structure of the game. The more coaches and players that come to understand that notation systems are going to improve the players' performance, their team's performance and especially the coaches' performance, then the better for sport in general.

Mike Hughes and Ian M. Franks

INTRODUCTION

WELCOME TO THE ESSENTIALS OF PERFORMANCE ANALYSIS

In this book we aim to deliver a 'Level One' textbook to fill the gap in the market. The theme of the book will be to provide a ready manual for beginners in performance analysis.

The book is written for the sports scientist, the coach, the athlete, or for anyone who wishes to apply analysis to any aspect of a performance operation, but in the simplest way. Although this book is applied directly to sport, performance analysis is a procedure that can be used in any discipline that requires assessment and analysis of performance, e.g. nursing, surgical operations, skilled manufacturing processes, unskilled manufacturing processes, haute cuisine, and so on.

To cater for the anticipated spectrum of readership, the book is written to balance the needs for a practical approach, with plenty of examples, and yet provide a sound basis for the scientific analysis of the subject area. In this way, it is hoped that both the practitioners of sport, the athletes, coaches and sports scientists will find the book useful.

ABOUT THIS BOOK

Like most texts, the information within this book is presented in an order that is considered logical and progressive. It is not totally necessary however to use the book in this way. It is anticipated that at times, certain sections will need to be used for immediate practical requirements. At the start of each chapter is advice on how to use that chapter and also which chapters, if any, which require reading and understanding beforehand. All the references for the book, including all those in each chapter, are collated in the Bibliography at the end of the book.

ORGANIZATION OF THIS BOOK

Chapter 1: The need for feedback
Dana Maslovat and Ian M. Franks

Historically, coaching intervention has been based upon subjective observations of athletes. However, several studies have shown that such observations are not only unreliable but also inaccurate. Although the benefits of feedback and KR are well accepted, the problems of highlighting, memory and observational difficulties result in the accuracy of coaching feedback being very limited. Video (and now DVD) analysis has been shown to benefit advanced athletes but care must be taken when providing this form of feedback to any other level of athlete. To overcome these problems, analysis systems have been devised. In developing these systems, it was necessary to define and identify the critical elements of performance and then devise an efficient data entry method, such that in certain situations a trained observer could record these events in real time. When the demands of the complexity of the systems are such that real-time notation was not possible, then post-event analysis has been completed using the slow motion and replay facilities afforded by video (and DVD). The benefits of using computers to record human athletic behaviour in this way can be summarized in terms of speed and efficiency.

Chapter 2: What is performance analysis?
Mike Hughes and Roger Bartlett

Based on the essays of Mike Hughes and Roger Bartlett, written for the UKSI website, on 'What is Performance Analysis', the aim of this chapter is to provide a full and complete understanding of the breadth of performance analysis and its possible applications. It summarizes the similarities of approach of biomechanics and notational analysis, and how through the application of motor control theories these different types of objective feedback can help the performer and their coaches or managers.

XXiii

introduction

Chapter 3: The provision of information
Nicola J. Hodges and Ian M. Franks

By examining the research recently completed on feedback, and the different forms it can take, conclusions are drawn to the best ways of providing feedback to the learning or competing athlete. The objectivity and accuracy with which trained and expert observers can provide feedback is reviewed and the consequences of this research analysed in a direct and applied way.

There are many principles based on theory and research in the field of psychology and more specifically, motor learning, that the coach can use to guide their methods of instruction. It is hoped that we provide a simple analysis of these general principles based on theories of the skill acquisition process and experimental studies where specific information sources have been manipulated.

Chapter 4: Video feedback and information technologies
Dario G. Liebermann and Ian M. Franks

The use of technology to enhance coaching and performance has been recognized as an important and effective undertaking (Katz 2001). However, many of the available tools are not orientated toward the coaches who will be using the technology. Focusing on the users' needs and tasks is not a new idea. 'Know the user' was the first principle in Hansen's (1971) list of design engineering principles (reported in Shneiderman 1987). Developments that focused mainly on the technology or the machine itself, rather than on the needs and the tasks of the end-users have been criticized by many researchers (e.g. Norman 1993). In Norman's (1993) words: 'We need to reverse the machine-centered point of view and turn it into a person-centered point of view. Technology should serve us' (Preface: xi). Norman (1998) also pointed out that an inappropriate 'machine-centered' approach might result in frustration and inefficiency for the end-users. Fischer (1998) agrees, and points out that the adoption of a machine-centered approach is responsible for the perception that computers are 'unfriendly', 'uncooperative', and time consuming.

Moreover, sport scientists and coaches, or anyone analysing performance, must prepare themselves in order to be successful in an ever more complex and constantly changing world. In order to keep up with the changes, it is necessary for sport scientists and coaches to review and update their knowledge and skills more frequently than in the past. Technology can play a role in providing quality information in a timely fashion. This information should be easily accessible and provide the user with the opportunity to store, retrieve and utilize the data when required. However, in order for most analysts to consider using a particular technology tool, it must be relevant, easy to use, time saving, visually appealing and cost-effective. Additionally, the potential user's experience and the perceived characteristics of the innovation will influence the individual's decision on whether or not to adopt a technology (Norman 1998).

Chapter 5: An overview of the development of notational analysis
Mike Hughes

This chapter is written in the form of a selective and applied literature review of the research work already published in this field. Great strides have been made in the last 15 years, with seven world conferences in performance analysis providing a platform for the development of ideas and further research. These new research initiatives will enhance this chapter for the analyst. Although this is written for, and by, sports scientists, it is hoped that anyone with an interest in this rapidly growing area of practice and research will find it equally interesting and rewarding.

The review is aimed at being as practical as possible and it is structured to follow the main developments in notational analysis. After tracing a historical perspective of the roots of notation, the application of these systems to sport is then developed. These early systems were all hand notation systems, their emerging sophistication is followed until the advent of computerized notation. Although the emphasis is given to the main research developments in both hand and computerized notational systems, where possible the innovations of new systems and any significant data outputs within specific sports are also assessed. These applications will be examined for the main team, racket and individual sports only.

Chapter 6: Sports analysis
Mike Hughes

The aim of this chapter is to provide an insight into how different sports can be broken down into a series of decisions represented by a limited number of actions and their possible outcomes. These logical progressions provide the inherent structure within each sport. The construction of flowcharts of different sports is examined, together with the definition of key events in these respective sports. The next step is to design a data collection and data processing system, so anyone interested in designing a notation system should read this chapter first.

Chapter 7: How do we design simple systems? How to develop a notation system
Mike Hughes

This chapter enables the reader to be able to develop their own hand notation system for any sport, no matter how simple or complicated you wish to make it – the underlying principles apply. If the reader is hoping to develop a computerized system, the same logical process must be followed, so this section is also a vital part of that developmental process.

Chapter 8: Examples of notation systems
Mike Hughes

The best way to appreciate the intricacies of notational analysis is to examine systems for the sport(s) in which you are interested, or sports that are similar. Presented here are a number of examples of different systems for different sports. They have been devised by students of notational analysis and are therefore of differing levels of complexity and sophistication – but there are always lessons to be learnt even from the simplest of systems. Some of the explanations and analyses are completed by beginners at notational analysis, coaches of these sports should not therefore be irritated at the simplistic levels of analysis of the respective sports. The encouraging aspects about these examples is the amounts of information that the systems provide – even the simplest of these.

Chapter 9: Analysis of notation data: reliability
Mike Hughes

It is vital that the reliability of a data gathering system is demonstrated clearly and in a way that is compatible with the intended analyses of the data. The data must be tested in the same way and to the same depth in which it will be processed in the subsequent analyses. In general, the work of Bland and Altman (1986) has transformed the attitude of sport scientists to testing reliability; can similar techniques be applied to the non-parametric data that most notational analysis studies generate? There are also a number of questions that inherently recur in these forms of data-gathering – this chapter aims to demonstrate practical answers to some of these questions. These ideas have been developed over recent years and represent a big step forward in our understanding the reliability of systems in this area of sports science.

The most common form of data analysis in notation studies is to record frequencies of actions and their respective positions on the performance arena, these are then presented as sums or totals in each respective area. What are the effects of cumulative errors nullifying each other, so that the overall totals appear less incorrect than they actually are?

The application of parametric statistical techniques is often misused in notational analysis – how does this affect the confidence of the conclusions to say something about the data, with respect to more appropriate non-parametric tests? By using practical examples from recent studies, this chapter investigates these issues associated with reliability studies and subsequent analyses in performance analysis.

Chapter 10: Qualitative biomechanical analysis of technique
Adrian Lees

Qualitative analysis is descriptive, usually based on video but with no measurements. In teaching or coaching, it can provide the learner with detailed feedback to improve performance. This has two-stages: first, observation to identify and diagnose the causes of any discrepancies between the desired and observed movement patterns; second, instruction to try to eradicate these discrepancies. In performance analysis, it can be used to differentiate between individuals when judging performance, e.g. in gymnastics. It can also be used in descriptive comparisons of performance. The recommended approach uses hierarchical models to identify the basic mechanical principles underlying the specific sports movement. Qualitative analysts need a good grasp of the techniques involved, experience of specific sport and exercise activities, and the ability to relate to coaches and athletes.

Chapter 11: Time–motion analysis
Peter G. O'Donoghue

Performance analysis involves the investigation of actual sports performance or training. Performance analysis can be undertaken as part of academic

investigations into sports performance or as part of applied activities in coaching, media or judging contexts. There is considerable overlap between performance analysis and other disciplines as most performance analysis exercises are concerned with investigating aspects of performance such as technique, energy systems or tactical aspects. What distinguishes performance analysis from other disciplines is that it is concerned with actual sports performance rather than activity undertaken in laboratory settings or data gathered from self reports such as questionnaires or interviews. There are a variety of methods that can be used to gather data for performance analysis exercises, ranging from highly quantitative biomechanical analysis to qualitative analysis. There are cases where laboratory based biomechanics exercises can count as performance analysis. If the technique under investigation is an important skill within the sport of interest then there is an argument that detailed biomechanical analysis of the technique is performance analysis. This is an especially strong argument where a skill such as running stride, golf swing or tennis serve is critically important to success in the sport and where the detailed data required cannot be gathered during actual competition. Notational analysis is a method of recording and analysing dynamic and complex situations such as field games.

Chapter 12: Probability analysis of notated events in sport contests: skill and chance
Tim McGarry

In this chapter, we present some examples to introduce the idea that the behaviours and outcomes in sports contests can usefully be analysed on the basis of chance (or probability). On first consideration from sports experience, the viewpoint that sports actions and sports outcomes might be thought of, and even explained, with reference to chance might seem questionable and, for some perhaps, objectionable. Nonetheless, in the following sections, we demonstrate that considerations of sports contests from the perspective of chance, using probability analysis, is a useful way of analysing and informing on sports behaviours. To do this, we first consider some definitions.

Chapter 13: Rule changes in sport and the role of notation
Jason Williams

Any sporting event is defined and played within a predetermined framework of rules and the number and complexity of these rules may differ significantly. The

process for changing them occur within the environment of a governing body or administrators, but little is known about why they occur. Traditional sport that is played today is the product of many years of evolution and development, but little is known as to why these rules change. This chapter reviews literature regarding rule changes in sport and will identify and categorize why rules change in sport and will investigate the use of notation in tracking the changes.

Chapter 14: Performance analysis in the media
Nic James

Performance analysis is usually thought of in terms of providing feedback for players and coaches to enable improvement in sports performance. This is not necessarily so, as media coverage of sport often adds statistical detail to their reporting of events for the purpose of informing the sports fan. Consequently, two separate explanations for carrying out performance analysis can be seen to exist, i.e. by those involved in a sport for performance improvement and by media groups for the enlightenment of sports fans. Identifying this distinction also raises the interesting question as to what extent these two performance analysis tasks differ or indeed are similar. This chapter focusses on presenting performance analysis as commonly depicted in the media. Some reference will be made to academic and professional sports teams' use of similar information; although this will not be exhaustive since other publications offer more of this type of information. For example, students of sport have been well served by previous books edited by Hughes and Franks (1997, 2004) as well as original research published in scientific journals, e.g. electronic *International Journal of Performance Analysis in Sport*. Soccer players and coaches have also had a book written for them (Carling *et al.* 2005) detailing the types of analysis performed at elite clubs. There have also been books aimed at the general public, one which achieved bestseller status in the USA (Lewis 2003), told the account of how Billy Beane, a highly talented but low achieving baseball player became gene-ral manager of the Oakland Athletics and transformed the team's fortunes by picking new players solely on the analysis of their playing statistics rather than trusting his scouts' reports and recommendations.

Newspaper, television and internet coverage of sporting events usually presents performance analysis in the form of summary statistics or 'performance indica-tors' to use the terminology of Hughes and Bartlett (2002). These statistical insights are often debated over in the television studio by the assembled pundits or form the basis of in depth analysis in the newspapers. However, they may also be used as the basis of the topic of conversation in school playgrounds, university cafeterias and business meeting rooms all over the world. Indeed, these statistics are now so common that it would be surprising if anyone with an interest in sport was not familiar with this form of performance analysis, although they might not recognize it as such.

This chapter will review the type of information portrayed in the various forms of media and discuss the extent to which they achieve their aim of describing the events of the sport in question. Potential limitations of these methods are also discussed with suggestions given for how performance analysts working for sports teams or undertaking research might amend or apply these methods.

Chapter 15: Notational analysis of coaching behaviour
Kenny More

A primary function of every coach is to provide athletes with the opportunity to acquire, refine and learn skills that will produce a successful performance in competition. This requires the coach to:

1   Identify the technical and strategic skills required for successful performance.
2   Observe and analyse their athlete's competence in the execution of these skills.
3   Design training opportunities to assist the acquisition and learning of these skills.
4   Provide instruction and feedback on these skills in the training environment.

In relation to these requirements, previous chapters have provided guidance and methods on how to identify, then systematically observe and analyse key aspects of individual and team performance, while National Governing Bodies and coaching materials typically provide the coach with support in the design of appropriate training content, and guidance on their instructional behaviour.

The coaching skills of observation, planning and delivery naturally flow from athlete performance, and the position of notational analysis as a means of supporting innate observation is well documented. However, less well established is the role of notational analysis in monitoring the instruction and feedback the coach delivers during training.

If we consider the significant time devoted to the formal analysis of performance, followed by the careful and informed selection of training content, it would seem folly to have no rationale for, or means of, monitoring effectiveness in providing instruction and feedback.

This chapter describes how, on a theoretical and practical level, coaching behaviour in the training environment can be observed and analysed to improve coaching effectiveness. In particular, the chapter will inform on the sequential development of systematic observation and analysis for the measurement and modification of verbal coaching behaviour.

ACKNOWLEDGEMENTS

Ian M. Franks acknowledges funding support from the Social Science and Humanities Research Council of Canada.

CHAPTER ONE

THE NEED FOR FEEDBACK

Dana Maslovat and Ian M. Franks

In this chapter we:

■ aim to explain the need for feedback including intrinsic and extrinsic feedback.

■ highlight the importance of a well designed notational analysis system to ensure sport performance is effectively and efficiently evaluated.

1.1 INTRODUCTION: FEEDBACK

Participation in sport is typically undertaken with the intent to improve performance. One of the most important variables affecting learning and subsequent performance of a skill is feedback. Feedback involves sensory information resulting from a particular movement. One source of feedback is from the athlete's own sensory channels (i.e. sight, hearing, touch), known as intrinsic or inherent feedback. Although some information from intrinsic sources provides clear information (i.e. the ball missed the goal), more detailed information (i.e. coordination of joint activity, amount of force produced) often requires experience from the performer to evaluate. A second source of feedback usually comes from an outside source, typically a coach, and is meant to complement the intrinsic feedback. This information is known as extrinsic feedback and helps the athlete compare what was done to what was intended. For most complex skills, it is thought that extrinsic information accelerates the learning process and may be necessary to assist the athlete in reaching optimal performance levels. Presumably, the experience and background of the coach allows him or her to provide useful information about a given movement to aid in the development of that skill along with error detection and correction mechanisms. Thus extrinsic feedback can be thought of as a complement to intrinsic feedback.

Extrinsic feedback can be delivered in two main forms: knowledge of results (KR) and knowledge of performance (KP). KR involves information pertaining to the *outcome* of the action, while KP involves information pertaining to the *movement pattern* that caused the result. The majority of feedback from the coach involves KP, as often KR is inherently obvious from the athlete's own feedback sources. However, the coach still has a number of decisions regarding how and when the feedback is presented. One consideration is the mode of presentation. Although most feedback is provided verbally, coaches can also use demonstrations and modeling, video feedback or even biofeedback, which involves information about the person's bodily processes (i.e. heart rate, breathing, sweat rate, even brain activity). The coach must also consider the precision of feedback. More precise feedback seems to be of more benefit; however this does seem to be dependent on the skill level of the athlete. As the athlete's skill level increases, so too must the precision of the feedback. Also dependent on skill level appears to be the amount of feedback. Although high amounts of feedback may be beneficial early on in the learning process, too much feedback later in learning may actually impair performance. It is thought that high frequency feedback may result in a dependence on that feedback by the athlete, and therefore not allow him or her to perform correctly when the extrinsic feedback is no longer present (i.e. a competition situation). Thus, error detection and correction mechanisms may develop faster with reduced feedback or feedback that guides the athlete to the correction rather than simply changing behavior. Another important consideration in the presentation of feedback is the timing of when feedback is presented. Feedback during a skill will often interfere with performance as the athlete's attention is divided between the feedback source and the skill itself. It also appears that feedback immediately following performance may not be optimal. Once an athlete performs a skill he or she should be encouraged to evaluate the performance and then compare the intrinsic feedback to the desired (even predicted) result. Providing feedback during this 'self-reflection' timeframe can interfere with this process and in some cases may retard skill development, again by disrupting internal error detection and correction mechanisms. Thus although presentation of feedback is a critical role of the coach, there are many considerations to ensure this feedback is given correctly to maximize learning for the athlete. More on the topic of feedback presentation is outlined in Chapters 2 and 3.

2

1.2 THE COACHING PROCESS AND ITS PROBLEMS

To provide meaningful feedback, the coach must somehow observe and evaluate performance. Traditional coaching intervention often involves subjective observations and conclusions based on the coach's perceptions, biases and own previous experiences. However, a number of studies have revealed that subjective observations are potentially both unreliable and inaccurate. Human memory systems have limitations, and it is almost impossible to remember accurately all the meaningful events that take place during an entire competition. Studies have shown international level soccer coaches could only recollect 30 per cent of the key factors that determined successful soccer performance and were less than 45 per cent correct in the post-game assessment of what occurred during a game (Franks and Miller 1986, 1991). Another study found no difference between novice and experienced gymnastic coaches in distinguishing differences between two performances (Franks 1993). In fact, the experienced coaches were more likely to report a difference in performance when none existed, and were very confident in their decisions, even when incorrect!

If we consider how humans process information, the above results are not particularly surprising. Committing data to memory and then retrieving it at a later time is a complex process with many opportunities for interference. Distinctive portions of a competition (i.e. controversial decisions, exceptional technical performances, actions following stoppages in play, etc.) are often easily remembered by coaches and spectators alike, while non-critical events are more like to be forgotten. This form of *highlighting*, when combined with emotions and personal bias of the observer, may cause a distorted perception of the game in total. Furthermore, our processing system has limitations which make it near impossible to view, assimilate and store all actions taking place in the playing area. This results in the coach focussing attention on a limited area of play (usually what is considered to be the most critical area) with the peripheral action largely ignored.

Interestingly, the inaccuracies of subjective coaching observations are very similar to eyewitness reports during criminal situations, which are also typically considered to be unreliable and often incorrect. Errors in eyewitness reports have been attributed to increased arousal level (Clifford and Hollin 1980), improper focus of attention (Wells and Leippe 1981) or bias of the observer (Malpass and Devine 1981). These factors may also be present in a coaching environment. While accurate eyewitness testimony is of critical importance during a criminal investigation, the same can be said of coaching observations during competition situations, as this information forms the basis of feedback presentation by the coach.

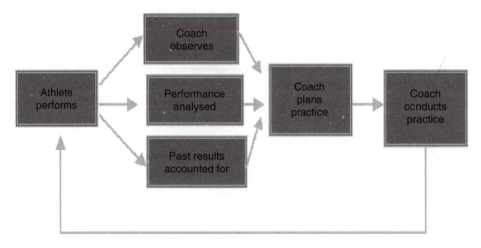

Figure 1.1 A simple schematic diagram representing the coaching process (from Franks *et al*. 1983a)

The coaching process can be thought of as an ongoing cycle of performance and practising, as shown schematically in a flowchart in Figure 1.1 (from Franks *et al*. 1983a). During and following athletic performances, it is the responsibility of the coach to observe and analyse the performance and combine this information with previous results and observances. This forms the basis for planning and implementation of upcoming practices to improve performance. Thus a successful coaching process hinges on the accuracy of collection and analysis of performance. Hopefully, the previous paragraphs have provided rationale why subjective evaluation will not provide an accurate assessment of performance and highlight the fact that a different tool is necessary for coaches to effectively instigate observable changes in athlete performance.

1.3 THE NEED FOR OBJECTIVE INFORMATION

Surprising, given the importance of observation and analysis in the coaching process, there does not seem to be a standard or pre-defined system to monitor and evaluate performance. If reliance on the human information processing system is problematic, we must determine another way to collect information during athletic performances. It should be apparent from the previous discussion that it is paramount that this information be objective, unbiased and as comprehensive as possible. This can be achieved by creating a sport evaluation system, through the use of notational analysis. The purpose of this book is to provide the reader with information pertaining to the development and implementation of such a system to improve coaching and performance in sport.

Recent advances in technology have made the development of a notational analysis system a much less onerous task. Computers and videotaping tools allow for almost limitless storage, retrieval and analysis of data from a sporting competition in real time. Although these technologies will be further discussed in upcoming chapters, we introduce them now to highlight the importance of collecting objective information. Obvious benefits of video analysis are that information can be replayed to the athlete and performance can be reviewed numerous times, resulting in reduced observer bias and the gathering of much more information. However, given all these potential benefits, there is surprising little research providing support for the effectiveness of video feedback (see Rothstein and Arnold 1976 for an excellent early review of experiments that examined the effectiveness of video feedback). In fact, some laboratory-based studies have even shown a decrease in performance following presentation of video feedback (e.g. Ross et al. 1985). It has been suggested that a potential drawback of video is that too much information may be presented and the learner may not be able to concentrate on the important details of the skill. Thus, effective presentation of video feedback likely involves *cueing* from a coach to highlight salient features during the viewing (Kernodle and Carlton 1992). Other alternatives include editing the videotape before showing it to an athlete or using slow motion to reduce the attention demands of the viewer. Use of video - feedback also may change with skill level of the learner. Athletes in an early stage of learning will likely need much more instruction from an outside source to ensure they pay attention to the critical skill features and not be overwhelmed by the volume of information presented.

If the coach's role in video feedback is to provide cueing information, it is imperative the coach determine the critical elements of successful performance. Once these elements are identified, they must be recorded and analysed. Again, we argue this can be most effectively done via a notational analysis system, ideally using a computer to store the collected data. Computers offer the obvious advantages of rapid analysis and large storage capacity but designing an effective way to enter and store information from a dynamic sport environment can provide a challenge. Numerous researchers have developed computer-aided sport analysis systems that have overcome this challenge, and provided invaluable information to coaches (see Chapters 5–7 for a more detailed summary). Once it is determined which information is most important, the next challenge is one of an efficient data input process. This will allow the trained observer to record all pertinent activities such that they can be retrieved and analysed when needed. Although preferable, real-time data input may be not be possible due to the high complexity of sport performance. In these situations, we can combine video and computer technologies to allow for post-event analysis using replay and slow motion. This would result in an extremely comprehensive, unbiased analysis of performance. A further benefit of this type of analysis is that the performance data can be linked directly to a video image that corresponds to the athletic behaviour. This may also streamline any cueing or editing processes undertaken by the coach. The advantages of using an interactive computer-video analysis system were originally outlined by Franks and Nagelkerke as early as 1988, including necessary procedures and hardware requirements. One vital component of such a system is that each recorded activity also be coded with a time stamp, allowing for a real-time re-creation of the competition.

The analytical requirements differ greatly from sport to sport, thus resulting in a potentially very different notational analysis system. For example, the coaching intervention for a team sport may differ greatly than for an individual sport. Furthermore, individual *closed* skills (in which events or the environment are predictable) may differ in their analysis when compared to individual *open* skills (in which events or the environment are unpredictable). For individual sports involving closed skills (i.e. diving, gymnastics, golf), the focus of the evaluation typically revolves around how the pattern of movement is performed, as this is what primarily determines success in the sport. This is often achieved by comparing the movement pattern to a set criterion in order to determine where differences occur. To ensure this comparison is effective, clear criteria must be established and performance must be viewed from an angle allowing a clear view of all key points or multiple angles. Time delays between performance and assessment should be minimized as should the delays between assessment and the next performance. In addition, the athlete should be involved in the analysis, such that they can improve their error detection and correction mechanisms to assist them with future attempts of the skill, when extrinsic feedback may not be present. When examining individual sports involving open skills (i.e. tennis, boxing, squash), in addition to the performance of the specific skills, decision-making and tactics should also be included in the analysis. Tactics play a much larger role in team sports. Therefore the evaluation of performance should reflect this fact. For example, if we consider the involvement of the 22 players during a 90 min soccer game, it becomes apparent that each player spends a majority of the time not in contact with the ball. It is critical that information related to 'off the ball' behaviour be taken into consideration.

Typical computer-aided analyses collect data on relatively gross behavioural measures of performance such as shots on net, penalties, turnovers, etc. While this information is certainly useful, it is often limited in the analysis of total performance during times when the ball is not involved. Newer systems allow for digitization of the video image, resulting in the ability to track the movement and actions of every player throughout the entire match (this is further discussed in Chapter 3). This provides a much more detailed analysis of performance and is not limited to specific areas of play. However, as with all computerized video - feedback systems, the wealth of data comes with a corresponding increase in time the coach must dedicate in determining and examining the information that is most critical to an improvement in performance. This again, highlights the importance of a well designed notational analysis system to ensure sport performance is effectively and efficiently evaluated.

SUMMARY

Extrinsic feedback provided by a coach has the potential to greatly affect performance by the athlete. Coaches should carefully consider how and when they will provide feedback to maximize learning. Historically, coaching intervention has been based on subjective observations, which have been shown to be problematic. Bias, highlighting, limitations of memory and observational difficulties are just a few of the pitfalls associated with a subjective evaluation. Thus, successful coaching hinges on the collection and analysis of unbiased, objective data.

The definition of critical elements of performance and the establishment of an efficient method of data entry is the foundation for an effective data collection and analysis system. Data entry should not only contain the pertinent action but also a time stamp for each event, so that the competition can be re-created later if necessary. Although this can be performed effectively with limited equipment, new technologies now allow for a much greater volume of data collection and analysis. Video recording devices and computers are valuable tools allowing for evaluation of performance during a complex, dynamic sport environment. Video and DVD recordings also allow for slow motion replays and much more detailed analysis in all areas of activity. However, for all the advantages new technologies afford, there is a potential downside. The wealth of information provided by video and computer analysis can overwhelm the coach and athlete, resulting in no change or even a decrement in performance. Thus it is critical the coach approach the analysis of sport with a clear understanding of what activities will lead to successful performance. We argue this is best achieved by a well designed, notational analysis system.

CHAPTER TWO

WHAT IS PERFORMANCE ANALYSIS?

Mike Hughes and Roger Bartlett

In this chapter we:

- aim to provide a comprehensive description of performance analysis, its purpose and its broad possible applications.
- summarize the similarities of approach of biomechanics and notational analysis, and will show how, through the application of motor control theories, these two different approaches to of objective feedback can combine to help the sports performer, coach and manager.

2.1 INTRODUCTION

This presentation will consider what performance analysis is, what biomechanical and notational analysis have in common and how they differ. The main focus will be how they have helped, and can better help, coaches and athletes to analyse and improve sports performance.

Biomechanics and notational analysis both involve the analysis and improvement of sport performance. They make extensive use of video analysis and technology. They require careful information management for good feedback to coaches and performers and systematic techniques of observation. They have theoretical models – based on performance indicators – amenable to AI developments and strong theoretical links with other sport science and IT disciplines. They differ in that biomechanists analyse, in fine-detail, individual sports techniques and their science is grounded in mechanics and anatomy. Notational analysis studies gross movements or movement patterns in team sports, is

8

primarily concerned with strategy and tactics and has a history in dance and music notation.

The practical value of performance analysis is that well-chosen performance indicators highlight good and bad techniques or team performances. They help coaches to identify good and bad performances of an individual or a team member and facilitate comparative analysis of individuals, teams and players. In addition, biomechanics helps to identify injurious techniques while notational analysis helps to assess physiological and psychological demands of sports.

Drawing on a range of sports examples, we will argue here that performance analysts require a unified approach, looking at interactions between players and their individual skill elements. Of fundamental importance is the need for us to pay far greater attention to the principles of providing feedback-technique points that a coach can observe from video and simple counts of events are unlikely to enhance individual or team performance. We should also address the role of variability in sports skills and its implications for coaching. We must pay more attention to normalization of performance indicators to aid coaches. Finally, further development of IT- and AI-based coaching tools by performance analysts is a high priority.

2.2 NOTATIONAL ANALYSIS

2.2.1 Introduction

Notational analysis is an objective way of recording performance, so that critical events in that performance can be quantified in a consistent and reliable manner. This enables quantitative and qualitative feedback that is accurate and objective.

No change in performance of any kind will take place without feedback. The role of feedback is central in the performance improvement process, and by inference, so is the need for accuracy and precision of such feedback. The provision of this accurate and precise feedback can only be facilitated if performance and practice is subjected to a vigorous process of analysis.

Augmented feedback has traditionally been provided by subjective observations, made during performance by the coaches, in the belief that they can accurately report on the critical elements of performance without any observation aids. Several studies not only contradict this belief, but also suggest that the recall abilities of experienced coaches are little better than those of novices, and that even with observational training, coaches' recall abilities improved only slightly. Furthermore, research in applied psychology has suggested that these recall abilities are also influenced by factors that include the observer's motives and beliefs. The coach is not a passive perceiver of information, and as such his or her perception of events is selective and constructive, not simply a copying process. This importance of feedback to performance improvement, and the limitations of coaches' recall abilities alluded to above, implies a requirement for objective data upon which to base augmented feedback, and the main methods of 'objectifying' this data involve the use of video/notational analysis (Hughes and Franks 1997: 11).

Coaches have been aware, consciously or unconsciously, of these needs for accuracy of feedback and have been using simple data gathering systems for decades. More recently, sports scientists have been using notational analysis systems to answer fundamental questions about game play and performance in sport. An early work, over some decades, on analysis of soccer was picked up by the then Director of Coaching at the Football Association, and this had a profound effect on the patterns of play in British football – the adoption of the 'long ball' game. Generally, the first publications in Britain of the research process by notational analysis of sport were in the mid-1970s, so as a discipline it is one of the more recent to be embraced by sports science. The publication of a number of notation systems in racket sports provided a fund of ideas used by other analysts. Because of the growth and development of sports science as an academic discipline, a number of scientists began using and extending the simple hand notation techniques that had served for decades. This also coincided with the introduction of personal computers, which transformed all aspects of data gathering in sports science. Currently hand and computerized notation systems are both used to equal extents by working analysts, although the use of computer databases to collate hand notated data post-event makes the analyses much more powerful.

The applications of notation have been defined as:

1   tactical evaluation
2   technical evaluation
3   analysis of movement
4   development of a database and modelling
5   for educational use with both coaches and players.

Most pieces of research using notation, or indeed any practical applications working directly with coaches and athletes, will span more than one of these purposes.

10

2.2.2 The applications of notation

2.2.2.1 Tactical evaluation

The definition of tactical patterns of play in sports has been a profitable source of work for a number of researchers. The maturation of tactics can be analysed at different levels of development of a specific sport, usually by means of a cross-sectional design. The different tactics used at each level of development within a sport will inevitably depend upon technical development, physical maturation and other variables. The 'maturation models' have very important implications for coaching methods and directions at the different stages of development in each of the racket sports. These tactical 'norms' or 'models', based both upon technique and tactics, demonstrate how the different applications, defined above, can overlap.

Sanderson and Way (1977) used symbols to notate seventeen different strokes, as well as incorporating court plans for recording accurate positional information. The system took an estimated 5–8 h of use and practice before an operator was sufficiently skilful to record a full match actually during the game. In an average squash match there are about 1,000 shots, an analyst using this system will gather over 30 pages of data per match. Not only were the patterns of rally-ending shots (the Nth shot of the rally) examined in detail, but also those shots that preceded the end shot (N-1) to a winner or error, and the shots that preceded those (N-2) to a winner or error. In this way, the rally ending patterns of play were analysed. Not surprisingly, processing the data for just one match could take as long as 40 h of further work. The major emphasis of this system was on the gathering of information concerning 'play patterns' as well as the comprehensive collection of descriptive match data. Sanderson felt that 'suggestive' symbols were better than codes, being easier for the operator to learn and remember. The main disadvantages of this system, as with all longhand systems, was the time taken to learn the system and the large amounts of data generated, which in turn needed so much time to process it.

The 1980s and 1990s saw researchers struggling to harness the developing technology to ease the problems inherent in gathering and interpreting large amounts of complex data. Hughes (1985) modified the method of Sanderson and Way (1977) so that the hand-notated data could be processed on a mainframe computer. Eventually, the manual method was modified so that a match could be notated in-match at courtside directly into a microcomputer. This work was then extended to examine the patterns of play of male squash players at recreational, county and elite levels, thus creating empirical models of performance, although the principles of data stabilization were not thoroughly understood at the time. This form of empirical modelling of tactical profiles is fundamental to a large amount of the published work in notational analysis. By comparing the patterns of play of successful and unsuccessful teams or players in elite competitions, world cup competitions, for example, enables the definition of those performance indicators that differentiate between the two groups. This research template has been used in a number of sports to highlight the tactical parameters that determine success, and it has been extended in tennis to compare the patterns of play that are successful on the different surfaces on which the major tournaments are played.

Most of the examples for tactical applications of notation could appear in the other sections of direct applications of notational analysis, but their initial aims were linked with analysis of tactics. The interesting theme that is emerging, from some of the recent research, is that the tactical models that are defined are changing with time, as players become fitter, stronger, faster, bigger (think of the changes in rugby union since professionalization in 1996), and the equipment changes – for example, the rackets in all the sports have become lighter and more powerful. Over a period of less than 15 years, the length of rallies in squash, for elite players, has decreased from about 20 shots, to about 12 shots per rally. An excellent review (Croucher 1996) of the application of strategies using notational analysis of different sports outlines the problems, advantages and disadvantages associated with this function.

2.2.2.2 Technical evaluation

To define quantitatively where technique fails or excels has very practical uses for coaches, in particular, and also for sports scientists aiming to analyse performance at different levels of development of athletes.

Winners and errors are powerful indicators of technical competence in racket sports and have often been used in research in notational analysis of net-wall games. It has been found that, for all standards of play in squash, if the winner : error ratio for a particular player in a match was greater than one, then that player usually won. (This was achieved with English scoring and a 19-inch tin!) Although this ratio is a good index of technique, it would be better used with data for both players, and the ratios should not be simplified nor decimalized. Rally end distributions, winners and errors in the different position cells across the court, have often been used to define technical strengths and weaknesses. This use of these distributions as indicators is valid as long as the overall distribution of shots across the court is evenly balanced. This even distribution of

12

shots rarely occurs in any net or wall game. Dispersions of winners and errors should be normalized with respect to the totals of shots from those cells. It would be more accurate to represent the winner, or error, frequency, from particular position cells, as a ratio to the total number of shots from those cells.

Similarly, performance indicators, such as shots, are insufficient and need to be expressed with more detail, for example shot to goal ratios (soccer). Even these, powerful as they are, need to be viewed with caution and perhaps integrated with some measure of shooting opportunities? In rugby union, simple numbers of rucks and mauls won by teams may not give a clear impression of the match, the ratio of 'rucks won' to 'rucks initiated' is a more powerful measure of performance. This too could be improved by some measure of how quickly the ball was won in critical areas of the pitch?

Many coaches seek the template of tactical play at the highest level for preparation and training of both elite players and/or teams, and also for those developing players who aspire to reach the highest position. Particular databases, aimed at specific individuals or teams, can also be used to prepare in anticipation of potential opponents for match play. This modelling of technical attainment has been replicated in many sports and form the basis of preparation at the highest levels by the sports science support teams.

2.2.2.3 Movement analysis

Reilly and Thomas (1976) recorded and analysed the intensity and extent of discrete activities during match play in field soccer. With a combination of hand notation and the use of an audio tape recorder, they analysed in detail the movements of English first division soccer players. They were able to specify work-rates of the different positions, distances covered in a game and the percentage time of each position in each of the different ambulatory classifications. Reilly has continually added to this base of data enabling him to clearly define the specific physiological demands in not just soccer, but all the football codes. This piece of work by Reilly and Thomas (1976) has become a standard against which other similar research projects can compare their results and procedures, and it has been replicated by many other researchers in many different sports.

Modern tracking systems have taken the chore out of gathering movement data, which was the most time-consuming application of notational analysis, and advanced computer graphics make the data presentation very simple to understand. Modelling movement has created a better understanding of the respective sports and has enabled specific training programmes to be developed to improve the movement patterns, and fitness, of the respective athletes.

2.2.2.4 Development of a database and modelling

Teams and performers often demonstrate a stereotypical way of playing and these are idiosyncratic models, which include positive and negative aspects of performance. Patterns of play will begin to establish over a period of time but the greater the database, the more accurate the model. An established model provides for the opportunity to compare single performance against it. The modelling of competitive sport is an informative analytic technique because it directs the attention of the modeller to the critical aspects of data that delineate successful performance. The modeller searches for an underlying signature of sport performance, which is a reliable predictor of future sport behaviour. Stochastic models have not yet, to our knowledge, been used further to investigate sport at the behavioural level of analysis. However, the modelling procedure is readily applicable to other sports and could lead to useful and interesting results.

Once notational analysis systems are used to collect amounts of data that are sufficiently large enough to define 'norms' of behaviour, then all the ensuing outcomes of the work are based upon the principles of modelling. It is an implicit assumption in notational analysis that in presenting a performance profile of a team or an individual that a 'normative profile' has been achieved. Inherently, this implies that all the variables that are to be analysed and compared have all stabilized. Most researchers assume that this will have happened if they analyse enough performances. But how many is enough? In the literature there are large differences in sample sizes.

These problems have very serious direct outcomes for the analyst working with coaches and athletes, both in practical and theoretical applications. It is vital that when analysts are presenting profiles of performance that they are definitely stable otherwise any statement about that performance is spurious. The whole process of analysis and feedback of performance has many practical difficulties. The performance analyst working in this applied environment will experience strict deadlines and acute time pressures defined by the date of the next tournament, the schedule and the draw. The need then is to provide coaches with accurate information on as many of the likely opposition players, or teams, in the amount of time available. This may be achieved by the instigation of a library of team and/or player analysis files, which can be extended over time and receive frequent updating. Player files must be regularly updated by adding analyses from recent matches to the database held on each player.

Finally, some scientists have considered the use of a number of sophisticated techniques, such as neural networks, chaos theory, fuzzy logic and catastrophe theory, for recognizing structures, or processes, within sports contests. Each of these system descriptions, while incomplete, may assist in our understanding of the behaviours that form sports contests. Furthermore, these descriptions for sports contests need not be exclusive of each other, and a hybrid type of description (or model) may be appropriate in the future, a suggestion that remains only a point of conjecture at this time.

2.2.2.5 Educational applications

It is accepted that feedback, if presented at the correct time and in the correct quantity, plays a great part in the learning of new skills and the enhancement of performance. Recent research, however, has shown that the more objective or quantitative the feedback, the greater effect it has on performance. However, in order to gauge the exact effect of feedback alone, complete control conditions would be needed in order to minimize the effect of other external variables, which is by definition impossible in real competitive environments. This experimental design is also made more difficult because working with elite athletes precludes large numbers of subjects.

Hughes and Robertson (1997) were using notation systems as an adjunct to a spectrum of tactical models that they have created for squash. The hand notation systems are used by the Welsh national youth squads, the actual notation being completed by the players, for the players. It is believed that in this way the tactical awareness of the players, doing the notation, are heightened by their administration of these systems. This type of practical educational use of notation systems has been used in a number of team sports, soccer, rugby union, rugby league, basketball, cricket, and so on, by players in the squads, substitutes, injured players, as a way of enhancing their understanding of their sport, as well as providing statistics on their team.

2.3 BIOMECHANICS – WHAT IS THE BIOMECHANICAL VIEW OF PERFORMANCE ANALYSIS?

When the British Olympic Association (BOA) set up the Performance Analysis Steering Group, bringing together biomechanists and notational analysts, there was some scepticism as to whether these two groups of sport scientists had enough in common to make the Group meaningful. After all, sports biomechanics is concerned with fine detail about individual sports techniques while notational analysts are more concerned with gross movements or movement patterns in games or teams. Furthermore, notational analysts are more concerned with strategic and tactical issues in sport than with technique analysis and the two disciplines do not share a common historical background.

However, the similarities between the two groups of performance analysts are far more marked than the differences. A crucial similarity is evident when we look at the other sport science disciplines: sports psychology and physiology (including nutrition) essentially focus on preparing the athlete for competition. Performance analysts, in contrast, focus on the performance in competition to draw lessons for improving performance and this is true of both notational and biomechanical analysis. Both are fundamentally concerned with the analysis and improvement of performance. Both are rooted in the analysis of human move-ment. Both make extensive use of video analysis and video-based technology. Although both evolved from manual systems, they now rely heavily on com-puterized analysis systems. Both have a strong focus on data collection and processing. Both produce vast amounts of information – this is sometimes claimed to be a strength of both sports biomechanics and notational analysis, however, it often requires careful attention in providing feedback to athletes and coaches.

In addition, biomechanists and notational analysts both emphasize the develop-ment of systematic techniques of observation. This is more obvious in notational analysis and, perhaps, in the somewhat-neglected 'qualitative' analysis approach of biomechanics than in fully quantitative 'computerized biomechanical analy-sis', which seems somewhat out of fashion with coaches at present. Both have a strong focus on the provision of feedback to the coach and performer to improve performance and each group is now learning and adopting best practice from the other.

Biomechanics and notational analysis are, somewhat mischievously if with some justification, accused by other sports scientists of lacking theoretical foundations and being over-concerned with methodology: this might explain the attraction of notational analysis and qualitative biomechanical analysis to coaches as they are immediately seen as being of practical relevance. However, theoretical models do exist in both biomechanics and notational analysis. These can also be effectively represented graphically – by flowcharts for notational analysis and hierarchical technique models for biomechanics (Bartlett 1999; Hughes and Franks 1997). Both disciplines have 'key events' as important features of their theoretical foundations. This again helps to present information clearly and simply to coaches and sports performers, as evidenced by the current popularity of 'coach-friendly' biomechanical analysis packages, such as Silicon COACH (http://www.siliconcoach.com) and Quintic (http://www.quintic.com). These theoretical models can, at least in principle, be mapped onto the sophisticated approaches of artificial intelligence, such as expert systems and neural net processing, hopefully offering exciting developments in performance enhancement by the middle of this decade. The theoretical models are highly sport, or technique specific but with general principles, particularly across groups of similar sports or techniques. Both have strong theoretical and conceptual links with other areas of sport science and information technology, for example the dynamical systems approach of motor control.

Many practical issues, which impinge strongly on performance improvement, are common to biomechanics and notational analysis. These include optimizing feedback to coaches and athletes, the management of information complexity, reliability and validity of data and future exploitation of the methods of artificial intelligence. Sharing of approaches and ideas has already begun to have mutual benefits as was evident in the very successful NCF/BOA High-performance Coaches workshop held in Cardiff in 1999, which was highly acclaimed by many of the coaches attending.

But, you might ask, is performance analysis really helpful in improving performance? Perhaps your sport uses sports psychologists, nutritionists, physiologists and conditioning consultants but no performance analyst of either 'hue'. Well, biomechanics are employed in the World Class Performance Plans (WCPPs) for athletics, gymnastics, swimming and speed skating. Notational analysts are employed in WCPPs, for example, for netball, badminton, hockey, squash, sailing, cycling, canoeing, badminton, Tae Kwon Do and disability basketball. Cricket, from the ECB to county cricket clubs, uses the services of biomechanists and notational analysts, as do many other sports, such as golf and tennis (biomechanics) and rugby and soccer (notational analysis).

As to their value for the coach, biomechanics identifies the features of performance that relate to good and bad techniques, thereby helping to identify how techniques can be improved. It also facilitates comparative analysis of individual performers and helps to identify injurious techniques. The latter is well exemplified by the contribution made by biomechanists to establishing the link between low back injury and the mixed technique in cricket fast bowling (for a brief review, see Elliott *et al.* 1996). Notational analysis identifies the performance indicators that relate to good and bad team performance and identifies good and bad performances of team members. It, therefore, facilitates comparative analysis of teams and players. In addition, it helps to assess the physiological and psychological demands of various games (for examples, see Bartlett 2001).

Of all the sports sciences, performance analysis is the one most influenced by technological changes. Digital video and improvements in computer processing speeds and capacities have transformed biomechanical and notational analysis almost beyond recognition in the last 10 years, allowing far faster turnaround times for feedback and far more realistic feedback to coaches and performers. The latter is evident, for example, by comparing crude 'stick figure' displays (Figure 2.1) of earlier biomechanical analyses (often only produced weeks after filming) by the models available in real-time from modern optoelectronic systems such as SIMM (Figure 2.2) (from the Motion Analysis Corporation of Santa Rosa, CA: http://www.motionanalysis.com) and Vicon (from Oxford Dynamics: http://www.vicon.com). These systems are not yet routinely used by coaches and performers, but this is changing rapidly. The Sport and Recreation Association

Figure 2.1 Stick figure

what is performance analysis?

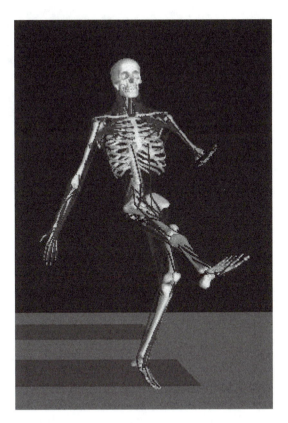

Figure 2.2 SIMM skeleton and muscles

(SRA) is looking to install such a system for training and feedback in the squash centre in Manchester, where the English Institute of Sport Regional Centre has a staff of five analysts who use both notation and biomechanical software with a variety of sports, but mainly squash and cycling.

SUMMARY

The use of systematic observation instruments provides researchers with a method of collecting behavioural data on both the coach and the athlete. These data can be analysed and processed in a variety of ways to provide a descriptive profile that can be used for giving both the athlete and the coach feedback about their actions. Advances in both computer and video technology can make this observation process more efficient and also provide the coach with audio-visual feedback about their interactions with athletes. The next phase of solving these problems in their entirety is translating the use of these objective observation systems into practice. The presentation here attempts to exemplify some of the better practical uses of analysis by elite coaches and athletes. The next step is to be able to describe in generic terms the whole process, of performance analyses and their applications to the coaching process, so that it can be applied to any type of sport.

CHAPTER THREE

THE PROVISION OF INFORMATION

Nicola J. Hodges and Ian M. Franks

In this chapter we:

- aim to provide a discussion of general motor learning principles and relate these principles to coaching and instruction. The coach has a critical role to play in the learning process. However, an area of continued debate is how active should the coach's participation in the learning process be?
- review how information provided before, during and after motor performance affects the quality of learning.

3.1 INTRODUCTION

In Chapter 1 we discussed the sources of information that are available to the learner during performance. It should be clear from this discussion that information feedback, whether this is provided through intrinsic or extrinsic sources, alerts the performer to error. Information plays an important *error-alerting* role. In addition to error-detection, the performer also requires information about how to correct error. Information therefore can play an important *error-correcting* role. Seeing that a putt was missed contains little or no information about how the shot should be changed or corrected on the next attempt. At a very basic level, the performer might know that a correction to the right will be needed if the ball goes too far left, but how to control the ball to effect this change needs to be discovered through practice and taught by a coach. This error-correcting role can at a very basic level be encouraged through outcome feedback alone (i.e. I missed, therefore I need to do something different next time), but more

21

frequently instructions and demonstrations are provided to alert more specifically as to what to change. Combining demonstrations with verbal cues is one technique for alerting to specific errors and also to ways of correcting these errors. Combining demonstrations with video feedback may help the performer evaluate what to change to perform more like a skilled performer.

Figure 3.1 illustrates how augmented information affects performance and subsequently learning, through the processes of error detection and correction. As will become clear through the rest of this chapter, the intentions and goals of the performer are influenced by feedback about the just performed action (both intrinsic and extrinsic feedback) and also by augmented information in the form of demonstrations, instructions and verbal and visual cues usually provided by the coach or instructor.

In the following sections, we evaluate these augmented information sources in terms of their potentially positive and negative roles in the learning process. Various methods are compared to find out how effectively they alert the performer to error throughout performance and how effectively they help change performance. What should be clear from this review is that more information is not necessarily better than less and what might work in one situation for one

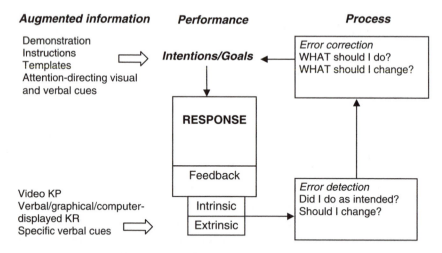

Figure 3.1 Schematic diagram to illustrate how the learning process is affected by various augmented information sources. Error-detection and correction processes are informed by augmented information in the form of feedback and pre-practice information. This information influences the intention and goals of the performer and subsequently the movement response

person will not necessarily be the most effective under different conditions and at a different level of skill.

3.2 AUGMENTED FEEDBACK

Feedback provides both a motivational and informational role. That is, feedback can help to encourage repeated performance and also to reduce the discrepancy between a desired and an actual outcome. It is this second, informational role that is of most concern here. Although the motivational role of the coach is undoubtedly important to performance change, it is the type of information that is delivered and how it is delivered that is most important in encouraging specific changes in performance.

3.2.1 Positive effects

It has been proposed that both KR and KP (extrinsic information sources) help to confirm a person's own judgement about outcome success that is based on intrinsic information sources. Alerting to success of an outcome will lead to continued performance if the result was successfully achieved and a change in performance if it was not (see Figure 3.1). We can distinguish between two different ways of providing feedback about outcome success. This feedback can be *qualitative* or *quantitative*. A general statement alerting to the success of the action, such as 'good' or 'bad' or 'too much' or 'too little', would be considered qualitative in nature. This information is typically not as precise as quantitative feedback. A more specific statement referring to the amount of error, such as 'you missed by 25 cm' would be considered quantitative. The amount of information conveyed by either source will also be somewhat dependent on the motor skill, and the knowledge of the performer. There have been many experiments where the precision of outcome-based feedback has been examined. Generally, early in practice, qualitative and quantitative KR typically have similar effects on performance. After an initial period of practice (which would depend on the difficulty of the task), more precise quantitative information can be used more effectively to reduce error.

In general, the positive effects of outcome-based feedback, typically KR, have been observed during the practice or what we refer to as the acquisition or performance phase of skill learning. Repeated feedback from trial to trial will lead or guide the learner to the correct response. The learner is provided with enough information to promote change in performance across practice such that goal-attainment can be achieved. KR and KP can help to alert the learner to errors such that corrections can be made. It has been shown that so powerful are the effects of outcome feedback that even when this feedback is incorrect and contradicts valid information from intrinsic sources such as vision, learner's prioritise this extrinsic information and erroneously correct performance (see Buekers et al. 1992). This finding is of course worrying if there are errors with measurement tools or with the coach's perception (as was discussed in Chapter 1).

As long as the learner knows whether an error has been made, there is a strong likelihood that changes in performance will be observed. Even withholding KR can be informational if the performer realizes that error information is only provided once performance falls outside a certain criteria or bandwidth. For example, if feedback is only provided when an archer misses the target board, then the learner also knows that on the trials when feedback is not provided that she or he was successful. If a change in a response is not encouraged through KR and the skill has not been performed to the degree of required success then the information is probably not specific enough and therefore not sufficient.

3.2.2 Negative effects

It is also important to note that precise, quantitative information about performance and frequent feedback can also impact negatively on performance during the practice phase causing variable (unstable) performance. Knowledge of an error, whether this is within 1 s, or 1 ms, could lead to an over-correction of performance. If the level of feedback is too specific for the level of control, which the performer is able to exert over the skill, then this feedback could prevent stable performance and hinder outcome success. The level of feedback provided should therefore be appropriate for the skill level of the individual and appropriate to the level of control they have over their performance. Despite this instability, which might result from frequent provision of precise KR, very rarely are negative effects from providing KR observed during the practice phase of learning.

However, true learning can only be effectively assessed at a later time period. Performance changes during practice might be only temporary and not relatively permanent long-term adjustments (see Schmidt and Lee 2005). To separate these temporary or transient effects from more long-term effects, the acquisition or practice phase has been distinguished from the retention phase (could be equivalent to competition for athletes). In laboratory-based studies, this retention phase is introduced at least 24 h after the last practice session and typically without augmented feedback. During the retention phase of testing, conditions should match those that will be encountered by the performer during evaluation. For example, a long-jumper who is provided with augmented feedback about error in footfall, in relation to the take-off board during practice, will not typically have this information available under competitive conditions. In contrast, outcome information concerning the length of the jump remains during the test phase, so the assessment of the skill with this information is a valid and realistic measure of learning. In view of the need to adequately assess what has been learnt by the performer, we need to examine the relationship between performance and learning under different conditions of augmented feedback. As we will show, the effects of feedback are remarkably dependent on the type of assessment. In fact, these effects are so strong that researchers have shown conflicting performance and retention effects, such that the greater the benefits of feedback seen during the practice phase of skill acquisition, the greater the detriments observed in the test or retention phase (see Salmoni et al. 1984 for more details).

One of the most serious effects of regular performance feedback is that the learners who receive it become dependent on it. This dependence leads to poor performance when the feedback is withdrawn. This has been referred to as the guidance hypothesis of feedback (Salmoni et al. 1984; Winstein and Schmidt 1990). One of the consequences of receiving extrinsic feedback on every performance attempt is that the learner does not need to evaluate their own intrinsic feedback, such as evaluating how the movement felt. They do not engage in a form of self generated error detection. When extrinsic feedback is no longer available the learner is unable to judge the accuracy of their movements.

The amount of feedback and when it is delivered could have a significant impact on how dependent the performer will be on this information for accurate performance. Very generally, feedback provided at the same time the skill is being performed, referred to as concurrent feedback, has been found to be more guiding and promote greater dependency than feedback about task success provided after the movement has been completed, referred to as terminal feedback. Vander Linden and colleagues (1993) found that concurrent feedback about the amount of force expended during an elbow extension task was more helpful at reducing error in acquisition when compared with terminal feedback. However, when performance was assessed in retention, the concurrent feedback group performed with the most error. Concurrent feedback *guides* the performer to the correct response such that they do reduce error based on other sources of intrinsic information. There is no incentive to engage in error-detection and actively work out why an error occurred and what changes in the movement led to the correction of this error.

Similar to the negative effects of concurrent feedback, feedback provided immediately after the movement has also been shown to discourage the learner from being actively involved in the error detection process and interpreting intrinsic information sources. Although feedback needs to be provided very soon after the actual movement, when it is provided too soon after movement completion, negative effects in retention are likely to result.

Finally, there have been a number of studies on the frequency of providing KR which have demonstrated that a high frequency of instructor-provided augmented feedback is detrimental for later performance in retention tests. Again, the mechanisms behind frequent KR appears to be related to a decreased reliance on other natural, intrinsic information sources available from performing the action (such as the feel and the visual consequences of the movement) and a failure to spontaneously evaluate how effective the actions were in achieving the desired outcome.

As should be clear from all of these studies, the negative effects of feedback in retention can in most cases be quite simply overcome by reducing the frequency of feedback during practice and increasing the time delay between feedback and successive practice attempts. Even encouraging learners to evaluate their own performance in the interval between the end of the action and KR can help to overcome potentially negative consequences in retention. Such reduction in frequency measures include: (1) an overall reduction in the relative frequency of feedback, for example, providing feedback on 50 per cent of the trials; (2) fading schedules of feedback, whereby the frequency is gradually reduced as a function of practice; (3) bandwidth feedback, which is only provided when error falls markedly outside performance guidelines (which might work in a similar way to a fading schedule as the frequency of feedback is reduced as participants' learn); (4) summary feedback, provided after a block of practice trials relating to all the trials in a general manner (such as mean performance), or perhaps only the previous trial; and finally, (5) self-selected feedback, whereby the learner determines when feedback is needed and when it is not.

Knowing the optimal amount of feedback to provide is difficult to prescribe accurately. Very generally, it is the reduction in the relative frequency of KR that is more important than the actual amount of feedback. There is also an important balance to be maintained in that providing feedback too infrequently has been shown to be somewhat equivalent to providing feedback after every trial. An optimal frequency allows for self-directed (intrinsic) error detection, but does

26

not allow performance to depart too markedly from the goal or criterion. A slightly slower rate of acquisition, as a result of a reduction in feedback, will result in enhanced performance in retention relative to a performance when feedback is provided every trial. This reduction in feedback frequency will also prevent the over-correction of errors during practice that can lead to instability in responses.

3.2.3 Additional factors to consider when providing feedback

Although we have discussed potential negative consequences associated with providing too much feedback, there are instances when frequent feedback in practice is actually desirable for learning (and hence retention). Generally, it has been shown that more frequent feedback is beneficial for acquiring features of a movement that change across different skills of a similar class of action, referred to as the absolute features of a movement. For example, in shooting a basketball, the overall force of a throw will change across similar shots from different distances outside the key. However, a reduction in feedback benefits the learning of the more stable or relative features of the shot (i.e. the throwing action, which might be indexed by the consistent relative timing of the knee bend, body straightening and release of the ball). There is also evidence that the effects of feedback are dependent on the complexity of the skill. It seems that for tasks that are rich in intrinsic information about how the movement feels, frequent feedback helps the learner know how to relate the intrinsic feedback to outcome success. In this way, the learner is able to make more refined judgements about success.

As a result of this research and similar studies, Swinnen (1996) has recommended that optimal summary length should become close to every trial as the complexity of the task increases. Although there is no specific criteria that can describe a task as more complex than others, typically more complex tasks require the learning of new relationships between a number of body segments, they are rich in intrinsic feedback and might involve more degrees of freedom (such as whole body movements) in comparison to more simple tasks. Wulf and Shea (2004) have suggested that because of these differences between complex and simple skills feedback provided in more complex skills typically serves less of a guiding role. Knowing that a shot cleared the top goal post by 1 m in soccer does not guide the learner to the correct solution for reducing this error. There are many features of the movement that can be changed to reduce the height of the ball (such as the positioning of the head and trunk when the ball is struck, the follow through of the kicking leg, the force imparted on the ball). In contrast, if the movement is constrained to one limb moving in one dimension (i.e. horizontally as is typical in many simple target aiming experiments), then feedback about the error in displacement guides the performer in terms of what to change on the next trial (i.e. the extent of the contraction). These dual roles of augmented information as a description of what was done and a guide as to what should be done (Figure 3.1) are elaborated on below, when we discuss the role of demonstrations and instructions in the motor learning process.

3.3 DEMONSTRATIONS AND INSTRUCTIONS

Before change in a movement, and hence learning can be observed, some knowledge that change is required is necessary. Feedback (whether this is intrinsic or extrinsic) usually provides this error-alerting role as discussed above. Extrinsic feedback also has another role to play in the learning process, that of establishing a goal (or goals) for the movement. If a learner is provided feedback about the movement technique and a particular feature of the movement, such as bending the knees during a basketball free-throw shot, then the learner's goal becomes one of changing this aspect of the movement on the next trial. As should be clear in this example, the learner might have a number of performance goals at any one time (e.g. getting the ball through the hoop and bending the knees), but feedback can change the importance of these goals. Additional goal-related information can be given through verbal instructions, demonstrations or movement templates. We will refer to this second type of goal information as pre-practice information. Pre-practice information serves to provide an error-correcting role in the learning process. We will evaluate the positive and negative effects of this type of augmented information below.

3.3.1 Positive effects

3.3.1.1 Providing a reference-of-correctness

There is no doubt that one of the important components of motor skill acquisition is adequate goal-related information. People need to have guidance as to what is required such that their performance attempts remain goal-directed. Various environmental and task constraints will *indirectly* dictate how a skill is to be performed (e.g. certain equipment will constrain how a person can stand, hold an object or impart force onto an object). More often, however, additional constraints will be needed in terms of instructions or demonstrations, which more *directly* limit the manner of attaining a task goal.

Movement goals conveyed through instructions, demonstrations and criterion templates (e.g. computer displays such as those in simulators and virtual reality devices) help to provide a reference-of-correctness, so it is possible for the performer to judge whether their actions matched what was required. This comparison across various information sources (i.e. intrinsic and extrinsic feedback and demonstrations and instructions) is an important and necessary process in learning. There are specific types of actions which have no immediate outcome goal(s), but rather have as their goal a specific technique or movement pattern. For example, a pike jump on the trampoline, a cartwheel in gymnastics or a choreographed dance sequence. For these and similar skills some sort of reference information is needed (usually a demonstration). In these situations, feedback has decreased value in terms of bringing about an appropriate change in the movement. The feedback cannot be adequately evaluated against a standard. For example, Kernodle and colleagues (2001) found that verbal information, which alerted participants as to errors (i.e. what a desired throw should look like) and how to correct them, was more beneficial for acquiring a desired throwing pattern than only providing video feedback. The authors concluded that because no reference information was provided to the video feedback group, they were unable to perform comparisons and thus detect errors in performance over and above their existing knowledge concerning how to throw over-arm. It is important to note therefore that the potential benefits of video - feedback is improved if the coach can direct the learner to the specific errors of performance that need correcting. This is discussed in more detail later.

3.3.1.2 Effective demonstrations

Some of the most convincing research showing that demonstrations help to convey important features of a movement, which are then translated into effective motor reproduction, comes from Carroll and Bandura (1982, 1985, 1990). These researchers have used two measures of performance to assess how demonstrations facilitate motor learning. Through assessment of visual recognition, the authors were able to determine whether a performer has developed an understanding of what is required (i.e. a reference-of-correctness). Assessment of performance, what they refer to as recall, allows the instructor to assess the ability of the learner to transfer this information effectively into movements.

These researchers have shown that a discrete sequence of arm movements (similar to those used by air-traffic controllers) can be learnt via a series of demonstrations. Repeated demonstrations help the learners encode the information, such that errors can be detected (i.e. desired performance is correctly determined as assessed through measures of recognition and recall) and subsequently corrected (as assessed through recall). Very few researchers have tried to untangle these two components of learning even though the issue of conceptual understanding, that is, the ability to determine the task requirements and understand the critical features of a demonstration, is especially pertinent with young children. Not only will the inexperience of young children affect their ability to correctly discern what to do, but also underdeveloped cognitive skills (i.e. attention span, verbal skills, memory capacity) will cause problems in understanding. Additional information is sometimes required, such as feedback or visual cues to help learners extract the important information from a display.

3.3.1.3 Conveying a strategy

Demonstrations and instructions also help to convey a strategy. In some instances, the success of a skill is not automatically determined by its closeness to a particular movement ideal. For example, the success of a throw may be judged by its end-result, whether it reached the intended target, not whether the technique matched a desired criterion. In fact, sometimes the method for attaining a goal is not always clear cut and may depend on many factors such as the novelty of the task, the strength and height of a performer, the environmental conditions on the day. Therefore, one of the roles of instructions and demonstrations is to relay a strategy for achieving success, which might be in terms of a general technique or form (e.g. how to throw a javelin) a specific cue (e.g. the position of the arm during the backswing of a javelin throw) or a reliable method (e.g. the cascade method of juggling). In some early research, looking at the effectiveness of visual demonstrations in teaching an unusual motor skill (i.e. shoot-the-moon task where a ball had to be moved to the top of two hand-held rods) Martens and co-authors (1976) found that demonstrations alerted participants to an effective strategy for achieving the task goal (i.e. a ballistic, rather than creeping strategy). In this way, ineffective strategies and perhaps valuable practice time were avoided so that practice could be devoted to refining a technique.

3.3.1.4 Comparing pre-practice methods

There have been a number of experiments comparing across these different mediums to examine which method is the most effective for encouraging correct technique and successful performance. For example, Magill and Schoenfelder-

Zohdi (1996) showed that demonstrations were more effective at encouraging the acquisition of a rhythmic-gymnastic's rope-skill, than a series of instructions which contained essentially the same information. The authors concluded that for skills with complex features, visual demonstrations most effectively conveyed these features and the relationships between components. It is the general consensus that more information can be conveyed more simply by a visual demonstration than by verbal instructions. It has also been shown that taking information from a visual display requires less attention in comparison to written or verbal instructions. What is perhaps important to think about when comparing across these two types of mediums is how well verbal or written instructions are able to generate a visual image. Annett (1993) has suggested that if verbal instructions can activate an image of the action to the same degree as a visual demonstration, the value of these two mediums will be similar.

There has also been evidence that a combination of verbal and visual information aids the retention and subsequent recall of an act (Hall et al. 1997). Adults and skilled learners often spontaneously label an action (or parts of an action) but there is evidence that children do not spontaneously attach verbal labels to actions which causes difficulties in recall (Cadopi et al. 1995). In addition, children appear to have a more pronounced tendency than adults to focus on the outcome effects, or success of an action, rather than the actual movements required to attain them. If this is the case, then verbal or visual cues might help children attend to important features of the movement when technique-based information is important. If a specific movement form is the intended goal of instruction then additional information might be required to direct people (and young children in particular) to this information. The combination of visual and verbal cues would also help later recall of these features.

3.3.2 Negative effects

3.3.2.1 Movement strategies

One of the critical information roles of pre-practice information is to alert to a strategy. Strategies help to limit the choice of possible movement solutions. Although this can be beneficial, early constraints can also be harmful, especially if it discourages variability in practice attempts. Early variability in practice attempts is especially important when a learner needs to resist or break away from previously learnt or pre-existing behaviours or habits. Further, the strategy alerted from a demonstration or instruction might not be one intended or anticipated by a coach or teacher.

Strategy or technique information can also be detrimental for performance and learning in tasks where the desired movement is not the goal of the action. For example, in a kicking skill, the goal is usually to hit a ball a particular distance rather than demonstrate a certain technique (as with the throwing example we gave earlier). The reason why this type of pre-practice information might not be helpful in these situations is that it may cause the performer to trade-off performance in one at the expense of the other (i.e. concentrate on moving correctly at the expense of kicking the ball the desired distance). Evidence for this was shown by Vereijken (1991). She found that individuals learning to perform slalom ski-movements on a simulator, where success in achieving fast and wide movements was not dependent on a specific method, were more successful when they did not watch, as opposed to did watch, a skilled model. Again, constraints imposed by demonstrations or instructions had a negative impact on task success.

This study underscores the importance of adequately conveying, either directly (through instructions) or indirectly (though feedback), the desired performance goals(s) to the learner. If outcome attainment is the only requirement of a skill, such as is the case with a javelin throw, then additional technique goals can interfere with attainment. As should be clear, however, coaches often have dual goals of attaining a specific outcome, in a specific manner, perhaps as a result of experience with other athletes, mechanical principles or aesthetics. In these conditions, the coach needs to be clear as to the critical goal, perhaps at different points in acquisition. Although there have been very few empirical studies where instructions have been manipulated at different points in the learning process, a possible method for instruction might be to encourage outcome goals initially, then to follow-up this method with technique-based instruction, if success is not forthcoming.

In summary, strategy information can act to detrimentally constrain performance, which is a particular issue early in practice of difficult skills. Second, in many sporting skills, the success of the action is not directly dependent on the technique and movement form. Again, early in practice, very rarely are success and technique perfectly in tune. As such, trade-offs in performance might result due to augmented information directed to one, rather than another. Learning is a process of discovering how movements and effects are related, not the acquisition of one in isolation (see also van Rossum 1987).

3.3.2.2 Searching for the critical information

One of the critical questions in observational learning research concerns what information is selected and used by the learner to perform the skill as required.

Some researchers have proposed that the critical information relayed by a demonstration is the relative motions of the limbs or joints (i.e. how the limbs or joints move in relation to one another). Despite this proposal, there has only been relatively weak support in favour of this hypothesis and there is evidence that this *higher-order* information is not easily detected in unfamiliar and complex movements. Collier and Wright (1995) showed that extraction of relative timing information might only be possible for simple, more natural movements such as walking and running and that for unusual or sport-specific tasks, other information might be more important. Horn *et al.* (2002) showed that in learning a soccer-chip shot, model groups appeared to pick up more on information about the approach to the ball (e.g. number of steps), rather than the coordination pattern between the hip, knee and ankle as indicated through copied behaviours. There is also evidence that performers tune in to end-point features of the movement (such as the foot in a kicking skill or the hand in grasping skills), suggesting that the guiding information in a display may be more specific (or local) rather than global. Thus, although we might recognize the movements of a spin bowler, an overhead kick in soccer, the scaling of a hurdle, or a complicated turn on the ice or in the air by a figure skater, whether we understand what we see (i.e. the relationship between the joints and the relative motions in general) and can effectively relate what we see to our own bodies, is questionable. Indeed, the perceptual skill of differentiating across different spins or gymnastic stunts takes experience and knowledge of how these actions are performed. Further, although there might be evidence that a practised performer shows movements that are similar to a model in terms of the relationships across joints, the pattern of movement might have emerged as a consequence of trying to implement a strategy or copy the motions of one limb, not because of the pick-up and use of the relative motion information.

Further evidence that demonstrations fail to alert the naïve learner to the desired movement was shown in a two-handed coordination study where augmented feedback was withheld such that participants only saw a movement demonstration (Hodges *et al.* 2003). The authors used recognition tests after practice to determine whether the learners could discriminate the desired movement (i.e. the frequently presented demonstration) from non-desired, yet similar coordination movements. A number of individuals were unable to differentiate the required movement pattern from incorrect, yet similar movements. Therefore, not only was an undesirable strategy adopted due to difficulties performing the required movements, but participants were not aware that the movements were wrong. Interestingly, video feedback about the learner's own movement helped to overcome some of these difficulties in error detection and subsequently correction. If the performer is able to compare and contrast across information sources (i.e. this is what I should do and this is what I did), then subtle differences in the information content of the two displays should help make salient the required features of the movement. There are many examples in sports and arts where demonstrations need to be supplemented with video or mirrors to alert the performer as to discrepancies between their performance and that which is required.

3.3.2.3 Attentional focus

Another important mechanism influencing the effectiveness of instructions and demonstrations is that of the type of attentional focus encouraged by augmented information. There has been considerable evidence to show that limb-related instructions are actually harmful to performance and learning. In a series of experiments, Wulf and colleagues (see Wulf and Prinz 2001, for a review) manipulated attentional focus to either encourage attention to the limbs or *internal* features of the movement, or to the effects of the action on the environment, referred to as an *external* focus of attention. In skills such as pitching and putting a golf ball, serving a shot in tennis and volleyball, an attentional focus onto the club, racket or the ball and its effects was more beneficial for performance and learning than an attentional focus onto the limbs, such as the arms or hands. Even in skills requiring balance and slalom-like movements on a ski-simulator, again a focus onto an external cue, such as the apparatus or even a marker placed in a position far, rather than near a participant's feet, facilitated performance relative to a focus on the feet or a near cue.

As an instructor, the skill in delivering information is in focussing attention onto task success and external features of the movement, whilst also offering some prescriptive information concerning how to perform a task or what to change. In an experiment designed to both prescribe what to change, but also to decrease the attentional focus on to the limbs Hodges and Franks (2000) provided movement demonstrations in conjunction with instructions that directed the performer's attention to the feedback and the relationship between their arms and the feedback (i.e. external focus instructions). This type of instruction coupled with a demonstration was more beneficial for learning a coordination skill than a demonstration only. However, there was no significant benefit of this combined information over that of a control group who only received feedback. This finding leads to the suggestion that attentional focus might play a role in the effectiveness of pre-practice information but that this factor is not sufficient to explain why demonstrations fail to

34

lead to understanding of the desired movement especially for more complex, novel tasks.

One method which has shown to have some success in conveying a movement strategy, while keeping the learners focus externally directed, has been to provide a dynamic template of the external action effect. In serving a tennis ball, this could be the movements of the racket from a skilled performer (rather than the more traditional demonstration of the server's motion) or in kicking a soccer ball, this would be the desired ball flight. With this external template information the performer is able to focus on an external cue, but also refine their movements from trial to trial based on the degree of discrepancy between their trajectories and the trajectories of an expert. Todorov and colleagues (1997) found that providing the trajectory of a player's paddle and ball concurrently with those of a skilled player's paddle and ball (through a computer simulation) facilitated performance relative to a group provided with verbal feedback statements. Hodges *et al.* (2006) directly compared demonstrations and feedback relating to either movement form or ball trajectory in a soccer-chip shot. In retention, the ball-trajectory group was more accurate in achieving the height and distance requirements of the task, than the movement form group. Moreover, analysis of knee and hip angles showed that regardless of the type of presentation (a model or the ball), the types of movements displayed were similar (although only the form group adopted the same approach to the ball in terms of the number of steps). Similarly, Wulf and colleagues (2002) found that externally-related feedback statements provided during volleyball training improved service accuracy relative to internal or limb-related feedback statements, but that both types of feedback produced similar improvements in movement form. Further research is required to determine the effectiveness of these techniques in both the attainment of outcome success and bringing about a desired movement technique.

3.3.2.4 Implicit learning/re-investment

A final consideration is necessary when considering how and when to instruct during skill acquisition. There has been increasing evidence that the conditions where performance will be assessed will have a bearing on how successful various instructional approaches will be. Under conditions which promote competitive stress or anxiety people have been shown to show performance decrements when they had previously practised in an explicit compared to a less explicit or implicit manner (see Masters and Maxwell 2004, for a review). Explicit learning is promoted when explicit rules, instructions or detailed feedback are given which encourages the learner to think in a cognitively aware fashion about their performance. In contrast, implicit learning hinders the ability of the learner to formulate explicit rules about the motor skill. This is usually achieved through methods where the learner is required to perform a secondary, attention-demanding task during acquisition, therefore preventing the learner from thinking about the primary task during practice. Conditions where instructions are withheld are generally presumed to be less explicit in nature than environments where instructions or rules are provided, but these conditions might still result in the formulation of some rules which cause a more explicit than implicit type of learning strategy.

In an early study where performers practised golf putting, the explicitly instructed and non-instructed groups performed more accurately than the implicit group. This is perhaps not surprising in view of the additional attention demands required of implicit learning groups during practice. However, under manipulations designed to elicit stress in retention, the implicit group and to a somewhat lesser degree the non-instructed group, were less or not affected by this stress manipulation, in comparison to the explicitly instructed group (Masters 1992). It has been suggested that the mechanism responsible for these effects under stressful performance conditions is *re-investment* of knowledge into the control of actions. Once a skill is learnt or begins to improve there is evidence that the individual begins to worry less about how to perform the skill and monitoring performance in comparison to early in practice. As such, it is believed that the level of control switches as a function of practice (or at least is less conscious in nature after practice). However, under conditions of stress, it is proposed that the learner may start to think again about their performance, which is particularly detrimental if they have explicit rules to draw upon, causing a regression in performance.

Despite the fact that implicit learning results in performance benefits under conditions of anxiety, this condition of learning is somewhat impractical, not only because of the difficulty learning under secondary task conditions, but also the research has failed to show that implicit learning groups are able to acquire the skills as well as explicit groups. In an effort to rectify this position, Liao and Masters (2001) required participants to learn a table tennis serve with either explicit instructions, implicitly (while performing a secondary task), or by analogy (that is they were asked to imagine coming up the hypotenuse of a right angled triangle with the racket during the serve). The analogy learning group was not affected by the stress manipulation, which interfered with the performance of the explicit learning group. Additionally, the learning encouraged by analogy did not affect acquisition performance in contrast to the implicit learning manipulation. In the most recent review of this research, Masters and Maxwell (2004) suggest that learning with visual demonstrations, rather than verbally-based instructions, should be less impervious to this reinvestment under stress because of the role of verbally-based memory processes interfering with the control of motor performance. To date this has not been tested. Although this research is somewhat limited, what is an important message for teachers and coaches is that the conditions where the motor skill is to be evaluated need to be considered when assessing the benefits of a particular method of teaching. This research shows that knowledge-rich strategies for conveying information are not the most effective for later performance under competitive conditions.

3.3.3 Overview of instructions and demonstrations

Information which specifies what to do and how a movement should be changed can be beneficial to learning under conditions where it (a) dictates what the goal of the action should be, (b) when it provides a clear and obtainable reference-of-correctness such that comparisons can be made and (c) when valuable practice time can be circumvented by a strategy that has been shown to be the most effective and/or only way for performing the skill. Some of the negative effects of demonstrations and instructions relate to the fact that an unintended strategy might be conveyed in complex tasks where individuals have difficulty extracting the critical information and understanding the requirements. Even when this information can be adequately perceived and used by a performer, there are situations where it might be ineffectual or indeed detrimental to success on the task (such as when outcome success is not dependent on a specific technique or strategy). The fact that augmented information also directs attention is an important consideration when deciding how best to facilitate learning. The work of Wulf and colleagues (2002) strongly cautions against providing information which directs the learner's attention to the movement (i.e. internally), at the expense of a more effects-related, external focus of attention onto the apparatus, implement or even the augmented feedback. Moreover, an overly explicit, rule-based method of learning can result in performance detriments under conditions of competitive stress.

3.4 CONCLUSIONS

While it should be clear that feedback plays a primarily error-detection role and instructions and demonstrations play an error-correcting role, these roles are not always effectively served unless certain conditions are also met. For example, feedback presented on every trial during practice of a relatively simple motor skill will fail to encourage self-generated error-detection mechanisms necessary to ensure effective production when that information is no longer available. Even though a demonstration might effectively convey a strategy for performing a motor skill, under conditions where many different techniques can lead to successful performance or the technique is complicated such that little understanding is gained by merely watching, demonstrations alone are unlikely to facilitate learning and may fail to adequately alert to the desired movement and subsequently error. Combining different forms of augmented information might help to increase the saliency of desired movement features as has been suggested in earlier reviews of the feedback literature (e.g. Rothstein and Arnold 1976), and also the combination of verbal and visual information might benefit later retention and recall.

Although we have discussed a number of reasons why instructions, demonstrations and feedback might have negative consequences for performance and learning, what is important to remember is that all these mechanisms might be operating during the learning process. If a performer is unable to effectively work out what the task requirements are from a demonstration, then an ineffective strategy might be implemented on the basis of this information. This strategy could lead to a decrease in early variability in initial movement attempts, hindering the discovery of the required movement or a successful strategy for attaining task success. Additionally, the information conveyed could lead to a detrimental focus onto the movements and away from the effects of the movement on the environment. If the information is conveyed through detailed task instructions, under competitive situations performance might breakdown, in comparison to the performance of athletes whose practice conditions were less knowledge-heavy.

Often feedback will indirectly specify to the performer what needs changing without the need for additional instruction or demonstration. However, if change is not forthcoming from feedback alone, supplemental information will be needed. Whether this needs to relate to a desired form so that a reference-of-correctness can be formulated will be somewhat dependent on the type of skill to be acquired and perhaps the experience of the learner and conditions under which the skill will be required. Other, less knowledge-rich methods of instruction which encourage variability, problem-solving and attention to intrinsic sources of error might be effective for encouraging outcome and/or movement success. Indeed, although we have made little discussion as to the importance of cognitive effort in aiding memory and later retention, there is considerable

the provision of information

research in the field of education to show that active, problem-based methods of instruction and learning are more effective at encouraging long-term retention of information (Ramsden 1993). Discovery-based methods of instruction, where the learner is encouraged to find the solution or strategy for task success should help promote a deeper level of learning and understanding and later recall and transfer to new skills.

SUMMARY

What has been highlighted in this somewhat brief review of the literature on augmented information, is that there are no easy, hard and fast rules for effectively providing information to individuals wishing to acquire motor skills. What might be beneficial to performance in one situation, might not necessarily be beneficial in another and therefore it is critical to consider both the conditions of practice and later testing conditions where the skill will be required. The cognitive processes underlying improvements in practice, especially when a skill is being refined through augmented feedback, might be impaired in later conditions when the skill is required in the absence of the augmented information.

CHAPTER FOUR

VIDEO FEEDBACK AND INFORMATION TECHNOLOGIES

Dario G. Liebermann and Ian M. Franks

In this chapter we:

- discuss the popular use of video with regard to the effects on the skill acquisition process.
- suggest that video technology may be used to augment sensory input as well as enable the calculation of higher-order abstract information.

4.1 INTRODUCTION

Information technologies (IT) in general, and those that are based on video in particular, are today strongly associated with motor skill acquisition. IT enables an efficient management of movement-related information based on the assumption that feedback enhances the learning process. Although normal healthy individuals (Crossman 1959) or even patients (Taub *et al.* 2002) may naturally improve motor skill even without feedback (simply by practising), feedback affects learning. The evolution of the learning process over time depends on the quantity and the quality of the feedback provided to the performer during the motor training (Schmidt and Lee 2005). IT may act as 'feedback facilitators', which shorten acquisition time and exert influence on the rate of learning (i.e. the shape and slope of the learning curve). Although coaches are the main facilitators of feedback in daily training conditions, technologies aid not only in enhancing the augmented feedback provided by the coach but also its administration. Today, diverse feedback modes are integrated in IT, allowing for richer and more intense training experiences. Naturally, under such conditions performers are expected to achieve better results. The current chapter is concerned with the question of whether or not this is always the consequence of using IT. As example of the implementation of IT, the popular use of video will be presented with regard to the effects on the skill acquisition process.

4.2 EXTRINSIC AND INTRINSIC FEEDBACK IN SPORTS

Elite athletes and certainly novices improve motor performance based on the extrinsic or intrinsic feedback received about the movement errors. However, some individuals are able to translate such information to motor performance almost immediately, while others are not. It is assumed that learning time may be shortened while IT is implemented. But, why are some individuals better able to correct performance more efficiently and more effectively than others? The time it takes to adapt and master a skill may be regarded as a criterion for discriminating between different potential athletes.

A possible answer for the differences among individuals may be found in the individual capability to use the information available and the capability to associate the information provided with the actual movement performance. Information about 'how we actually performed' together and in parallel with information about 'how we feel about our motor performance' arrives to the central nervous system (CNS) via different neural paths. Cues about the outcomes of one's performance may arrive from outside, for example, via visual and/or auditory senses. On the other hand, cues about how one feels about a performance arrive from within the system, via kinaesthetic sensors and, in particular, via proprioceptive afferents. Accordingly, modifications in a movement are done by comparison between what we do (i.e. the actual motor act) and what we should do (i.e. a forward model or a virtual plan of how to perform). Specifically, such comparisons may be carried out by cerebellar structures (Miall et al. 1993). Matching motor plans with actual movements implies a correlation process. Lack of correlation between expected and actual performance is interpreted as a motor error, and thus, the movement should be corrected. In parallel, the plan should be updated via an internal close-loop process (feedback-dependent). Such learning models seem to be supported by neurobiological and neuroanatomical evidence (von Holst and Mittelstaedt 1950). Sperry's experiments (see Trevarthen 1990, for a review of his work) were among the first to show a functional correlation between neuroanatomy and performance. The behavioral studies of Held (1965) showed adaptation processes that may involve the previously hypothesized neural structures. In those adaptation experiments, performers received distorted visual input and this was enough to induce passive motor adaptations. Nevertheless, the greatest and sometimes irreversible sensorimotor changes were produced when the performers were active. This has been clearly shown in kittens in a series of classical experiments (Held and Hein 1958, 1963). Proprioceptive information arriving from within is then correlated with the visual input, and this implies an active type of learning and adaptation processes. While vision captures external events (including the outcomes of our own motor actions), proprioception relates to our internal motor experience. The former allows for 'a posteriori' corrections of motor errors while the latter enables online corrections during a motor performance. Reliance on vision may induce a dependence on external information, while reliance on proprioception enhances autonomic learning (i.e. independent of external sources of information). It should be mentioned that proprioception is a main sensory channel facilitating feedback. Proprioceptive information arrives via different sensors in the skin, muscles and joints during either static or dynamic conditions of self-motion of body segments or the whole body. The machinery encapsulated within the proprioceptive perception is suited to capture force, velocity, displacement and/or posture (i.e. static configurations of one segment relative to another or relative to the gravity vector). In brief, proprioception allows for sensing a movement (kinesthetic sense) via information about muscle tension, balance and exerted force (i.e. the sense of effort).

It should be mentioned that IT may be used to strengthen the link between movements and our internal experience about them. That is, feedback-based technologies play a role in facilitating the shift from dependence on extrinsic information (e.g. augmented feedback provided by a coach) to an independent performance that relies mainly on intrinsic sources (i.e. an autonomous performance).

4.3 VISUAL FEEDBACK, VIDEO AND MOTOR LEARNING

Visual information is massive and complex, and thus, it requires higher-order CNS involvement for processing and interpretation of the input. Vision enables the brain to recognize environmental features, faces and objects via centrally-located rode-cells (sensitive to colours) that are largely concentrated within the fovea. On the other hand, spatiotemporal features (e.g. an object's movement velocity) are mediated mainly by sensors in the periphery of the retina (outside the area of the fovea) where cone-cells (suitable for capturing minor changes in light-dark conditions) are widely dispersed. However, seeing is more than just sensing. Visual perception is intricate and involves higher-order cognitive processes. Learning via observation may, therefore, result in a slower process that should be accompanied by expert guidance about the specific events where to focus attention.

Video technology has significantly developed lately, and it is often a rich source of visual and auditory information for coaches and athletes. Video has significantly influenced movement evaluation and movement training methods. It is relatively low cost, it is accessible and portable. Using video, coaches can pinpoint the relevant information and, although athletes watching video of their own performances are passive observers, they can make use of the information in the future. Accompanied by a coach's supervision, athletes can focus on specific motor events recorded on video, watch the replays as many times as required, and later attempt to correct the errors.

One question that is of concern however, is: how should video-feedback be provided to make its application more efficient in sport situations? Trainers often use video replays of previous performances as training aids, but for the inexperienced athlete, the information provided by such a medium should always be re-directed to general performance parameters (e.g. general posture, timing errors). For the more experienced athletes, video-feedback and guidance should be specific and as close as possible to the real event (e.g. errors in implementation of a tactic, errors in specific positions during a skill, information about the center of mass kinematics).

Further to the popular use of video replay as we know it today, coaches may use video as a tool for the provision of elaborated feedback. For instance, coaches observe team performance and then analyse and quantify individual and group performances. A major setback is that such information is often provided after a performance has long ended. Some athletes may find it difficult to associate the expected movement pattern with the previous errors.

In some instances, video-based IT may even benefit coaches more than their own athletes because coaches are able to elaborate more on the performances and strategies. Athletes have to gain experience in order to use video information appropriately to correct motor skill or game situations. From video-based IT, coaches extract information about the qualitative aspects of performance and can extract quantitative information as well if they can access suitable software. The athlete then only receives the pre-processed information and is not involved in its analysis.

As discussed in detail in this text, technologies used for notational analyses in sports enable the integration of relevant applications (database, digital video coding and data storage) into a single system (PC and software) that allow an efficient shift from a data collection process to a data analyses stage, and from the latter to a synthesis of the performance. Some questions that still remain to be answered are: Should athletes participate in notational analyses as part of their skill training process? Is it beneficial for the athlete to get involved in biomechanical analyses of their own performances? Should the athlete become a coach of his/her own? More research is required in this regard, but given that notational analysis software and video technologies are widespread and athletes may be as suitable to handle them as their own coaches, it is possible to say that athletes with only minor expertise could operate and understand the information facilitated by such sport applications and further implement the feedback they elaborate to improve their skill.

4.4 QUALITATIVE FEEDBACK AND QUANTIFICATION OF PERFORMANCE USING VIDEO-BASED TECHNOLOGIES

One common learning strategy that enhances motor performance is observation and comparison. Demonstration and imitation may be fundamental to motor development and to motor learning because most movement features are expressed as extrinsic (external) kinematic variables that are observable. These features are naturally perceived via vision (e.g. movement duration, movement path geometric features and their temporal evolution). Imitation of an observed movement might actually reduce complexity of the motor learning process by allowing a performer to bypass the dynamic aspects of a motor plan (i.e. the muscle moments and joint torques required to move; Wolpert et al. 1995).

Software developed for implementing motor imitation is readily available in sport. Basic hardware technology coupled with appropriate software enables users to split a computer screen in two halves. In one half, the actual performance is observed and in the other half a model performance is presented. The same technology enables a user to superimpose two synchronized video footages. Each video-taped performance can be viewed as continuous replays or as single frames (one frame after the other).

In recent years, improvements in the interface between video cameras and PCs have facilitated the process. Video-feedback for example can be provided at the training site to the extent that comparisons are immediate, at the end of the last motor performance. The number of such video-based technologies in sport has grown significantly, and consequently, learning by comparison is now

44

popular. The readers are encouraged to search the web for keywords such as 'video analysis sports', 'video technology sports' or any other combination of relevant words to witness the growing number of companies and uses of video-based systems at the service of sport. Given the wide range of options, it is recommended to focus on those technologies that allow a fast digital blending of images (i.e. a superposition of two appropriately scaled, translated and rotated video sequences). Such software tools enable performers to compare their own movements and, eventually, to match themselves to elite athletes simply by retrieving performances from a 'video repository'. This may prove to be a power-ful motor learning tool, whereas essential differences between two observed performances are exposed.

Consistency is a feature of well-learned movements. Athletes should aim at maintaining the same correct motor performance. Nevertheless, no two per-formances are identical and certainly no two athletes are equal. Therefore, what is optimal for one athlete is not for another (Bartlett 1999). Comparison and imitation of performances has not yet been validated as a general learning strat-egy, and only highly competitive athletes and experienced coaches may be able to take advantage of such technologies. As mentioned earlier, visual feedback provided via video or other means may sometimes be too complex, and there-fore, beginners may find the use of video and comparison of performance quite ineffective. Finally, one should remember that video images are only two-dimensional representations of a three-dimensional reality. In fact, all move-ments take place in three-dimensions. Only experienced people may be able to reconstruct a three-dimensional movement sequence in their mind and even mentally rotate the imagined performance, after receiving only a series of two-dimensional views that are kept in memory for a few seconds. Such a process is indeed complex, and cannot allow for immediate feedback. With further complexity of an imagined three-dimensional rotation, processing time becomes longer (Shepard and Metzler 1971; Cooper and Shepard 1973). Cog-nitive involvement in such tasks has been specifically addressed in Shepard's early experiments. Shepard and colleagues also showed that a gradual mental rotation of an object increases the response time during the actual performance, while anticipatory mental rotation of the same object (before starting the motor performance) reduces the response time.

Quantitative information provided to novice performers via video raises similar concerns as regards qualitative movement information. The major concern is the complexity of the quantitative information. There are many video-based systems today that enable biomechanical analyses of sport performances. These can be based either on two-dimensional views or on combinations of such views into three-dimensional simulations of motor performances via Direct Linear Transformation (DLT) algorithms. Such systems synthesize movement to its essential mechanical characteristics. For example, they may provide information about the direction and magnitude of the centre of mass of the performer. However, one may wonder what the meaning of such information is for the inexperienced athlete. The level of abstraction of such feedback is high. We should assume that the more complex and abstract the information, the less efficient such feedback would be. Only simple and specific kinematic variables may be appropriate for most individuals. Although video analysis technology makes such feedback readily available, the coach should be selective about what information to provide to the athlete.

Temporal features of movement, for example, are available using any affordable video cameras. Commercially available cameras generally use time-codes based on temporal accuracies of a 50 Hz or 60 Hz frame/s (0.016–0.02 s between each recorded frame, respectively). Frame-by-frame movement features (such as the postural set, as defined by joint angles) could be provided to any athlete. Video-analyses systems allow for immediate measurements of simple quantitative information such as the approximate time of a performance (e.g. temporal asymmetries between the two legs during the swing phase while walking). Such information could be extracted easily and provided to the athlete immediately as KR feedback.

4.5 QUANTITATIVE FEEDBACK DERIVED FROM COMPLEX SIMULATIONS

An alternative use of kinematic information, aside from the general and simple descriptive information previously mentioned, is for building models and for simulating optimum sport techniques. Models allow coaches to become aware of potentially unnoticed weaknesses of a motor performance. The information retrieved from models may not be directly applicable for an athlete. Only the experienced coach could use such a feedback once it is understood, interpreted and translated. In this case, the coach acts only as a venue to transmit and explain complex information to the performer. Modelling and simulation based on video-based recorded performances enables creating optimized movements (e.g. What would a swim stroke look like if we reduced energy expenditure?) or creating maximized performances (e.g. What would a maximal-distance hammer throw look like if energy expenditure were reduced to a minimum?). Models are based on equations of constraint that limit the endless number of solutions available to the motor system while producing a movement. The computer is only a mean for fast calculation and visualization of the virtual movement (i.e. the simulation). Computer graphic power is therefore important in the process. In fact, it may be the main goal of the modelling and simulation strategy because visual comparisons between real and computer-simulated (optimized) performances are essential. A major problem with such an approach is its complexity and the time-consuming processes involved. Provided that only essential features of a movement are calculated by the model, results and visualizations can be provided immediately. Hubbard and Alaways (1989) were among the first that reported an implementation of such an approach. They measured simple kinematic variables at release during a javelin throws and optimized the flight path by instructing the performers to change the angle of release, the angle of attack and the pitch rate, and provided feedback about actual and expected results after each throw.

It appears that the costs of the quantification of sport motor performance may not be justified. The technologies and expertise required for creating models and running simulations is 'overkill' for most sports. The reality is that most coaches and athletes would simply rely on their hands-on experience and their intuition rather than on information provided by biomechanical models. However, this does not imply that such an approach should not be used. Perhaps in the future, some of the complexity can be overcome and simple understandable models could be developed.

4.6 WATCHING VERSUS PERFORMING MOVEMENTS IN THREE-DIMENSIONS: VIRTUAL AND REAL ENVIRONMENTS

A common assumption of learning by imitation or comparison from video images is that athletes are able to translate two- or three-dimensional simulated feedback into action. However, in reality we live in a three-dimensional world and we move relative to three-dimensional surroundings. Therefore, a relatively new application of video-based technologies is the generation of virtual environments where the subject perceives a three-dimensional world and feels as if performance were in realistic conditions of training. Specific performance technology (e.g. a racing bicycle) may be temporally coupled with stereo views of the environment that enables creating three-dimensional effects. The principle is simple. Each eye receives a slightly different perspective of the same virtual images, and fusion of the two planar views (one for each eye of the same object) takes place in higher brain centres. This is known as an augmented virtual reality that is used for training movements in different sport- and non-sporting scenarios (Feiner 2002). A potential advantage of using virtual environments is that a coach may manipulate feedback to enhance motor learning by allowing training in unknown conditions or using exaggerated feedbacks that cause motor compensation. Some technologies have specifically been developed to enhance feedback in three-dimensional virtual settings. Research suggests that feedback during virtual reality training may accelerate the learning process compared to standard coaching techniques (Todorov et al. 1997). However, for precise actions (as opposed to the gross movements cited above), this is not recommended way to train.

To summarize, training in virtual reality settings may enhance motivation to learn, at least while the conditions challenge the performer. Sometimes the mere practice in a novel setting is just enough to captivate some individuals (e.g. children and young athletes). It should be mentioned that in spite of the widespread use of virtual reality training, the information about its effectiveness in sports is limited. In clinical conditions, in some industry application and in the military the results are positive. However, further research is required to support the use of such virtual settings in sports.

4.7 VIDEO TECHNOLOGY AND TEMPORAL FEEDBACK

It has been suggested previously that video technology enables coding time information. Such information can be useful for the improvement of motor skill under the assumption that timing or rhythmical constraints solve spatial aspects of movement. The duration of the movement, for example, seems to be perceived and learned better than other aspects even when the performer does not pay attention (Liebermann et al. 1988). Temporal feedback or rhythmical cueing may prescribe the spatial configuration of a movement. Thus, the use of time information conveyed via visual or auditory feedback is often used in practice. Coaches whistle or clap their hands to convey information about how to perform. Temporal information about one's performance may be extracted from simple time codes inherent in the video frames and this information can be reduced to a rhythmical structure of the movement, as suggested in the previous section. The fact that humans are able to extrapolate from temporal information a spatial configuration of a movement became evident in the early experiments of Johansson (1975). This researcher showed that visual perception, which includes higher-order cognitive processing, may be used to reconstruct a complete movement pattern from limited visual inputs. Johansson showed that a body in the dark, as defined by markers attached to the joints of the performer, may be easily used to identify a type of movement (e.g. dancing or walking). The same information may even be used to discriminate among people of different identities or gender, by simply looking at the moving markers (Johansson 1975).

Using a reverse engineering approach, a mechanically-optimal movement pattern like a whip-like action (Chapman and Sanderson 1990) may be characterized by the specific inter-joint timing that can be transformed into identifiable and harmonic auditory cues (i.e. a motor melody). A rhythmical structure that corresponds to an idealized mechanical system could lead to the use of the appropriate inter-segmental coordination underlying for example actions that resemble catapult or whip-like motions (Wilson and Watson 2003). In the past, such an approach has been implemented by Liebermann (1997) for improving the tennis serve of elite athletes.

4.8 IMMEDIACY AS A PRE-REQUISITE FOR THE EFFECTIVE USE OF FEEDBACK DURING SKILL ACQUISITION

Coaches may often assume that immediate feedback is a pre-requisite to improve skills. Thus, it is also assumed that technologies providing immediate feedback are beneficial for learning. However, this may not always be the case. Sometimes, it may be just as effective to give feedback information after some long delay, in a specific and limited manner. This is because too much information interferes with performance and sometimes athletes need time to assimilate the information (Salmoni et al. 1984). Augmented feedback that is provided after each trial is counterproductive in the sense that the athlete becomes dependent on such external information instead of becoming independent. Recall that in order to learn movement based on intrinsic feedback the subject must educate proprioception. This is a process whereby movement outcomes are associated with the afferent information. Feedbacks of different kind become only indispensable at the beginning of the learning process. As skill acquisition progresses, and performers gain experience, augmented feedback is not essential (Winstein and Schmidt 1989; Hodges and Franks 2002). That is, as skill improves, feedback allowance should be reduced progressively until only specialized and elaborated summary feedback enhances performance (Schmidt et al. 1990).

SUMMARY

The present chapter suggests that video technology may be used to augment sensory input as well as to enable the calculation of higher-order abstract information. Information technologies not only enhance feedback but also make it more efficient. IT oriented to sport have converged into efficient and easy to use notational analyses applications and software that allow for feedback regulation and immediacy of feedback provision. IT makes feedback information manageable, efficient and specifically adjusted for each individual need. Some of the new software technologies are relatively inexpensive. However, the hardware that may be used to convey objective information (biomechanical-related feedback) may still involve very high costs. Among the most common and useful technologies presented and recommended in this chapter were video-based technologies. Coaches might still need training in order to make efficient use of video. Combinations of video with appropriate notational analysis software are available. The gains of such technologies are various but the main advantages are objectivity and accuracy of the information, visualization power, image comparison and blending features and primarily the ease by which these new technologies allow administering feedback that ultimately are expected to enhance motor performance.

CHAPTER FIVE

AN OVERVIEW OF THE DEVELOPMENT OF NOTATIONAL ANALYSIS

Mike Hughes

In this chapter we:

- aim to offer as much information about notation systems as possible.
- have written the chapter in the form of a literature review of the research work already published in this field. Although this is written for, and by, sports scientists, it is hoped that anyone with an interest in this rapidly growing area of practice and research will find it interesting and rewarding.

5.1 INTRODUCTION

It is not possible to trace the work of all those coaches and sports scientists who have contributed in one way or another to notational analysis. A large number of these innovative people did not see the point of publishing the work that they did, regarding it as merely part of their job and consequently cannot receive the just acclaim that they deserve here in this compilation. There is no doubt that all the published workers mentioned within the following chapter could cite five or six other 'unsung' innovators who, either introduced them into the field, or gave them help and advice along the way.

Literature in notational analysis has been difficult to find until recently. Researchers have had to find different types of journals that would accept their papers, and so they are spread throughout many different disciplines. This chapter should help initiate a search for information on a specific sport or technique.

There are a number of texts that contain sections devoted to research in notational analysis. The best of these was, until recently, copies of the proceedings of four conferences on football (Reilly 1997; Reilly et al. 1993, 1997, 2001) and racket sports, respectively (Reilly et al. 1995; Lees et al. 1998). There is also a book Science of Soccer, again edited by Reilly (1997), which is a compendium of contributions by different sports scientists on the application of their own specialisms to soccer. There are three chapters in this book that are based on notational analysis and review current developments and ideas in the field.

A big step forward, to enable notational analysts to share their research and ideas, has been the introduction of world conferences on notational analysis of sport. The proceedings of these conferences offer an invaluable compilation of notational analysis. The presentations of the first two conferences, that were in Liverpool and Cardiff, respectively, are compiled in one book, Notational Analysis of Sport I & II (Hughes and Franks 1997) and the first section has a number of keynote speakers who present a varied but enlightened overview of different aspects of notational analysis. The third conference was in Turkey; Hughes (2000a) edited the proceedings, Notational Analysis of Sport III. The fourth was in Porto, Portugal and the book Notational Analysis of Sport IV was produced by Hughes and Tavares (2001). 'Pass.com' are the proceedings of the Fifth World Conference of Performance Analysis of Sport, which was combined with the Third International Symposium of Computers in Sports Science (Hughes and Franks 2001). Over the 18 months preceding this conference, biomechanists and notational analysts had come together, at the request of the British Olympic Association, to explore common areas of interest and had agreed on a generic title of 'performance analysis' – hence the change in the title of the world conference. Each of these books of proceedings are sectionalized; first the keynote presentations and then into different sports or equipment development, for ease of access for the reader. The keynote speakers at pass.com presented their papers and they were reviewed and edited into the first edition of the International Journal of Performance Analysis of Sport (eIJPAS) (http://ramiro.catchword.com). This is organized and managed by the Centre for Performance Analysis in UWIC, Cardiff. So now we have, at last, a research journal that is for performance analysis. At that moment in time, not many biomechanists were using it, so it was principally concerned with notational analysis. Since then however, the number of editions per year has increased to three, so there is a growing number of publications each year. The two most recent world conferences, in Belfast, 2004 and in Hungary, 2006, also increased proportionately in size and this is reflected in the breadth and quality of the proceedings (O'Donoghue and Hughes 2004; Dancs et al. 2006).

This review is not aimed at being as comprehensive as possible, there are many reviews in the literature (Hughes and Franks 2004; O'Donoghue *et al.* 2003; Hughes and Hughes 2005; James 2006) but it is structured to follow the main developments in notational analysis. After tracing a historical perspective of the roots of notation, the applications of these systems to sport are then developed. These early systems were all hand notation systems; their emerging sophistication is followed here until the advent of computerized notation. Although the emphasis is given to the main research developments in both hand and computerized notational systems, where possible the innovations of new systems and any significant data outputs within specific sports are also assessed.

5.2 THE DEVELOPMENT OF SPORT-SPECIFIC NOTATION SYSTEMS (HAND NOTATION)

The earliest publication in notation of sport is that by Fullerton (1912), which explored the combinations of players batting, pitching and fielding and the probabilities of success. But probably the first attempt to devise a notation system specifically for sport analysis was that by Messersmith and Corey (1931), who attempted to notate distance covered by specific basketball players during a match. Messersmith lead a research group at Indiana State University that initially explored movement in basketball, but went on to analyse American football and field hockey. Lyons (1996) presented a fascinating history of Messersmith's life for those interested in understanding the man behind the work.

The first publication of a comprehensive racket sport notation was not until 1973, when Downey developed a detailed system which allowed the comprehensive notation of lawn tennis matches. Detail in this particular system was so intricate that not only did it permit notation of such variables as shots used, positions, etc. but it catered for type of spin used in a particular shot. The Downey notation system has served as a useful base for the development of systems for use in other racket sports, specifically badminton and squash.

An alternative approach towards match analysis was exemplified by Reep and Benjamin (1968), who collected data from 3,213 matches between 1953 and 1968. They were concerned with actions such as passing and shooting rather than work-rates of individual players. They reported that 80 per cent of goals resulted from a sequence of three passes or less. Fifty per cent of all goals came from possession gained in the final attacking quarter of the pitch.

Bate (1988) found that 94 per cent of goals scored at all levels of international soccer were scored from movements involving four or less passes, and that 50–60 per cent of all movements leading to shots on goal originated in the attacking third of the field. Bate explored aspects of chance in soccer and its relation to tactics and strategy in the light of the results presented by Reep and Benjamin (1968). It was claimed that goals are not scored unless the attacking team gets the ball and one, or more, attacker(s) into the attacking third of the field. The greater the number of possessions a team has, the greater chance it has of entering the attacking third of the field, therefore creating more opportunities to score. The higher the number of passes per possession, the lower the total number of match possessions, the total number of entries into the attacking third, and the total chances of shooting at goal. Thus, Bate rejected the concept of possession football and favoured a more direct strategy. He concluded that to increase the number of scoring opportunities a team should play the ball forward as often as possible; reduce square and back passes to a minimum; increase the number of long passes forward and forward runs with the ball and play the ball into space as often as possible.

These recommendations are in line with what is known as the 'direct method' or 'long-ball game'. The approach has proved successful with some teams in the lower divisions of the English League. It is questionable whether it provides a recipe for success at higher levels of play, but these data have fuelled a debate that continued through several decades. Hughes and Franks (2005) tried to demonstrate that perhaps these analyses of the data were too simplistic and that broader non-dimensional analyses give a different answer.

The definitive motion analysis of soccer, using hand notation, was by Reilly and Thomas (1976), who recorded and analysed the intensity and extent of discrete activities during match-play. They combined hand notation with the use of an audio tape recorder to analyse in detail the movements of English First Division soccer players. They were able to specify work-rates of the players in different positions, distances covered in a game and the percentage time of each position in each of the different ambulatory classifications. They also found that typically, a player carries the ball for less than 2 per cent of the game. Reilly (1997) has continually added to this database enabling him to define clearly the specific physiological demands in soccer, as well as all the football codes. The work by Reilly and Thomas has become a standard against which other similar research projects can compare their results and procedures.

Several systems have been developed for the notation of squash, the most prominent being that by Sanderson and Way (1977). Most of the different squash

an overview of the development of notational analysis

Shot Codes

Drive	|
Xdrive	/
Drop	•
Boast (B'hand)	⊂; (F'hand) ⊃
Volley	V
Lob	L
Serve	S

Combinations

e.g.   Xdrop   /·
        Volley-Lob   VL

Figure 5.1 The shot codes, or suggestive symbols, used by Sanderson (1983) for his data gathering system for squash

notation systems possess many basic similarities. The Sanderson and Way method made use of illustrative symbols to notate seventeen different strokes, as well as incorporating court plans for recording accurate positional information. The major emphasis of this system was on the gathering of information concerning 'play patterns' as well as the comprehensive collection of descriptive match data. Sanderson felt that 'suggestive' symbols were better than codes, being easier for the operator to learn and remember, and devised the code system shown in Figure 5.1. These were used on a series of court representations, one court per activity, so that the player, action and position of the action were all notated (see Figure 5.2). In addition, outcomes of rallies were also recorded, together with the score and the initials of the server. The position was specified using an acetate overlay with the courts divided into 28 cells. The system took an estimated 5–8 h of use and practice before an operator was sufficiently skilful to record a full match actually during the game. Processing the data could take as long as 40 h of further work. Sanderson (1983) used this system to gather a database and show that squash players play in the same patterns, winning or losing, despite the supposed coaching standard of '. . . if you are losing change your tactics'. It would seem that the majority of players are unable to change the patterns in which they play.

Most of the data that Sanderson and Way presented was in the form of frequency distributions of shots with respect to position on the court. This was then a problem of presenting data in three dimensions – two for the court and one for the value of the frequency of the shots. Three-dimensional graphics at that time were very difficult to present in such a way that no data were lost, or, that was easily visualized by those viewing the data. Sanderson overcame this problem by

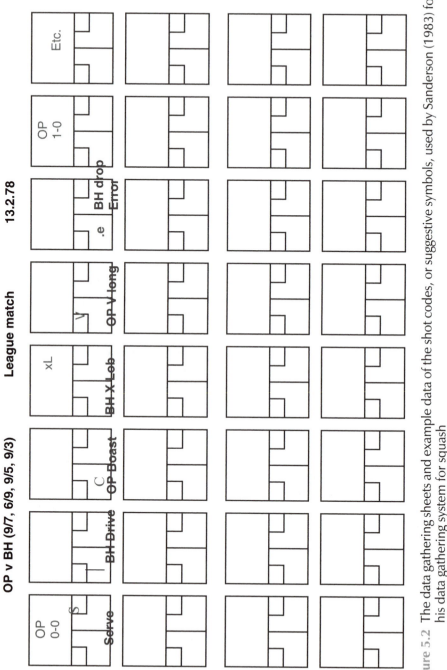

Figure 5.2 The data gathering sheets and example data of the shot codes, or suggestive symbols, used by Sanderson (1983) for his data gathering system for squash

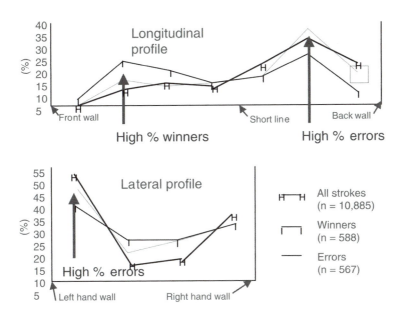

Figure 5.3 Example from some of Sanderson's data showing frequency distributions of all shots, winners and errors

using longitudinal and lateral summations (Figure 5.3). Not only were the patterns of rally-ending shots examined in detail, but also those shots (N-1), that preceded the end shot, and the shots that preceded those (N-2). In this way, the rally ending patterns of play were analysed. The major pitfall inherent in this system, as with all long-hand systems, was the time taken to learn the system and the sheer volume of raw data generated, requiring so much time to process it.

Penalties are now a subject of myth, romance, excitement, dread, fear and pressure – depending upon whether you are watching or taking them. They have either helped careers of footballers or destroyed them. Yet little research has been completed on penalty kicks. Using a hand notation system, Hughes and Wells (2002) notated and analysed 129 penalties with an intention to examine:

■ the time in preparing the shot
■ the number of paces taken to approach the ball
■ the speed of approach
■ the pace of the shot
■ its placement and the outcome.

In addition, the actions of the goalkeeper were notated – position, body shape, movements as the player approached, his first movements and the subsequent direction, the outcome. Not all video recordings enabled all of these data to be notated, so in the subsequent analyses some of the totals are 128 and 127.

A summary of their findings are presented below:

- One in five penalties were saved (20 per cent; 3/15), one in 15 missed (7 per cent; 1/15) and three in four resulted in a goal (73 per cent; 11/15)
- Players using a fast run up had 25 per cent of their efforts saved, because the player then tried either 50 per cent or 75 per cent power
- Best success ratios are from an even run up of 4, 5 and 6 paces
- There is no laterality in the success ratios – left footers and right footers have the same success percentages
- No shots above waist height were saved
- In every case, the goalkeeper moved forward off the line before the ball was struck
- Although there is only a small data set, the goalkeepers who did not dive to either side while the striker approached the ball, had the best save and miss ratios.

This is a good example of hand notation providing accurate data in this age of computers, in fact the data were then entered into Access, and analysed through this database, a method used more and more. In addition, because of the nature of these data, and a performance analysis of what is virtually a closed skill situation, the data analysis provides a clear picture of the most efficient ways of penalty taking and saving.

5.3 INTRODUCTION TO COMPUTERIZED NOTATIONAL ANALYSIS

Using computers does introduce extra problems of which the system-users and programmers must be aware. Increases in error possibilities are enhanced by either operator errors, or hardware and software errors. The former type of error is when the system-user unintentionally enters incorrect data, e.g. presses the wrong key on the keyboard. Any system is subject to perception-error where the observer misunderstands an event, or incorrectly fixes a position but the computer-operator interface can result in the operator thinking the correct data is being entered when it is not. This is particularly so in realtime analysis when the data must be entered quickly.

Hardware and software errors are introduced by the machinery itself, or the programs of instructions controlling the operation of the computer. Careful programming can eradicate this latter problem. To minimize both of these types of problems, careful validation of computerized notation systems must be carried out. Results from both the computerized system and a hand system should be compared and the accuracy of the computerized system quantitatively assessed.

Computers have been used by notational analysts since PCs became available – and even before then, Hughes (1985) was executing post-event analysis of hand notation data gathered on squash. Notational analysis readily embraced the advantages that computers brought and, as a discipline, has strived to keep abreast of the technological advances in the electronic industries, utilizing the new developments in video and computing to ease data collection and enhance the interpretation of data analyses. Franks *et al.* (1983a) maintained that these forms of technology are likely to enhance manipulation and presentation due to improved efficiency. This postulation is supported by the work of Hughes (1985).

Four major purposes of notation have been delineated they are:

1   Analysis of movement
2   Tactical evaluation
3   Technical evaluation
4   Statistical compilation.

Many of the traditional systems outlined above are concerned with the statistical analysis of events which previously had to be recorded by hand. The advent of online computer facilities overcame this problem, since the game could then be digitally represented first, via data collection directly onto the computer, and then later documented via the response to queries pertaining to the game (Franks *et al.* 1983a). The major advantage of this method of data collection is that the game is represented in its entirety and stored in ROM or on disk. A database is therefore initiated and is a powerful tool once manipulated.

Team sports have the potential to benefit immensely from the development of computerized notation. The sophistication of data manipulation procedures available can aid the coach in their efforts to ameliorate performance. Many of the traditional systems outlined above are concerned with the statistical analysis of events which previously had to be recorded by hand. The advent of online computer facilities overcame this problem, since the game could then be digitally represented first, via data collection directly onto the computer, and then later documented via the response to queries pertaining to the game.

The information derived from this type of computerized system can be used for several purposes as suggested by Franks *et al.* (1983a):

1   immediate feedback
2   development of a database
3   indication of areas requiring improvement
4   evaluation
5   as a mechanism for selective searching through a video recording of the game.

All of the above functions are of paramount importance to the coaching process, the initial *raison d'etre* of notational analysis. The development of a database is a crucial element, since it is sometimes possible, if the database is large enough, to formulate predictive models as an aid to the analysis of different sports, subsequently enhancing future training and performance.

5.4 SOME RESEARCH USING COMPUTER SYSTEMS

One of the first developments in computerized notation has been the development of a mini system devised by Franks *et al.* (1983a). Franks configured a keyboard on a mini-computer to resemble the layout of a soccer field and designed a program which yielded frequency tallies of various features of play. The path of the ball during the game was followed, so off-ball incidents were considered extraneous. A video was time-locked into the system so that relevant sections of the match could be replayed visually alongside the computer analysis.

An essential pre-requisite of evaluation was that it must be carried out as objectively as possible. Franks *et al.* (1983b: 77) maintained that:

> 'if it can be measured – it is fact, if it cannot be measured – it remains opinion', also applies to the coaching arena

It was suggested as a result of the analysis, that it would be extremely beneficial to performance if coaches could advise players to keep the number of passes in sequence down to three of less. This application of the research could be improved and a more thorough analysis of the parameters would be required to enhance the result. Minimal consideration was given to the number of games to be notated prior to the establishment of a recognized system of play. This is an important point, since any fluctuation in the patterns and profile will affect the deduced consequences, particularly with reference to the match outcome. Teams may also vary their system and pattern of play according to opponents, although these factors are not considered. Furthermore, the existence of patterns of play peculiar to individual players was not illustrated. It is in this area that the study by Church and Hughes (1986) concentrated, in an attempt to investigate the presence of patterns of play in a soccer team and whether any reasons can be found to explain the results.

Church and Hughes developed a computerized notation system for analysing soccer matches using an alternative type of keyboard, called a concept keyboard. This is a touch sensitive pad that can be programmed to accept input to the computer. This permitted pitch representation to be graphically accurate and action and player keys to be specific and labelled. This considerably reduced the learning time of the system, and made the data input quicker and more accurate. The system enabled an analysis of patterns of play on a team and player level, and with respect to match outcome. An analysis of six matches played by Liverpool during the 1985/6 season resulted in a number of conclusions, the most important of which were:

1   A greater number of passes were attempted when losing than when winning.
2   Possession was lost more often when losing.
3   A greater number of shots were taken when losing than when winning.

Hughes and colleagues (1988) used the same concept keyboard and hardware system developed by Church and Hughes (1986), but with modified software, to analyse the 1986 World Cup finals. Patterns of play of successful teams, those teams that reached the semi-finals, were compared with those of unsuccessful teams, i.e. teams that were eliminated at the end of the first rounds. A summary of the main observations is as follows:

1   Successful teams played significantly more touches of the ball per possession than unsuccessful teams.
2   The unsuccessful teams ran with the ball and dribbled the ball in their own defensive area in different patterns to the successful teams. The latter played up the middle in their own half; the former used the wings more.
3   This pattern was also reflected in the passing of the ball. The successful teams approached the final sixth of the pitch by playing predominantly in the central areas while the unsuccessful teams played significantly more to the wings.

4   Unsuccessful teams lost possession of the ball significantly more in the final one-sixth of the playing area both in attack and defence.

Hughes (1985) modified the method of Sanderson and Way so that the hand-notated data then could be processed on a mainframe computer. The manual method was modified so that a match could be notated live at courtside using a microcomputer. Because of difficulties with the speed of the game and the storage capacity only one player was notated. Hughes established a considerable database on different standards of squash players and reviewed his work in squash in 1986. He examined and compared the differences in patterns of play between recreational players, country players and nationally ranked players, using the computerized notational analysis system he had developed. The method involved the digitization of all the shots and court positions, and entered these via the QWERTY keyboard.

A detailed analysis of the frequency distribution of shots showed that the recreational players were not accurate enough to sustain a tactical plan, being erratic with both their straight drives and their cross-court drives. They played more short shots, and although they hit more winners they also hit more errors.

The county players played a simple tactical game generally, keeping the ball deep and predominantly on the backhand, the weaker side of most players. They hit significantly more winners with straight drives. Their short game, consisting of boasts, drops and rally-drops, although significantly less accurate than the nationally ranked players, was significantly more accurate than the recreational players.

The nationally ranked players, because of their far greater fitness, covering ability and better technique, employed the more complex tactics, using an 'all-court' game. Finally, the serves of the county players and the recreational players, because of shorter rallies, assumed greater importance than the serves of the ranked players.

Hughes et al. (1989) were interested in analysing the motions of athletes of any sport, without having to resort to the long and arduous job of cinematographic analysis, nor the semi-qualitative methods associated with notational methods, used live or from video. They attempted to combine the best of both systems without the faults of either. They designed a tracking system that enabled the use of the immediacy of video, and, by using mixed images on the same VDU screen, accurate measurements of the velocities and accelerations of the players, usually associated with film analysis. A 'Power Pad' was used to gather positional data along with the time base. The playing area representation on the Power Pad was video-taped and its image mixed with that of the subject tape. Careful alignment of the images of the two 'playing areas', enabled the subject, and the tracking stylus on the bit pad, to be both viewed at the same time, and an accurate tracing of the movements of the player onto the simulated playing area in real time. A careful validation of the system showed its accuracy and the short learning time required by operators.

Hughes and Franks (1991) utilized this system and applied it to squash comparing the motions of players of differing standards. They presented comparative profiles for four different standards of players, spanning from club players to the world elite. The profiles consisted of analyses of distance travelled, velocities and accelerations during rallies. The work provides reference data against which physiological studies of squash play can be compared. In addition, the distance travelled during rallies by both recreational and regular club players was surprisingly short, the mean distance being approximately 12 m for both top club players and recreational players. Hughes and Franks were able to present suggestions about specific training drills for the sport. Their system could also compare the individual profile of a player to those of his peer group so giving a direct expression of his relative fitness, as an example they chose to analyse some of the reasons why Jahangir Khan has dominated squash for so long. This profile was of the 1989, and seven times World Champion Jehangir Khan, compared with the top six in the world (which data included his own profile). The data clearly showed the vast physical advantage that he has over the best athletes in the world at this sport.

A more recent innovation in attempting to solve the problems of data entry was the utilization of a new language, visual basic, which enables a graphical user interface, that is, the operator enters data by moving an arrow round the screen using the 'mouse' and clicking to enter a selected item. All IBM-compatible systems can run these software packages. This language was used to write a system for squash, which was used by Brown and Hughes (1995) to examine the effectiveness of quantitative feedback to squash players. While this system of data entry will not be as quick as the concept keyboard, when used by a fully trained and experienced operator, it is again very easy to use, attractive to the eye and the extra hardware requirements are nil. It was used by Hughes and Knight (1995) to examine the differences in the game of squash when played under 'point-per-rally' scoring as opposed to the more traditional English scoring. The former had been introduced to most senior international tournaments because it was believed to promote more 'attacking' play, shorter rallies and hence make the game more attractive. It was found that the rallies were slightly longer on average (not significantly), so that there were more winners and the same errors – this being attributed to the lower height of the 'tin' under these new rules.

A similar system was used Hughes and Clarke (1995) to analyse the differences in the playing patterns of players at Wimbledon, on grass, to those of players at the Australian Open, on a synthetic surface. They found very significant differences between the two surfaces, particularly with the ball-in-play time. This averaged about 10 per cent for the synthetic surface (14 min in an average match of just over 2 h), while it was as low as 5 per cent on grass (7 min in an average match of just over 2 h). This work, that of Hughes and Knight (1995) and some analyses of squash tournaments using tennis scoring, prompted Hughes (1995a) to analyse and recommend a new scoring system in squash to try to make the game more attractive. Hughes recognized the need to shorten the cycles of play leading to 'critical' points in squash – currently, it takes about 15–20 min to reach a game-ball – by having more, shorter games, more critical points will arise and this will raise the levels of excitement and crowd interest. Badminton has the same problems with its scoring systems and the ensuing activity cycles.

McGarry and Franks (1994) created a stochastic model of championship squash match-play, which inferred prospective from previous performance through forecasting shot response and associated outcome from the preceding shot. The results were restricted because it was found that players produced the same patterns of responses against the same opponent ($p > 0.25$) but an inconsistent response was found when competing against different opponents ($p < 0.25$). This contradicts earlier work by Sanderson (1983) who found that squash players played in the same patterns against different opponents, whether winning or losing, but this may well be a function of the finer degree to which McGarry and Franks were measuring the responses of the players. However, these results led to further analysis by these authors (1995) of behavioural response to a preceding athletic event and they again found the same results. They confirmed that sport analysis can reliably assume a prescriptive application in preparing for future athletic competition, but only if consistent behavioural data can be established. The traditional planning of match strategies from a priori sport information (scouting) against the same opponent would otherwise seem to be an expedient and necessary constraint. A review of work completed in the computerized analysis of racket sports (Hughes 1995b), together with a number of papers in match analysis of racket sports, is included in *Science and Racket Sports* (Reilly et al. 1995).

Murray and colleagues (1998) researched into the effect of computerized notational analysis as feedback on improving squash performance. This study used a similar method to that of Brown and Hughes (1995) on the effectiveness of quantitative and qualitative feedback in squash. It was concluded that both groups reacted positively to the feedback provided and the feedback from notational analysis accounted for an increase in the number of winners and a decrease in the number of errors. From this evidence, it is clear that notational analysis has its uses as an effective practical tool during the coaching of performance.

5.5 MODELLING

The modelling of competitive sport is an informative analytic technique because it directs the attention of the modeller to the critical aspects of data which delineate successful performance. The modeller searches for an underlying signature of sport performance which is a reliable predictor of future sport behaviour. Stochastic models have not yet, to our knowledge, been used further to investigate sport at the behavioural level of analysis. However, the modelling procedure is readily applicable to other sports and could lead to useful and interesting results.

(Franks and McGarry 1996c)

Some exciting trends are to be found in modelling performances and match play, using a variety of techniques. Many examples can be found in the Journals now available in these disciplines: *The International Journal of Performance Analysis of Sport* (electronic – eIJPAS) and *The International Journal of Computers in Sport Science* (electronic – eIJCSS). The simplest, and traditional, form is using empirical methods of producing enough performance data to define a performance profile at that particular level. Some researchers are extending the use of these forms of data bases to attempt to predict performances; stochastic probabilities, neural networks and fuzzy logic have been used, singly or in combinations, to produce the outputs. McGarry and Perl (2004) presented a good overview of models in sports contest which embraces most of these techniques. So far, results have been a little disappointing in practical terms. It does seem to have potential – perhaps if we added a dash of Feng Shui?

Early research of modelling in sport includes Mosteller (1979), who set out guidelines when he developed a predictive model, and these ideas are eminently practical and many researchers in the area use these, or modifications of these to delimit their models.

Other attempts to model team games (Ladany and Machol 1977) theoretically have tended to founder upon the complexity of the numbers of variables involved and, at that time, did not base their predictions upon sound databases. The advent of computer notation systems has enabled the creation of large databases of sports performances in different sports, these in turn have helped the development of a number of different techniques in modelling performance in sport. These will be discussed under the following generic headings:

1   Empirical models
2   Dynamic systems
3   Statistical techniques
4   Artificial Intelligence
    ■   Expert systems
    ■   Artificial neural networks.

5.5.1 Empirical models

Hughes (1985) pioneered using databases to create empirical models of tactics and technique. He used a PC to gather data and established a considerable database on different standards of squash players. He examined and compared the differences in patterns of play between recreational players, country players and nationally ranked players, using the computerized notational analysis system he had developed. The method involved the digitization of all the shots and court positions, and these were entered via the QWERTY keyboard. Hughes (1986) was able then to define models of tactical patterns of play, and inherently technical ability, at different playing levels in squash. Although racket developments have affected the lengths of the rallies, and there have been a number of rule changes in the scoring systems in squash, these tactical models still apply to the game today. This study was replicated, with a far more thorough methodology for the women's game by Hughes et al. (2000).

Fuller (1990) developed and designed a Netball Analysis System and focused on game modelling from a database of 28 matches in the 1987 World Netball Championships. There were three main components to the research: to develop a notation and analysis system, to record performance, and to investigate the prescience of performance patterns that would distinguish winners from losers. The system could record how each tactical entry started; the player involved and the court area through which the ball travelled; the reason for each ending; and an optional comment. The software produced the data according to shooting analysis; centre pass analysis; loss of possession; player profiles; and circle feeding. Fuller's (1990) intention of modelling play was to determine the routes that winning, drawing and losing teams took and to identify significantly different patterns. From the results, Fuller was able to differentiate between the performances of winning and losing teams. The differences were both technical and tactical.

The research was an attempt to model winning performance in elite netball and the more research needed in terms of the qualitative aspects i.e. how are more shooting opportunities created. The model should be used to monitor performance over a series of matches not on one-off performances.

Empirical models enable both the academic and consultant sports scientist to make conclusions about patterns of play of sample populations of athletes within their sport. This, in turn, gives the academic the potential to examine the development and structures of different sports with respect to different levels of play, rule changes, introduction of professionalism, etc. The consultant analyst can utilize these models to compare performances of peer athletes or teams to the performances of those with whom the analyst is working.

5.5.2 Dynamic systems

Modelling human behaviour is implicitly a very complex mathematical exercise, which is multidimensional, and these dimensions will depend upon two or three spatial dimensions, together with time. But the outcomes of successful analyses offer huge rewards, as Kelso (1999) pointed out:

- If we study a system only in the linear range of its operation where change is smooth, it's difficult if not impossible to determine which variables are essential and which are not.
- Most scientists know about non-linearity and usually try to avoid it.
- Here, we exploit qualitative change, a non-linear instability, to identify collective variables, the implication being that because these variables change abruptly, it is likely that they are also the key variables when the system operates in the linear range.

Recent research exploring mathematical models of human behaviour led to populist theories categorized by 'Catastrophe Theory' and 'Chaos Theory'.

At the First World Congress of Notational Analysis of Sport (1992), Downey talked of rhythms in badminton rackets, athletes in 'cooperation' playing rhythmic rallies, until there was a dislocation of the rhythm (a good shot or conversely a poor shot) – a 'perturbation' – sometimes resulting in a rally end situation (a 'critical incident'), sometimes not. A good defensive recovery can result in the re-establishment of the rhythm. This was the first time that most of us had considered different sports as an example of a multidimensional, periodic dynamic system.

The term 'critical incident' was first coined by Flanagan (1954) in a study designed to identify why student pilots were exhausted at flight school.

'The critical incident technique outlines procedures for collecting observed incidents having special significance and meeting systematically defined criteria'. The critical incident technique is a powerful research tool but as with other forms of notating behaviour there are limitations inherent in the technique. Flanagan (1954) admitted that 'Critical incidents represent only raw data and do not automatically provide solutions to problems'. But Flanagan also pointed to the advantages of such a technique:

> The critical incident technique, rather than collecting opinions, hunches and estimates, obtains a record of specific behaviours from those in the best position to make the necessary observations and evaluations.

These opinions sound very much like the debates that have surrounded notational analysis within the halls of sports science over the last decade.

Research in sport has addressed some of these issues and notation and movement analysis systems have been developed that can overcome some of these disadvantages. Since Downey's suggestions in 1992, some researchers have investigated the possibilities that analysing 'perturbations' and 'critical incidents' offer. McGarry and Franks (1996a, b and d) applied further research to tennis and squash. They derived that every sporting situation contains unique rhythmical patterns of play. This behavioural characteristic is said to be the stable state or dynamic equilibrium. The research suggested that there are moments of play where the cycle is broken and a change in flow occurs. Such a moment of play is called a 'perturbation'. It occurs when either a poorly executed skill or a touch of excellence forces a disturbance in the stability of the game. For example, in a game of rugby, this could be a bad pass or immediate change of pace. From this situation, the game could unfold one of two ways; either the flow of play could be re-established through defensive excellence or an attacking error, or it could result in loss of possession or a try that would end the flow. When the perturbation results in a loss of possession or a try, it was then defined as a 'critical incident', sometimes the perturbation may be 'smoothed out', by good defensive play or poor attacking play, and not lead to a critical incident. A more in-depth approach is essential in order to derive a system for analysing the existence of perturbations. In order to do so, entire phases of play must be analysed and notated accordingly.

Applying McGarry and Franks' (1995) work on perturbations in squash, Hughes *et al.* (1997a) attempted to confirm and define the existence of perturbations in soccer. Using 20 English league matches, the study found that perturbations could be consistently classified and identified, but also that it was possible to generate specific profiles of variables that identify winning and losing traits. After further analyses of the 1996 European Championship matches ($n = 31$), Hughes *et al.* (1997b) attempted to create a profile for nations that had played more than five matches. Although supporting English League traits for successful and unsuccessful teams, there was insufficient data for the development of a comprehensive normative profile. Consequently, although failing to accurately predict performance, it introduced the method of using perturbations to construct a prediction model. By identifying 12 common attacking and defending perturbations that exist in English football leading to scoring opportunities, Hughes *et al.* (1997b) had obtained variables that could underpin many studies involving perturbations. These 12 causes were shown to occur consistently, covering all possible eventualities and had a high reliability. Although Hughes *et al.* (1997a, b) had classified perturbations; the method prevented the generation of a stable and accurate performance profile. In match play, teams may alter tactics and style according to the game state; for instance a team falling behind may revert to a certain style of play to create goal-scoring chances and therefore skew any data away from an overall profile.

In some instances, a perturbation may not result in a shot, owing to high defensive skill or a lack of attacking skill. Developing earlier work on British league football, Hughes *et al.* (2000) analysed how the international teams stabilize or 'smooth out' the disruption. Analysing the European Championships in 1996, attempts were made to identify perturbations that did not lead to a shot on goal. Hughes *et al.* (2000) refined the classifications to three types of causes: actions by the player in possession, actions by the receiver and interceptions. Inaccuracy of pass accounted for 62 per cent of the player in possession variables and interception by the defence accounted for the vast majority of defensive actions

(68 per cent). Actions of the receiver (12 per cent) were dominated by a loss of control; however these possessions have great importance because of the increased proximity to the shot (critical incident). Conclusions therefore focussed on improvements in technical skill of players, however with patterns varying from team to team, combining data provides little benefit for coaches and highlights the need for analysing an individual teams 'signature'.

Squash is potentially an ideal sport for analysing perturbations and as such, has received considerable attention from researchers. It is of a very intense nature and is confined to a small space. The rhythms of the game are easy to see, and the rallies are of a length (mean number of shots at elite level = 14; Hughes and Robertson 1997) that enables these rhythms and their disruption, i.e. perturbations and critical incidents. In defining perturbations, it may help to understand the reasons for this occurrence – consider the simplest model of a dynamic oscillating system. What are the main parameters and do the equivalent variables in sports contests conform to the same behaviour?

Squash coaches often talk about players imposing their own rhythms on the game – can this be measured by identifying specific values, the frequency of play for specific players and how does this vary against different opponents? This could be repeated in different individual and team sports (see Figures 5.4 and 5.5).

Critical incident and/or perturbation analysis seems to offer a way of making sense of all the masses of data that is available from an analysis of a team sport

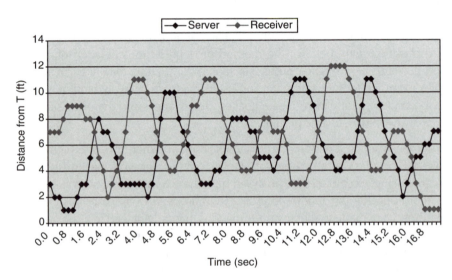

Figure 5.4 Distance–time graph for squash players (from Peakman 2001)

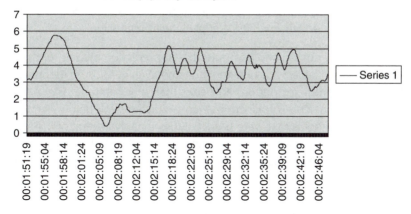

Distance (m) Rally 2, Player B

Figure 5.5 Example of a perturbation that was 'smoothed out' at time = 2.6:08

such as soccer – even a 'simple' sport such as squash will have 4,000–6,000 bits of data per match. The resultant data output can be so overwhelming that it leaves coaches and sports scientists struggling to see significant patterns among the thousands and thousands of bits of data. This method appears to direct analysts to those important aspects of the data that shape winning and losing models. Recent research had demonstrated that player profiles of perturbation shots are stable and differ from player to player (Hughes *et al.* 2007).

5.5.3 Statistical techniques

Historically, the prediction of sports performance has been a concept usually reserved for those associated with the betting culture. However, in reality, each and every person involved within sport will subconsciously process information to predict sports performance. Performance prediction could be described as the ability to draw conclusions upon the outcome of future performance based upon the combined interaction of previously gathered information, knowledge or data. For players and coaches, predictions are often made about forthcoming opponents based upon previous encounters and known traits. Therefore, is it not reasonable to assume that with valid and reliable information, using the correct techniques, the accurate prediction of performance should be possible? From a sports science perspective, the most common approaches to performance predication use large amounts of data and apply statistical techniques. Human predictions however, are entirely derived from one's underpinning knowledge and subjective bias, although the 'experts' are able to accommodate a greater understanding and opportunity for the element of chance and uncertainty, unlike computerized models of performance predication that are entirely statistically driven, such as Multiple Linear Regression.

In an evaluation of human and computer-based prediction models for the 2003 Rugby World Cup (Table 5.1), O'Donoghue and Williams (2004) identified that the best human predictor performed better than any computer-based model, although the mean score of all the human predictions fell below each of the computer-based models that were used; unquestionably a result of the subjectivity within human prediction. Interestingly, in a similar study during the 2002 Soccer World Cup (O'Donoghue et al. 2003), although the best computer-based models outperformed the human predictors once again, their overall effectiveness in predicting results was far inferior compared with the 2003 Rugby World Cup. Ironically, only the human-based focus group was able to predict four of the eight quarter-finalists and no method predicted more than one of the semi-finalists, whereas all of the computer-based models for the 2003 Rugby World Cup predicted seven of the eight quarter-finalists and three of the four semi-finalists.

However, this is understandable considering the inherent differences between soccer and rugby union. Very few upsets occur within rugby union and with only one drawn match during World Cup rugby from 1987 (O'Donoghue and Williams 2004), results generally go to form. Research by Garganta and Gonçalves (1997) led to the notion that among team sports, soccer presents one of the lowest success rates in the ratio of goals scored to the number of attacking actions performed, subsequently increasing the likelihood of drawn matches and upsets. This considered, unlike rugby union in which the number of points scored is far greater, the accurate prediction of soccer matches is far more difficult, a notion shared by O'Donoghue and Williams (2004) and demonstrated by O'Donoghue et al. (2003).

Making suggestions upon the types of data that should be used is difficult and ultimately reliant upon what is actually available. Historically, research in soccer, and similar team sports, that has attempted to identify the characteristics of a successful team has used game related performance indicators rather than factors such as distance travelled (Hughes et al. 1988; Yamanaka et al. 1993). By using process orientated data, such as pass completion, shots on target and entries into the attacking third for example, a more accurate picture of a team's abilities would be created which directly relates to the dynamic processes involved in soccer. Although large databases of such information are available, the validity of the data in terms of defining successful performance is questionable

Table 5.1 Marks awarded for each prediction

Method	Marks awarded					
	Group matches (40)	Quarter-finals (4)	Semi-finals (2)	3rd place play off (1)	Final (1)	Total (48)
Human-based methods						
Best individual human	39.00	4.00	2.00	1.00	0.00	46.00
Mean human prediction	35.63	3.45	1.17	0.26	0.31	40.66
Expert Focus Group	37.00	4.00	1.00	0.00	1.00	43.00
Computer-based methods						
Multiple linear regression (satisfies assumptions)	38.00	4.00	1.00	0.00	0.00	43.00
Multiple linear regression (violates assumptions)	38.00	4.00	1.00	0.00	1.00	44.00
Binary logistic regression	37.00	4.00	1.00	0.00	1.00	43.00
Neural networks with numeric input	37.00	4.00	1.00	0.00	1.00	43.00
Neural network with binary input – 4 middle layer nodes	34.00	3.00	1.00	0.00	1.00	39.00
Neural network with binary input – 8 middle layer nodes	34.00	4.00	1.00	0.00	1.00	40.00
Neural network with binary input – 16 middle layer nodes	36.00	4.00	1.00	0.00	1.00	42.00
Neural network with binary input – 32 middle layer nodes	37.00	4.00	1.00	0.00	1.00	43.00
Simulation program	38.50	4.00	1.00	0.00	1.00	44.50

and unsubstantiated. In order for performance prediction to move forward, not only within soccer, it is imperative that issues such as this are addressed, along with the continued development of valid and reliable methods of performance prediction.

By using MLR, a number of conditions must be accepted in considering its use as a prediction tool. The method is not based upon any 'artificial learning' process in order to generate predictions and predicts each game on its own merit without consideration for other factors. The simulation package used by O'Donoghue and Williams (2004) favoured Brazil to win the 2002 World Cup, rather than France who were the strongest team in the tournament. The model took into consideration the probabilities of qualifying from the group stages and then progressing through the knock-outs against different ranked opposition and predicted that Brazil had a greater chance of winning the fixture against France, should they have actually qualified from the group stages, because of the events preceding the potential tie. However, MLR would simply identify that France had both a superior rank and far less travelling distance than Brazil and would predict France to win the tie. This simplistic approach of MLR and indeed other algorithmic methods such as binary logistic regression is their fundamental drawback, although the results of these research papers quoted proved that even the most simplistic approach can be relatively effective.

5.5.4 Artificial Intelligence

Bartlett (2004) presented a broad overview of Artificial Intelligence (AI) encompassing speech recognition, natural language processing, computer vision (which would include online motion analysis systems that automatically track and assign markers, e.g. EVA real time, Vicon) and decision-making. He suggested that the intelligent core of AI included:

- Expert systems:
  - ☐ rule-based
  - ☐ fuzzy
  - ☐ frame-based and
  - ☐ their uses.

- Artificial neural networks (ANNs):
  - ☐ biological and artificial neural networks
  - ☐ the Perceptron
  - ☐ multi-layer neural networks
  - ☐ recurrent neural networks (we won't consider these here)
  - ☐ self-organizing neural networks and
  - ☐ their uses.

This is a fascinating area of research and applied theory and the potential developments for performance analysts is limitless.

5.6 CURRENT AREAS OF RESEARCH AND SUPPORT

Most of the support that is currently being offered to England Squash is based upon the work of Murray and Hughes (2001). During their research, they offered England Squash various types of feedback from information gathered using the SWEAT (Simple Winner and Error Analysis Technology — a simple data

74

gathering notation system) and the full analyses systems. Analyses ranging from simple winner and error ratios to complex rally ending patterns were produced from the computerized systems. Using the full analysis system (Brown and Hughes 1995) they analysed five matches of a particular player and pooled the data from these five matches into a single database. From these data the system is able to produce up to 300 different distribution graphs from the different combinations of shots and positions. This is far too much information for coaches and players to use. So Murray and Hughes (2001), using feedback from coaches and players and their years of experience, condensed the information into bullet points that were used as a storyboard to accompany an edited video of the player. After further feedback the information was normalized, converted into percentages and condensed further onto a representation of the court. The representation of the court was divided into 16 sections (in the same manner as the SWEAT system, see Hughes and Robertson 1997) with the areas of the court containing unusual data analysed with respect to shot type. These profiles could be created for winners, errors and N-1 and N-2 for winners and errors. The profiles were presented at a national squad and the players were very receptive of the style and content of the feedback.

The paper by Murray and Hughes (2001) was also the first to introduce the concept of momentum analysis. From the SWEAT analysis, they already had all of the information concerning winners and errors during a particular match. By writing a new program, they were able to give players a running score (momentum) during a match depending on the rally ending shots. A winning shot by a player was given a '+1' score, an error a '−1' score, and if the opponent hit the rally end shot, or it was a let, the score stayed the same. From this information, line graphs could be drawn to visually show any swings in momentum during a match. These line graphs can also be coupled with data regarding rally length to highlight whether any swings in momentum are perhaps fitness related. This work was born from conversations with the SRA psychologist who was interested to see whether extremes of body language had any effect on the outcome of the next three or four rallies. By matching up positive or negative forms of body language on tape with points on the graph, the psychologist was then able to see how these physical outbursts affected the momentum of the players.

The research into momentum analysis was furthered by Hughes et al. (2006) who analysed matches of elite squash players (n = 8 per player; 6 male and 6 female, all in top 40 in the world) to examine the length of the 'peaks' and 'troughs' of momentum in a match. Inevitably, large variations were found within each player's set of data, but all of these characteristics of the profiles stabilized to within 10 per cent of their respective means within six of the eight matches for all the players. The data from each match were summated and the average positive and negative increases in momentum were calculated. A Xi^2 analysis was used to test for inter-player differences and it was found that there were significant differences between patterns of peaks, peak lengths, troughs and trough lengths ($p<0.05$). Also both the male and female, world No.1 players had positive averages much higher than their peers.

Currently, the practical applications of these researches are being used with England Squash. Prior to the World Team Championships in November 2003, the England team were provided with player profiles of all possible future opposition, based on Hughes and Murray (2001). The only difference being that the profiles were created using the SWEAT analysis systems, rather than the full analysis system, due to time constraints and the large number of profiles that needed to be created. Compact discs containing edited video material of the unusual aspects of the relevant player profiles were provided to the players. They were created using the sports analysis package 'Focus'. Also English players

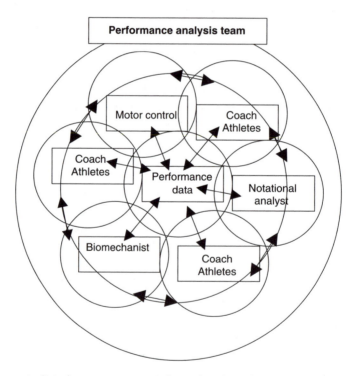

Figure 5.6 A digital systems approach to the data sharing that the interactive commercial systems have enabled for performance analysts working with coaches and athletes (from Hughes 2004)

76

competing in the World Championships or other major tournaments are provided with SWEAT analyses of their previous encounters with likely opponents and the respective momentum analyses of these matches.

This process is performed relatively quickly due to the large database of matches at the English Institute of Sport. The impressive use, and further recent developments, in feedback both for competition and training and coaching were presented by Murray and Hughes (2006) – an applied demonstration of the strengths and uses of the Focus, Quintic, Dartfish and SiliconCoach software, together with digital video, high-speed video and the best available VDUs for feedback. This 'digital' approach is represented schematically in Figure 5.6, and also exemplified by current approaches in badminton (see Figures 5.7 and 5.8).

One of the most exciting and potentially significant outgrowths of computerized sport analysis was the advent of interactive video technology. The ability of computers to control the video image has now made it possible to enhance existing sport specific analytical procedures. An inexpensive IBM-based system was described by Franks and colleagues (1989). The system operates in conjunction with an IBM XT (or compatible) and requires a circuit board to be resident within the computer. The system was designed to interact with a video cassette recorder (VCR) that has a 34-pin remote control outlet (some Sony and Panasonic AG and NV series). The interaction between the computer and the VCR was outlined as well the technical details of the circuit boards. In addition, several software programs were given that demonstrate the control features of the circuit board.

Franks and Nagelkerke (1988) developed such a system for the team sport of field hockey. The analysis system, described by Franks and Goodman (1986b), required a trained analyst to input, via a digitization pad, the game related data into a microcomputer. Following the field hockey game, a menu driven analysis program allowed the analyst to query the sequentially stored time-data pairs. Because of the historical nature of these game-related sequences of action, it was possible to perform both post-event and pre-event analysis on the data. That is to say, questions relating to what led up to a particular event or what followed a particular event could now be asked. In addition to presenting the sports analyst with digital and graphical data of team performance, the computer was also programmed to control and edit the videotape action of the game action.

The interactive video computer programme accessed from the stored database, the times of all specific events such as goals, shots, set plays, etc. Then, from a menu of these events, the analyst could choose to view any or all of these events within one specific category. The computer was programmed to control the

Analysis Guideline: Proposal

Preparation	**Performance Profiling** the starting point for tracking performance	Identify with the coach the areas of strength and areas for development for the player/pairs. This is information that the coaches will have already; it's just a case of making it accessible to me. This is set up using the performance profiling sheets distributed to the coaches. The results are then collated and put in an excel spread sheet format where any changes can be monitored and updated. Do the coach and player agree on strengths and weaknesses?
Technical analysis in Training and rehabilitation	Dartfish	Use of the Dartfish software to review technical aspect of training for player's personal development goals. This is set up courtside during training sessions. The players and coaches have access to review the technique as they progress through the session. Visual reinforcement assists the coach when giving feedback to the players, reduces the degree of discrepancy. This is available to the coaches and players whenever requested.
Match analysis	★ Focus X2 ★ Notation Sheets ★ Match reports ★ Stats	**Monitors if the areas identified for development are improving in matches after training.** Templates can be individually designed so that the information being drawn out is specific to the player/pair being analysed. Every bit of information is not always a productive use of time. Files can be created and data can be produced for performances against specific pairs. This information can also be fed into opponent analysis.
Review and feedback	★ CDs/DVDs ★ Review sessions with the coach	Relevant information and clips will be passed back to the player on a CD or DVD format depending on the size of the file. It is also possible to compress the data and send the information via email. Coach input is required to feedback to the player and me about which information to save for reviewing. From the analysis of the match, questions should be raised; Why did the player lose a certain match? What do they think, and do the results relate to this? Does the coach agree? Is it something that they have been working on in training? Should this aspect of training be included in the coaching plan? Can they use the strengths from this game in their next game? And so on......

↓

↔

Does any of the info here need to be fed back to the Physio/S&C?

Links can be made between technical and tactical analysis

↓

↔

↓

Figure 5.7 Analysis guideline proposals for the Badminton Association of England players and coaches (from Behan 2006)

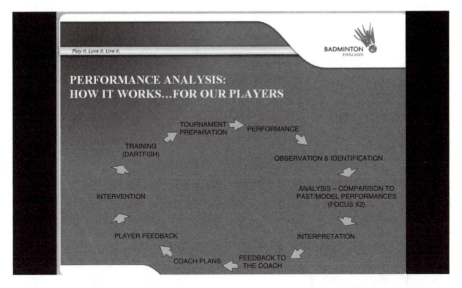

Figure 5.8 A schematic diagram of the analysis and feedback by the Badminton Association of England performance analyst (from Behan 2006)

video such that it found the time of the event on the video and then played back that excerpt of game action. It was also possible to review the same excerpt with an extended 'lead in' or 'trail' time around that chosen event. This system is at present being tested and used by the Canadian National Women's hockey team.

The system was modified for use to analyse and provide feedback for ice-hockey and soccer. A number of professional ice-hockey clubs are currently using it, as well as the national Canadian team.

There are now a number of commercial systems that are available for the notational analyst that can considerably enhance the power of feedback, through the medium of video replays and edited video clips. Some of the more successful are appraised by Hughes *et al.* (2002) and much more detail can be found on the appropriate websites for each system reviewed: Sportscode, Quintic, SiliconCoach, Tracksys and Purple VAIO.

5.7 RESEARCH INTO THE METHODOLOGY AND THEORY OF NOTATIONAL ANALYSIS

Recent research has reformed our ideas on reliability, performance indicators and performance profiling in notational analysis – also statistical processes

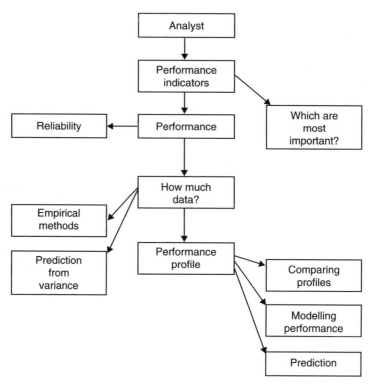

Figure 5.9 A schematic chart of the steps required in moving from data gathering to producing a performance profile (from Hughes 2004)

have come under close scrutiny, and have generally been found wanting. These are areas that will continue to develop to the good of the discipline and the confidence of the sports scientist, coach and athlete. If we consider the role of a notational analyst (Figure 5.9) in its general sense in relation to the data that the analyst is collecting, processing and analysing, then there a number of mathematical skills that will be required to facilitate the steps in the processes:

1 defining performance indicators
2 determining which are important
3 establishing the reliability of the data collected
4 ensuring that enough data have been collected to define stable performance profiles
5 comparing sets of data
6 modelling performances.

The recent advances made into the research and application of the mathematical and statistical techniques commonly used and required for these processes were discussed in detail by Hughes (2004), and are further analysed in different chapters of this book.

5.8 THE FUTURE OF NOTATIONAL ANALYSIS

In terms of technological development, notational analysis will undoubtedly move as rapidly as the developments in computer technology and video technology as we journey through the twenty-first century. The integration of these technological developments in computerized-video feedback will enable both detailed objective analysis of competition and the immediate presentation of the most important elements of play. Computerized systems on sale now enable the analysis, selection, compilation and representation of any game on video to be processed in a matter of seconds. The coach can use this facility as a visual aid to support the detailed analysis. Franks (1988) devised a more detailed model of the feedback process that could be possible with this type of technology. It is 15 years later that the top professional clubs in sports, and some National Governing Bodies, are implementing these ideas fully.

As these systems are used more and more, and larger databases are created, a clearer understanding of each sport will follow. The mathematical approach, typified by Eom (1988) and McGarry and Franks (1994, 1995), will make these systems more and more accurate in their predictions. At the moment, the main functions of the systems are analysis, diagnosis and feedback – few sports have gathered enough data to allow prediction of optimum tactics in set situations. Where large databases have been collected (e.g. soccer and squash), models of the games have been created and this has enabled predictive assertions of winning tactics. This has led to some controversy, particularly in soccer, due to the lack of understanding of the statistics involved and their range of application. Nevertheless, the function of the systems could well change, particularly as the financial rewards in certain sports are providing such large incentives for success. The following glimpse (Franks 1996b) into future integrated match analyses should help illustrate this point:

> The analysis from the match has been established and after reviewing a brief summary of the game statistics the coaching staff are concerned that late in the game crosses from the right side of the team's attack were being delivered behind the defenders and close to the opposing

team's goalkeeper. The result being that the front strikers were not able to contact the ball despite making the correct approach runs (information also gained from the match summary). The coaching staff call for videodisc (immediate recovery) excerpts of each crossing opportunity from the right side of the field in the last 15 minutes of play. Along with this visual information, the computer retrieves other on-line information that is presented in the inset of the large projected video image. This information relates to the physiological condition of the player(s) under review leading up to the crossing opportunity. In addition a 3-D analysis of the crossing technique is presented as each cross is viewed. One player had been responsible for these crosses. Upon advice from the consulting exercise physiologist the coaching staff have concerns about the telemetered respiration and heart rate of the player. A time–motion analysis of the player's movements in the second half of the game is called for, as well as a profile of the player's fitness level and physiotherapy report prior to the game. These are also retrieved from the same videodisc. After considering the information the coaching staff record their recommendations for team and individual improvement and move on to the next problem pro-vided by a comparison of the predicted data and real data. A computer programme running in the background is busy compiling instances of good performance (successful crosses) and poor performance that will make up an educational modelling programme for the individual player to view. Also the expert system of coaching practice is being queried about the most appropriate practice for remedial treatment of crossing in this specific setting. An individual fitness programme is prescribed when another expert system is queried. The final question that is asked of the mathematical model is 'given these changes are imple-mented, what is the likelihood that the number of crosses in the final fifteen minutes from the right side of the field will be more successful against our next opponent and what is their expected effect on match outcome?'

All aspects of the above scenario are either in place or are under investigation in notational analysis laboratories throughout the world.

Whether the most sophisticated and expensive of systems is being used, or a simple pen and paper analysis, as long as either system produces accurate, reliable results that are easy to understand, and they are based on performance indicators negotiated by the coach and the analyst, then coaches, athletes and sports scientists will gain objective, reliable data that will increase their insights into sport performance.

SUMMARY

To summarize the developments in computerized notational analysis, one can trace the innovative steps used in overcoming the two main problems of dealing with computers: data input and data output.

The initial difficulty in using a computer is entering information. The traditional method is using the QWERTY keyboard. But, unless the operator possesses considerable skills, this can be a lengthy and boring task. By assigning codes to the different actions, positions or players, that have some meaning to the operator, then the key entry can be easier. The next step is to assign areas of the keyboard to represent areas of the pitch, numbers for the players, and another section of the keyboard for the actions (see Hughes and Cunliffe 1986). An alternative to this approach is to use a specifically designed keyboard (Franks et al. 1983a; Fuller 1990) that has key entry designed ergonomically to meet the particular needs of the sport under analysis.

The major innovation, however, in this area, that eased considerably the problems of data entry both in terms of skill requirements and learning time, was the introduction of the digitization pad. In Britain, most workers have utilized the 'Concept keyboard', while in Canada, Ian Franks, at his Centre for Sport Analysis at UBC, Vancouver, has utilized another pad that has the trade name 'Power Pad' (Franks et al. 1986a). These are programmable, touch sensitive, pads, over which one can place an overlay that has a graphic representation of the pitch and aptly labelled keypad areas for the actions and the players. This considerably reduces the skill required for fast data entry, and the learning time required to gain this level of skill. These digitization pads have gradually given way to the use of the Graphical User interface (the mouse) and using on screen graphics, but this is not as quick as the use of the digitization pads, because of their easy 'point and click' demands. But the mouse is universal, and a lot more convenient than trying to get the extra 'add-on' hardware to work something which is not always 100 per cent compatible from country to country.

Another highlight, that is still awaited, is the introduction of voice entry of data into the computer Although Taylor and Hughes (1988) were severely limited by the amounts of funding for their research, they were still able to demonstrate that this type of system can and will be used by the computer 'non-expert'.

83

Although systems are expensive at the moment, computer technology is an environment of rapidly decreasing costs, even as the technology races ahead, so one can expect that this will be the next big step forward in the use of computers, in general, and sports systems in particular. It is strange, given the advance in electronic technology, that 15 years on from this research and the comments made above, that they are still true today.

Notational analysis, while having been the platform for considerable research, has its foundations in practical applications in sport. In these situations, it is imperative that the output is as immediate as possible and, perhaps more important, clear, concise and to the point. Consequently, the second strand of innovation that one can trace through the development of different systems is that of better output.

The first systems produced tables and tables of data, incorporated with statistical significance tests, that sport scientists had difficulty in interpreting, pity the coach or the athlete attempting to adopt these systems. Some researchers attempted to tackle the problem (Sanderson and Way 1977), but not everyone would agree that this type of presentation was any easier to understand than the tables of data. Representations of frequency distributions across graphics of the playing area, traces of the path of the ball prior to a shot or a goal (Hughes and Cunliffe 1986; Franks and Nagelkerke 1988), and similar ploys, have made the output of some systems far more attractive and easier to understand. The system developed by Hughes and McGarry specifically tackled this problem and produced some 3-D colour graphics that presented the data in a compact form, very easy to assimilate. Finally, the computer-controlled video-interactive systems (Franks et al. 1989) initiated the ideas that the users of analysis systems could utilize the potential of immediate analysis combined with the visual presentation of the feedback of the action. This has led now to the edited video image being the medium of feedback, the story-board of which is created by the detailed analyses provided by hand or computerized notation systems (or a combination of both) (see Murray and Hughes 2001).

CHAPTER SIX

SPORTS ANALYSIS

Mike Hughes

In this chapter we:

- aim to provide an insight into how different sports can be broken down into a series of decisions represented by a limited number of actions and their possible outcomes. These logical progressions provide the inherent structure within each sport.
- examine the construction of flowcharts of different sports, together with the definition of key events in these respective sports.
- suggest the next step is to design a data collection and data processing system, so anyone interested in designing a notation system should read this chapter first.

6.1 INTRODUCTION

Before discussing the work and research done in the field of notational analysis, including both manual and computerized systems, it is necessary to explore methods of applying analysis to sport in general. As stated in previous chapters, the very essence of coaching athletes is to instigate an observable change in behaviour. Methods of analysis used to measure these changes form the central focus of the remaining sections of this chapter. Objective performance measures should serve as the basis for future planning in any coaching process. While it is clear that both the quantification of performance and the assessment of qualitative aspects of performance are required, it would seem from the current research in these fields, that the former has been largely ignored, and the latter has many inherent weaknesses. This chapter therefore focuses on measures of performance that can be collected in order to analyse quantitatively the performance of an athletic event. First, analysis systems will be discussed with a view to applying them generally to either team sports or individual sports. In later chapters, these systems are then extended into data recording systems. Current research work, both pure and applied, is reviewed and assessed. Finally, the recent extension of these systems by the development of fast and inexpensive microcomputers, will form the nucleus of the final sections of the book.

6.2 CREATING FLOWCHARTS

The information that is available during a game is diverse and extensive. Continuous action and a dynamic environment make objective data collection difficult. Any quantitative analysis must therefore be structured. As there are so many ways in which to collect information about any sport, there are two very important points that should be considered:

1   consult with the best technical expert (i.e. coach) of the game to be analysed
2   the potential use of the information should guide how the system will be designed, i.e. make sure that what is required from the analysis system has been completely determined before starting anything else.

The first step is to create a 'flowchart' or logical structure of the game itself. This means defining the possible actions in the game and linking these actions with the possible outcomes, thus describing the sequential path the game can take. This is more easily explained by example. In a team sport, such as field hockey, Franks and Goodman (1984) described the game very simply by a two-state model. Either 'our' team has possession or the 'opposing' team has possession of the ball. This would be the top of what Franks and Goodman termed 'the hierarchy'. They then proposed that the next level of questions in the hierarchy would be:

1   Where on the field did our team gain and lose possession?
2   Can these areas be easily identified? (e.g. field divided into six areas)
3   Who on the team gained or lost possession?
4   How was possession gained and lost? (e.g. was it from a tackle, an interception, foul, etc.)

These questions can be included in the hierarchical structure as indicated in

sports analysis

BALL POSSESSION
/   \
GAINED   LOST
\   /
Where was it gained/lost?
|
Specify position.
|
Who was involved in
gaining/losing possession?
|
Specify player.
|
How was it gained/lost?
|
Specify action.

Figure 6.1 Hierarchical structure of a model for representing events that take place in a team game such as field hockey, soccer, basketball, water polo, etc.

Figure 6.1 (Note: For those interested in reading around the subject further, Franks and co-workers (1982) developed a series of detailed and more complex structures in which they modelled the decision-making processes of athletes engaged in team games. This work is very interesting from a modelling point of view, but as it approaches the problem from a perceptual point of view on behalf of the player, rather than an analytical view from the coach, it is not directly applicable here. However, it does provide a basis for a more thorough understanding of how to build up hierarchical structures.

The questions posed in Figure 6.1 can yield extremely useful information, although this level of analysis is obviously very simple. It is best to anticipate the form in which you wish to look at your data. Simple tabulated records are often the easiest to produce, and are easily translated to pictorial representations, which are always easier to assimilate. More detailed analyses might be concerned with the techniques individuals used during performance. It might also include physiological and psychological parameters that are mapped along a time axis during the performance. No matter how simple or complicated your intended analysis, always start as simply as possible and gradually add other actions and their outcomes bit by bit; in computing terminology this would be termed – the addition of more 'sub-routines'.

Franks and Goodman (1984) go on to suggest a simple series of steps or tasks in the evaluation of performance. The first one is based upon the above analysis and states:

TASK 1: Describe your sport from a general level to a specific focus.

The next step outlined by Franks and Goodman (1984) is fundamental in forming any evaluative analysis system:

TASK 2: Prioritize key factors of performance.

The final step in the process being:

TASK 3: Devise a recording method that is efficient and easy to learn.

The first two steps are discussed further with more examples in this chapter; the third task is given separate consideration in Chapter 7.

Consider our simple analysis of the team sport above in Figure 6.1. This can be made more sophisticated by considering, in more detail, the possible actions and their respective outcomes (Figure 6.2). These actions and outcomes can then be incorporated into a model for the events taking place in this team game, which happens to be soccer, but which could easily be transposed to any team sport. This is shown in Figure 6.3.

The natural sequential logic of the game can be followed. As possession is gained by one of the players, a number of choices of actions are presented to the player. The choice, and the outcome of the action, determines whether this side retains possession, scores a goal, gives away a free kick, etc. Inevitably, this system can be made more sophisticated still, which is always possible with any system. For example, the dribble, run, tackle, foul, etc. have not been included, nor have any actions when not in possession. The difficult decision to make in designing this type of model is knowing when the limitations of the model are acceptable within the terms of reference of the desired data.

The core elements: 'Player', 'Position', 'Action', in Figure 6.4 can be seen to be fundamental to analysis systems. If 'Time' is also included then this would represent the most complex of systems. These elements are rarely included in all systems, for example if we were analysing the attacking patterns of a hockey team, we would not need to record the players' identities, only the position on the pitch, the action and any outcomes (if any). If we were examining the work-rate of a player, then all we would be recording would be the position, the action

sports analysis

Action	Outcome	Effect on possession
Pass	Good	Retained
	Bad	Lost
Shot	High	Lost
	Wide	Lost
	Blocked	Retained or Lost
	Saved	Lost
	Goal	Lost
Cross	Good	Retained
	Bad	Lost
Corner Kick	Good	Retained
	Bad	Lost
Throw-in	Good	Retained
	Bad	Lost
Gk.'s Throw	Good	Retained
	Bad	Lost
Gk.'s Kick	Good	Retained
	Bad	Lost

free Kick – Pass, shot, etc. and their subsequent routines.

Penalty – Shot (subsequent routines).

Figure 6.2 Some actions, and their respective outcomes, for soccer

(stand, walk, jog, run, etc.) and possibly the time. These basic elements form the heart of any analysis of a sport.

Consider the game of squash as another example. This is a field invasive individual racket sport. Other than the definition of the playing area, the logic of this game could as easily be applied to tennis or to badminton, which are non-field invasive. The system in Figure 6.5 shows the simple logic needed to record and analyse the key elements of the performance. To include the scoring system would require considerable additions to this flowchart. The basis of the 'English' scoring, a similar system is used in badminton, is that the server receives a point if he/she wins the rally. If the non-server, 'handout' wins the rally, he/she does not receive a point. The winner of the rally serves for the start of the next rally. This simple logic to the game of squash is complicated a little by the concept of 'lets' and 'strokes'. A 'let' is when one player impedes the other in the process of his/her shot, this results in the rally being played again, no change in score, same server. A 'stroke' is given against a player when he/she prevents the opponent from hitting the front wall with a direct shot or prevents a winner. (The

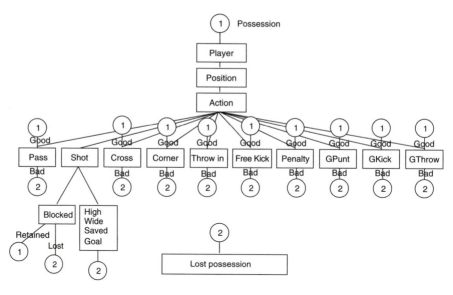

Figure 6.3 A simple schematic flowchart for soccer

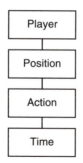

Figure 6.4 Core elements of any analysis system of performance

concept is a little more complicated than this, as all squash players will testify, but this explanation should suffice for non-combatants.) So a 'stroke' given against a player is equivalent to the player conceding an error.

Creating the model for the logic of the sequence of the shot production and respective positions is relatively straightforward (Figure 6.5). If the shot is a winner, then that player serves the next rally. Whoever hits an error, or receives a 'stroke' adjudged against him/her, does not serve the next rally. The 'let' ball decision results in the rally starting again. If none of these conditions apply, then the ball is still in play and the other player strikes his/her shot from the notated court position. In most simple systems for racket sports, analysts will start with a

90

sports analysis

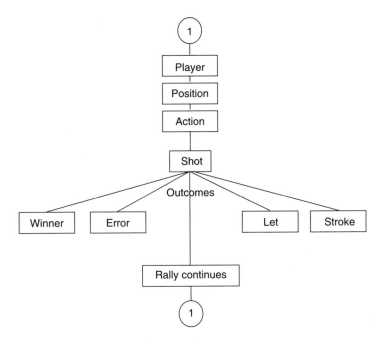

Figure 6.5 A simple flowchart for squash

'winner/error' analysis, recording the type of shots that were winners or errors and where on the court they were played.

One way of incorporating the logic of the scoring, and who serves, into the model of the action, is to keep the definition of the server and non-server throughout the rally. This helps clarify whether the score is increased at the end of the rally or not, depending upon who won. The selection of actions or, in this case, shots, to be inserted into these models, as in the previous examples, is determined by the detail of complexity required by the data collection. Sanderson and Way (1979) used a relatively complex menu of shots, which included:

> Straight drive; cross court drive; straight drop; cross court drop; volley drive; volley cross drive; volley drop; volley cross drop; boast; volley boast; lob; cross court lob; others.

Included in 'others' were infrequent shots such as cross-angles, cork-screw lobs, skid boasts, back-wall boasts, shots behind the player's back, etc. Perhaps this selection of shots does not look too complex at first sight, but consider the following facts. Sanderson and Way (1979) divided the court into 28 cells for definition of position. In the course of one match, they would record in the region of 4,500 items of information. Processing this data would take another 40 person-hours of work. In addition, the learning time to use the system 'in-match' was 5–8 h. This was a complex system, despite its apparent simplicity; it produced the data that its designers required. But it is only too easy to gather too much data. Be sure that your system gathers only the data needed.

Franks and Goodman (1986b), working with David Hart and John MacMaster of the Canadian Water Polo Association, developed a flow diagram of water polo. The design was attack-based, whereby the events, the player responsible and the reason, are recorded. By using this flow diagram, a computer program was constructed so the whole history of the game could be stored and produced for analysis.

6.3 LEVELS OF ANALYSIS – THE TEAM, SUBSIDIARY UNITS AND INDIVIDUALS

Although there are many facets of the team's performance that could be described, there are only a limited set of priority elements that serve a useful function with a view to improving performance. In deciding upon which infor-mation is useful, Franks and colleagues (1983a) suggested that the coach should be guided by three elements:

1   coaching philosophy
2   primary objectives of the game
3   database of past games.

For example, if a game objective has roots in the principle of possession, then the important questions to be answered should relate to possession (i.e. total number of possessions; where on the playing surface possession was lost and won; who was responsible for winning and losing possession, etc.). Coaching philosophy may also dictate certain defensive or offensive strategies to imple-ment at critical time periods during a game. If this is the case, then the analysis should be directed toward objective counts of defensive or offensive behaviours during these periods of play. It should be noted that Franks *et al.* (1983a) contend that:

> The most important of these three elements is the formation of a data base of past games. With such a data base it is possible to formulate a predictive model.

If one knew how, where and when goals or points were scored in past games, a probabilistic model could be constructed to aid future training and performance. Technical and tactical training could then be directed toward the high probability events. Coaching could then be directed at gradually modelling a team to more fully fitting a winning profile.

After all of the significant game-related questions have been defined by the technical expert, it is necessary to decide upon the level of analysis that is needed. Figure 6.6 illustrates a primary level of team analysis. The example extends the soccer model already used but it must again be emphasized that this can be equally be applied to other team games. Four areas are considered for information gathering: possession, passing, shooting and set pieces. However, within each of these categories, more detail is available. For example, when a shot is taken, this analysis should not only reveal if the shot was on or off target, but also, if it was on target, was it saved or was it a goal? Further information about the off-target shooting could also be gathered: was it high, wide or high and wide? This type of information is extremely important and should greatly influence subsequent coaching practices.

Franks et al. (1983b) stated, 'The information gained from set pieces (i.e. corner kicks, throw-ins and free-kicks) should be relative to some prescribed definition of success or failure'. Coaches should have expectations of performance at set pieces in a game such as soccer. Other games will have similar structured phases, where similar definitions of performance should be met, e.g. American football, yardage on a running play; field hockey, percentage of short corners converted to goals; rugby league, number of tackles made by specific positions, etc. The definition of performance in each case will depend upon the personal philosophy of the coach in relation to their sport. These expectations should be made clear to the players and should be practiced. For example, a free kick that is awarded in the defending third of the field should be delivered in less than three moves to the attacking third of the field, whereas a free kick that is awarded in the attacking third of the field should result in a strike on goal in less than three moves. If these expectations are not met, then the set piece is registered as a failure. Franks et al. (1983b) go on to say:

> It is important to note that these definitions of success and failure should be continually upgraded to correspond to the level of performance and realistic expectations of the coach. If the definitions are unrealistic then the evaluation will not be sensitive to the performance changes.

A detailed analysis of an individual player is illustrated in Figure 6.7. It would

```
┌─────────────────────────────────────────────────────────┐
│                   SOCCER EXAMPLE                          │
│                                                           │
│   1. POSSESSION INFORMATION.                              │
│                                                           │
│      (a) Total possessions.                               │
│                                                           │
│      (b) Where possessions were won and lost:             │
│          Defending 1/3, Mid-field 1/3, Attacking 1/3.     │
│                                                           │
│   2. PASSING INFORMATION.                                 │
│                                                           │
│      (a) Square passes.                                   │
│                                                           │
│      (b) Back passes.                                     │
│                                                           │
│      (c) Forward passes.                                  │
│                                                           │
│      (d) Consecutive passes.                              │
│                                                           │
│   3. SHOOTING INFORMATION.                                │
│                                                           │
│      (a) Opportunity.                                     │
│                                                           │
│      (b) On target.                                       │
│                                                           │
│      (c) Off target.                                      │
│                                                           │
│      (d) Blocked.                                         │
│                                                           │
│      (e) Shooting angle.                                  │
│                                                           │
│   4. SET-PIECE INFORMATION.                               │
│                                                           │
│      (a) Corner kick.                                     │
│                                                           │
│      (b) Free kick.                                       │
│                                                           │
│      (c) Throw in.                                        │
│                                                           │
└─────────────────────────────────────────────────────────┘
```

Figure 6.6 Primary level game analysis – team (from Franks and Goodman 1984)

take a very detailed and comprehensive recording system, involving a battery of experts, to gather the data for this sort of analysis. Franks et al. (1983b) have however, provided a very complete example of the way to go about defining the type of data required for an individual analysis. The player has two distinct categories of performance that can be evaluated, these are on the ball and off the ball behaviour. These behaviours could be recorded in a cumulative fashion, e.g. number of defensive recovery runs, or given a success/failure rating, e.g. 20 successful square short passes and ten unsuccessful short passes gives a success:failure ratio of 2:1. The area of the field in which events occur could, and should, be included in these computations to give the necessary spatial dimensions to the analysis. The division of the area of the pitch is again subject to the detail required, a simple division of the pitch into six equal areas would give a definition of the attacking, mid-field and defending one-third of the pitch. Other studies have used a finer definition overall, and then a finer definition yet again in the penalty area (Church and Hughes 1986; Hughes *et al.* 1988), so that these areas of specific interest have a finer degree of detail to them. Finally, further data relative to physiological requirements can be accessed in methods of measuring heart rate and physiological requirements can be accessed in methods of measuring heart rate and blood lactates during and/or after game action. These measures can be correlated to technical data and then inferences can be made about the complete performance of individuals within a team game.

The way of applying these analyses, demonstrated in this example, should be applied to units in a team as well as the whole team or individuals. The efficiency of attacking, mid-field or defensive groups of players within a team can be assessed. This is one objective way of selecting the best combinations of players within the tactical sub-groupings within a team and monitoring their continued performance.

For sports, such as tennis, golf, martial arts, etc., individual levels of analysis can be applied, using similar logical analyses as those shown in Figure 6.7.

SUMMARY

Logical analysis of the form and function of the events taking place in a sport is necessary before any analysis can take place. Franks and Goodman (1986) outlined three steps in forming any analysis system:

TASK 1:   Describe your sport from a general level to a specific focus.
TASK 2:   Prioritize key factors of performance.
TASK 3:   Devise a recording method that is efficient and easy to learn.

By elucidating tasks 1 and 2, the creation of a notation system becomes an easy and logical progression. Practising these logical definitions is not difficult but it is a skill that becomes easier and easier with practice.

The more complex the sport – team games like soccer or American football for

SOCCER EXAMPLE

OFF-BALL: Recovery runs
Diagonal runs
Overlap runs

Sprint   \
Jog   -   Further analysis
Walk   /

Heart rate

ON-BALL: Reception
Running with the ball
Dribbling

      / Backwards
Short passing - Forwards
      \ Square

      / Backwards
Long passing - Forwards
      \ Square
         / On target Goal
      / Taken
Shot opportunity   \ Off-target NO-goal
     \ Not-taken

     / Defensive
Heading
     \ Offensive

Pressurizing
Tackling
Covering
Screening

     /   Near post
     /   Far post
Crosses   -   Central
     \   Out of bounds
     \   Goalkeepers

Set pieces

Figure 6.7 Individual analysis (Franks and Goodman 1984)

example, then the more care that must be taken in deciding exactly what is required of the system. Which units of the team, or individuals, that are to be analysed, which actions and events that have the most relevance and so on.

The next step in analysis logic is to decide the level at which the analysis will take place. If it is a team game, then what units of the team are going to be analysed? Or are individuals to be monitored? Or the whole team? This type of decision does not apply in individual sports, but the level or degree of detail of output must be decided – and it is vital that these decisions are made early in the analytical process.

CHAPTER SEVEN

HOW DO WE DESIGN SIMPLE SYSTEMS? HOW TO DEVELOP A NOTATION SYSTEM

Mike Hughes

In this chapter we:

■ aim to enable you to begin to understand how hand notation systems are developed.

7.1 INTRODUCTION

No matter how simple or complicated you wish to make a data collection system, the same underlying principles apply. If you are hoping to develop a computerized system, the same logical process must be followed. Again, if you wish to go further down this design route then read Chapters 5 and 6 in Hughes and Franks (2004).

7.2 DATA COLLECTION SYSTEMS

There are several types of data collection systems that can be roughly divided into three categories, by the nature of the data collected:

1 Scatter diagrams
2 Frequency tables
3 Sequential systems.

7.2.1 Scatter diagrams

Scatter diagrams are usually simple and are most often used to gather data in-event and enable immediate feedback for the coach and athlete. They are usually used in the form of drawing a schematic representation of the playing surface of the sport in which you are interested on a sheet of paper, and then notating on this, the actions of interest, at the position at which they took place (and player number too, if needed). For example, consider a soccer coach who wants to know where his football team lose possession – a simple plan of the pitch enables the recording of these positions (Figure 7.1).

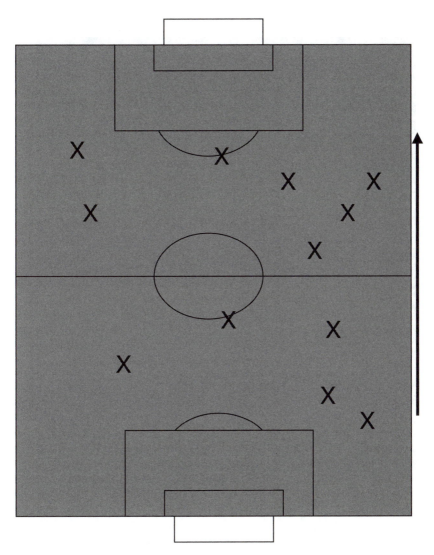

Figure 7.1 A simple scatter diagram for recording position of loss of possession in soccer

What else does the coach need to know: which of the players is offending most? This system can be made a little more sophisticated by adding the number of the player who lost possession (Figure 7.2).

What else might we need to know about our problem of loss of possession?

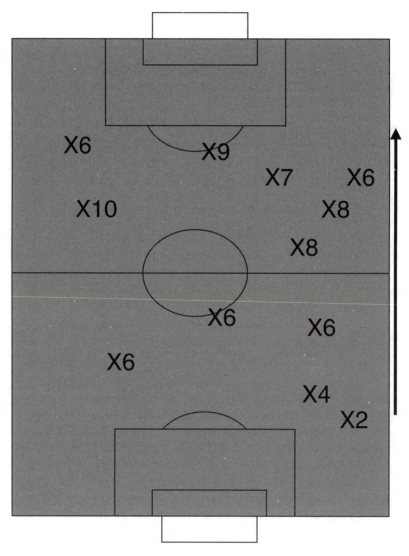

Figure 7.2 A simple scatter diagram for recording position of loss of possession, and the player involved, in soccer

Perhaps the actions that the players are executing might give us more insight into the relative merits of the performance of the players involved.

So let us also record the actions involved; for this we will need a simple definition of the most common actions and some symbols:

What action?

P – Pass
D – Dribble
C – Cross
S – Shot
K – Clear

Figure 7.3 shows an example of this form of data gathering. Because this is more complicated, to be able to do this at match speed might take a little practice. Scatter diagrams have a number of immediate advantages. They are:

- simple and quick
- accurate (with practice)
- usually 'in-event'
- able to give immediate feedback
- efficient, as usually there is no need to process data
- unable to know the order of events, so there is no 'sequentiality'.

But it must be noted that there are dangers in interpretation of these simple forms of data, not only because their accuracy is usually not very high, but also the simple data can only yield simple analyses. Attempts at further depth to analyses will only lead to problems.

7.2.2 Frequency tables

Frequency tables are another commonly used form of data gathering that enables quick, simple analyses of performance of athletes and teams. Let us consider an example of a basketball coach wanting to know which players have made which actions during a game. By using a frequency table like that shown in Table 7.1, the analyst can easily record the frequency of each of the actions by the players in the squad.

Like scatter diagrams, frequency tables have some obvious advantages and disadvantages:

- simple and quick

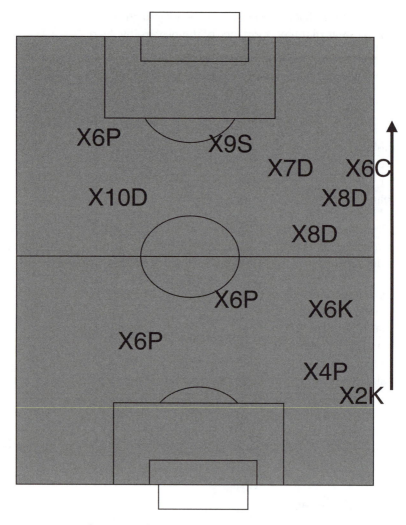

Figure 7.3 A simple scatter diagram for recording position of loss of possession, and the player and the action involved, in soccer

- accurate (with practice)
- usually 'in-event'
- able to give immediate feedback
- need to process data – not usually onerous
- unable to know the order of events, so there is no 'sequentiality'
- there are dangers in the interpretation of these simple forms of data.

Table 7.1 A simple frequency table for basketball.

Actions	1	2	3	4	5	6
Pass	★★★★★★★		★★★	★★★★		
Dribble	★★★		★	★★		
2-pt Shot	★★★★		★★★★	★★		
3-pt Shot	★★			★		
Assist	★★★★		★★★★	★		
Lost possession	★		★★			

7.2.3 Sequential data systems

Recording the sequence in which events occur enables the analyst to go to far greater depths in interpreting a performance. Now critical events, such as a shot at goal or a winning shot in a racket sport, can be analysed so that the events that led up to them can be examined for repetitions of patterns. These can be very informative for the coach, not only about their own players, but also the opposition. These patterns can also help the sports scientist understand different sports.

First step: You must decide what you want from your system before you begin to design the system.

This does sound a little obvious but the reason for this lies in the fact that notation systems provide masses of data. Unless you have a crystal clear idea about what data you wish to collect, then you will find that your system will collect confusing and sometimes irrelevant information. Keep in mind the old adage about not seeing the wood for the trees. Time spent working on what form(s) your output might take can save a great deal of frustration later. Most importantly, it also simplifies the job of defining input. Having once decided what you want, the process of designing your data collection system is simple and straightforward. Often, the most difficult part is making sense from the mass of data – this is true for all analysis systems. The simplest way of starting is to consider a basic example. A field hockey coach may wish to have more information about the shooting patterns, or lack of them, for the team. Consequently, this coach will need an output from his system consisting of:

1   Position of the pass preceding the shot (the assist)
2   Player who made the pass
3   Type of pass
4   Position from which the shot was taken
5   Which player made the shot

6   Outcome of the shot, i.e. goal, save, block, miss (wide), miss (high), corner
    . . . etc.

(*Note*: If field hockey is not a game with which you are familiar, this method will as easily apply to any field invasive team sport, such as basketball, soccer, water polo, lacrosse, etc.)

The data needed to be notated in this example is relatively simple. The next step is to assign notation symbols for each of the above variables. First, divide the pitch into segments or cells and give each one a code; this could be either a number or a letter, but there are usually advantages in using specifically one or the other. Deciding upon how the playing surface should be divided is not always as simple as it might appear. Using small cells does enable fine definition of the positions at which actions take place, but the more cells you have, the more data you have to collect in order to have significant numbers of actions in each cell. If in doubt, err on the side of simplicity – the most influential research on soccer was done with the pitch divided into three, the defending third, the middle third and the attacking third. The hockey pitch in Figure 7.4 is at the other extreme of definition, with a large number of position cells.

As position, player, action, etc. are notated, it is often useful to have the codes entered in the system alternating from letter to number to letter; this makes interpretation of the data much simpler. Any saving that can be made in the number of items entered, can also mean a large saving in time – often the difference in being able to notate 'in match' or not. It is easy to identify players by

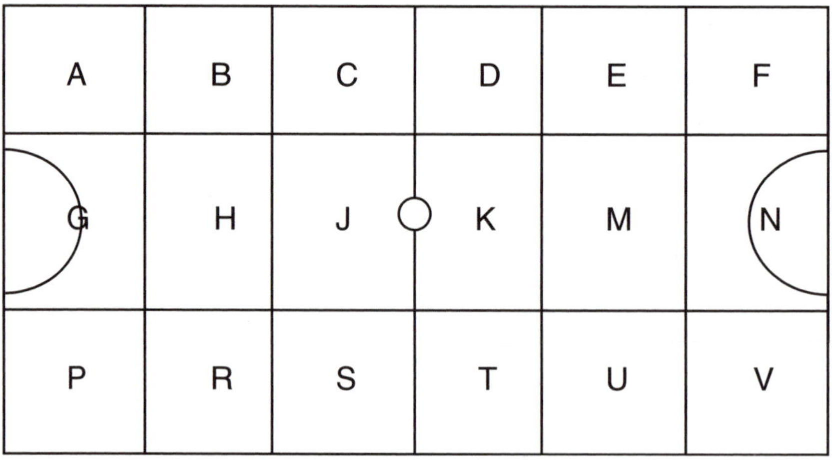

A	B	C	D	E	F
G	H	J	K	M	N
P	R	S	T	U	V

Figure 7.4 A definition of position on a representation of a field hockey pitch

how do we design simple systems?

their shirt number, but if there are more than nine in a team or squad, then you have to note two digits instead of one. Some systems in the past have employed letters for the players '10' and '11'. In Figure 7.4, letters have been used to differentiate between respective areas of the pitch rather than numbers. The significance of this is that, for each of the areas above, there is only a single item of information required to be written down, irrespective of which area. This may sound trivial, but when systems can be recording thousands of items of data, each small saving in design, at the developmental stage, will increase the effectiveness of the system many times over.

So let us assume that the coach has decided to use letters for pitch cell divisions and numbers for the players of the team. Does the coding of position cells in Figure 7.4 seem a reasonable layout? A number of potential problems present themselves. (The use of letters 'I', 'L' and 'O' could present some translational problems later. Most notation is done at speed, 'I' and 'L' can easily be confused both with each other and the number '1', and of course the letters 'O' and 'Q' with zero, '0').

The main problem with the representation of the playing area is one of definition. Will these pitch divisions give the coach sufficient information on the significant areas of the pitch from which his team are shooting well or poorly? It would seem unlikely. In this situation, previous researchers have used unequal divisions of the playing areas, making the definition finer in the areas of most interest. In this example, this will be around the goal. There are a number of ways of doing this. Figure 7.5 is one simple way using a representation of just half the playing area – this does however negate the possibility of notating shots at goal from the player's own half.

Another way of doing this would be to use arcs from the goal as shown in Figure 7.6. This has been used in a number of systems, both in basketball and soccer, to good effect. In both games, there is an optimum area from which to shoot, which is more easily defined in this way.

For our example, let us assume that the coach is using the area representation shown in Figure 7.6, and that players are identified by their shirt numbers. The two actions that we are notating are the pass and the shot. There are four different types of pass that our coach has defined:

Flick – F
Push – P
Arial – A
Hit   – H

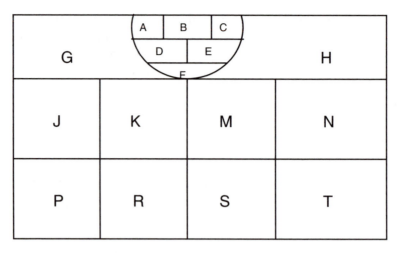

Figure 7.5 A definition of position on a representation of a field hockey pitch oriented to analysing attacking moves

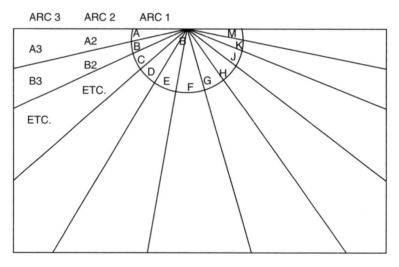

Figure 7.6 Another definition of position on a representation of a field hockey pitch oriented to analysing attacking moves

Now we only have to decide on the possible outcomes of the other action variable, the shot, and we have a notation system. The coach has decided at this stage not to differentiate between types of shot, so it is the outcome of the shots that need coding. As we are writing letter and then number as we notate position and player, let us use a letter code for the action outcome. A number of systems involve specifically invented symbols but, for the sake of keeping this example simple, let us stick to recognized numeric and alphanumeric symbols. A simple code would be:

Goal   – G
Saved   – S
Wide   – W
High   – H
Blocked   – B
Rebound – R

- The coach is now able to start notating a match. An example of the type of data obtained will be as shown below. In this way, the coach, or any other operator, can record the position from which the shot was made, who made it and the outcome. Because of the way that the data have been entered, a number, a letter, another number, and a separate line for each shot, interpretation of the data is relatively easy.
- Remember that the codes chosen here in this example were chosen for simplicity, a number of systems utilize invented symbols that represent actions or outcomes. This is a decision that can only be made by the individual designing the system. Use whatever you are most comfortable and familiar with. Above all, keep it as simple and as easy as possible.
- The only problem facing the coach now is processing the data. First, enough data will need to be collected to make it significant, then the distribution of the shots and their assists, with respect to players or position, together with their outcome, can be explored. This form of data processing is very important in most forms of analysis and feedback. Data analysis is a difficult part of notational analysis, a separate section is devoted to it later in Hughes and Franks (2004).
- The information above makes it easy to record the data, there is less chance of becoming confused, and it is easier to interpret the data once recorded. It also makes it easier for someone else to understand the data collection system, should that be desirable. Decide who is likely to use your system; if it is only for your own use only spend as much time 'dressing it up' as is necessary.

Note: Always remember that when other people either use your system or are presented with the data from your system, they will tend to judge the whole system by its appearance.

7.3 DATA COLLECTION SYSTEMS IN GENERAL

What can we learn in general terms about notational analysis from our example? In the most general form of notation, the following parameters are being recorded:

1 Position
2 Player
3 Action – and the subsequent outcome(s)
4 Time.

This is the most general situation possible in any match analysis – in most notation systems only two or three of these variables will be necessary. In individual sports, such as squash, tennis or gymnastics, the notation of which player is involved becomes easier. In team sports, it becomes more difficult, depending upon the analysis and the form of the output. In certain situations, perhaps where the movements of one particular player, are being recorded, it will be unnecessary to record that player because the notation is only about the one performer. The time variable is not used as frequently as the other variables in notation systems – it increases the complexity considerably, but there are some analyses which will require it. Analyses where velocities, accelerations and/or rates of work are the desired output from the data will use a time base. Reilly and Thomas (1976) completed what can be regarded now as a classical study of motion analysis in soccer, by using a combination of hand notation, with stop watches, and audio tape recorders. Position and action are nearly always involved in notation systems, although there are examples of systems not using one or other of these two. In summary then, most systems will use two or three of the above variables, there are very few instances where it is necessary to use all four.

In our example, we recorded position, player and then the outcome of the action (shot). The beginning and end of each sequence were indicated by using a new line for each event.

Position: The way in which the position was defined in the example was as good a way as any to record positional data. The needs of the system often dictate the definition required within the system. Obviously, the finer the definition the more accurate the information, *but* the finer the definition, the more data will need to be collected to make it significant. Be careful not to submerge yourself in too much data or too much data collection – notation is not an end in itself, the end-product has to justify the time spent on it. Notating position is always a compromise between accuracy and having manageable data.

Player: Recording which player executed the action cannot be very different in more sophisticated systems. In individual sports, the system may only be notating one player at a time, so differentiation will is not be necessary.

Action: What made our example a relatively simple one was that we were considering only two actions – the assist and the shot. But even so, the system still required four different types of pass (assist) and five possible outcomes of the shot to be notated. These again could have been more complicated since it may be useful to know whether possession was regained after the save or the block. Consider then the complexity of the situation when defining all the possible actions, and their respective outcomes, in a game such as soccer or hockey or basketball. It is this logical and structured analysis, coupled with a clear idea of the salient information that is required from the game, that forms the nucleus of any notation system. A sound system, that will produce consistent and meaningful data, must be based on a careful analysis of the sport to be notated. It is most important to be able to understand the logic of the game structure of the sport under study – a separate section is devoted to sport analysis.

The most important aspect of defining any action, or outcome, is ensuring that the 'Operational definition' of this term is clear and unambiguous. The operational definition of the action and outcomes enable you, and others, to consistently interpret events in the same way. We have found, with experience, that any problem with reliability (repeatability) of data gathering is nearly always associated with the clarity of the operational definitions.

SUMMARY

1   You must have a clear idea what information you want from the system.
2   Make the data collection, and the data processing, as simple as possible to start with. Build the complexity of your system in easy stages, adding on to what you know works and to what you can handle.
3   Test your system on a small part of a match or event using video. In this way you can practise and improve your notation skills, and also find out how accurate you are. Then practise some more; after that my advice is to practise some more. There is nothing worse than notating for some time, getting in a muddle and realizing you have made a mess of the whole thing (always after you have promised a detailed analysis to someone important).
4   Having tested the system, does it collect the data you wanted? It is easy to get carried away with the design stage, adding on little bits here and collecting a little more information there, until the whole structure has assumed

gargantuan proportions, and does not fulfil the original aims defined at the start.

5   The more complex your system, the longer it will take to learn. In addition, the amount of output increases immensely, which means considerably more work processing the data. For example, the notation system developed by Sanderson and Way (1979) involved 5–8 h learning time and also required 40 h of work to process the data of a single match.

Remember: Keep it simple

You can always add to your system and build up its complexity as you grow in experience, confidence and speed – and, most important, that you have fully processed the data output and have decided on additional forms of output.

6   Once you have arrived at the final version of your system, you find this out by continually testing the system to examine whether the data that you can gather provides the answers to the questions that you have about your sport, then you must test its reliability. This is not necessarily a complicated process, but it is very important to know the accuracy of your system.

CHAPTER EIGHT

EXAMPLES OF NOTATION SYSTEMS

Mike Hughes

In this chapter we:

- give a number of examples of different systems for different sports. They have been devised by students of notational analysis and are therefore of differing levels of complexity and sophistication – but there are always lessons to be learnt even from the simplest of systems.

8.1 INTRODUCTION

The best way to appreciate the intricacies of notational analysis is to examine systems for the sport(s) in which you are interested, or sports that are similar. The explanations and analyses are completed by beginners in notational analysis; coaches of these sports should not therefore be irritated at some of the simplistic levels of analysis for the respective sports. The encouraging aspects about these examples are the amounts of information that the systems provide – even the simplest of these. Examples 8.2.1–8.2.2 are for individual sports, while examples 8.3.1–8.3.4 are for team games. More examples can be found in *Notational Analysis of Sport* by Hughes and Franks (1997; 2nd edition 2004).

8.2 INDIVIDUAL SPORTS

8.2.1 A notation system for tennis

This system, for the notation and analysis of data for tennis, was designed to gather basic information on winners and errors. The court was divided up into

111

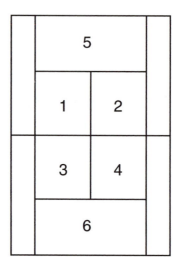

Figure 8.1 Division of the court into six cells for analysis of tennis

sections as shown in Figure 8.1. Six sections were chosen in order to keep the recording of position, and its subsequent analysis, as simple as possible. A singles match was to be notated which reduced the court size, removing the need for the tram-lines and simplifying the system.

Symbols were allocated for the basic shots to be recorded, these were as follows:

S   – Serve
F   – Forehand drive
B   – Backhand drive
V   – Forehand volley
<u>V</u>   – Backhand volley
L   – Forehand lob
<u>L</u>   – Backhand lob
Sm – Smash

Having established shot symbols, it was then necessary to devise 'result of shot' symbols, i.e. whether the shot was a winner, or whether a mistake was made.

These were as follows:

■   A dot ('.') following a shot symbol indicates that the shot was played into the net

112

- An arrow ('→') following a shot symbol indicates that the ball was played out of court
- A shot symbol followed by 'W', indicates that the shot was either an outright winner or that the opponents shot following this one was a mistake
- A single line indicates the end of a point
- A double line indicates the end of a game
- A triple line indicates the end of a set.

For the actual notation purposes, the construction of simple columns was used. One vertical column for each player. The play was notated by alternating from each column as the shots were played until the conclusion of the point. A single line was then drawn across both columns and the winning player's last shot ringed. An example of a game notated using this system is shown in Figures 8.2a, b.

8.2.1.1 Description of point

Smith served the ball wide and Jones returned the serve with a forehand that landed short. Smith moved in to play a deep cross-court backhand causing Jones to play a defensive backhand lob. This lob was not a good one and Smith had the chance to smash the ball, but he hit the ball out of court. Jones won the point and the score was 0–15.

The match chosen for analysis was the 1989 Ladies Wimbledon Final between Steffi Graf and Martina Navratilova. This selection was made to incorporate a wide variety of shots while at the same time displaying constructive rallies to analyse, but which did not continue for too long as is the case with some womens' matches, i.e. making notation strenuous.

Also the choice of a grass court surface would produce an exciting game without creating very short rallies as displayed in a men's game, with one player hitting a fast serve, which results in either a mistake or an outright winner from his opponent.

The aim of the notation was to devise a system which was simple enough to notate a match live without the use of video cameras. Therefore, although this match was viewed from video, it was notated continuously without pausing or rewinding the tape. An example of part of the notation is shown in Figure 8.3.

Smith	Jones
S4	F2
B6	L1
Sm →	

Figure 8.2 (a) Notation of data using the system for tennis

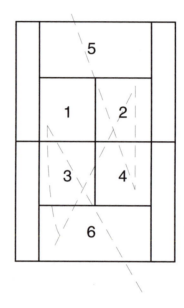

Figure 8.2 (b) Schematic representation of data used in (a)

examples of notation systems

WIMBLEDON LADIES FINAL 1989
Steffi Graf v Martina Navratilova

First Set (Graf won, 6–2)

STEFFI	MARTINA		STEFFI	MARTINA
	S4			S3
B2	V3		B	
F1 W	V →			S4
	S3		B	
B2	V̲4			S3
B2 W			B →	
	S4		1–0	
F5	V4		S4	B →
F2	V3 W		S3	B5
	S3		F6	F2
B			F6	B5
	S4		F4 W	|
B2 W	V		S4 W	
	S3		S3	F5
F5	V6 W		F4	B5
	S4		L̲	Sm2 W
F5	L̲6 W		S4	B
XF →			1–1	
	S3			S1
F1	V̲4		F3 W	
F2 W			Etc.	
	S4 →			
	S3 W			
B				

Figure 8.3 Example of the tennis data gathering system

A simple analysis of the data from this match is presented – more information could have been obtained from the data given more time.

Steffi Graf

Mistakes	Net	1 Forehand
		4 Backhands
	Out	2 Forehands
		3 Backhands
		2 Backhand lobs
Outright winners		5 Forehands
		4 Backhands
		1 Serve
		1 Lob
Points lost	Unforced errors	12
	Navratilova winners	12

Martina Navratilova

Mistakes	Net	3 Forehands
		5 Backhands
		4 Volleys
		1 Double fault
	Out	4 Forehands
		4 Backhands
		1 Volley
Outright winners		1 Forehand
		8 Volleys
		2 Smashes
		1 Serve
Points lost	Unforced errors	23
	Graf winners	11

8.2.1.3 Summary of results

If a performance indicator is defined as:

Tennis ratio = number of errors:number of winners

Graf tennis ratio = 12:11 (or nearly 1:1)

Navratilova tennis ratio = 23:12 (or nearly 2:1).

8.2.1.4 Discussion and conclusions

Analysis of the results showed that in this particular match, the loser, i.e. Martina Navratilova had a ratio of nearly 2:1 for unforced errors to winners. The players analysed were of the highest playing standard currently competing and therefore made relatively few unforced errors. Also, the fast grass court made rallies shorter than usual with many more winners played, in contrast to the 'waiting game' played on slow clay courts. Another reason for Navratilova's results could be related to the nature of her game. She plays a high powered attacking game aiming to control play from the net position as soon as possible. Consequently, her mistakes occurred in trying to get to that position but once there, very few unforced errors occurred and points were won by outright volley winners or by passing shots played by Graf.

8.2.2 A notation system for boxing

First, the types of punches have to be identified, together with other behaviour variables considered to be the important in defining a boxing match. These were considered to be:

1   Jabs
2   Hooks
3   Upper cuts
4   Misses (complete)
5   Front body punches
6   Side body punches
7   Holding
8   Hit guard (partial miss)
9   Foul punching

117

10 Ducking
11 On ropes
12 Knockdown
13 Knockout
14 Technical KO
15 Points decision.

As it can be seen, there are numerous actions which constitute:

■ offensive information
■ defensive information
■ positional information
■ fight outcome.

These provided too many variables to notate using a hand system, as many or all could be occurring simultaneously. It is suggested that, if both boxers are to be notated, only offensive actions and specific key features could be recorded. These could be identified as:

1 Jabs
2 Misses
3 Knockdowns
4 Hooks
5 Body shots
6 Uppercuts
7 Holding.

The system was now progressed to separating these factors into left and right sides depending on which side the punch was thrown from. (Knock downs remained universal as the final punch would be recorded.) The symbol denoting the jab, aims to represent the jab itself, i.e. a straight punch. Hence the symbol used was a straight line. The dash was placed either side depending on where it was thrown from, the left or right. This reasoning was then followed for the construction of the other symbols. Thus, the notation shown in Table 8.1 was devised.

For example, a boxer while holding his opponent with his left arm produces an uppercut which misses with his right; it would be notated as:

    <URm

Table 8.1 Symbols used in the data gathering system for boxing

Left	Right	Punch
–]	[–	Jab
(	)	Hook
UL	UR	Uppercut
m	m	Miss
B	B	Body punch
<	>	Holding
v	v	Knockdown

A chart (Table 8.2) was then devised to record a fight on which the punches of each boxer could be notated in sequential order.

This format of a vertical linear layout remains common in hand systems as it enables quickly translated and stored records. One line of the chart corresponds to one punch from each boxer. In situations where punches were thrown simultaneously, both were recorded on the same line to indicate they occurred within the time space of one punch.

It was decided that certain characteristics of a fight which might ease the notation task were as follows:

1   A heavyweight match in which the 'punch rate' is considerably slower than lower weight categories.
2   A fight which is relatively short in duration, so massive amounts of raw data are not produced.

The chosen match was: Mike Tyson vs Frank Bruno held in 1989 at the Hilton International, Las Vegas. This was a five round fight between two heavyweight boxers.

Notating the fight involved first watching the fight through completely, to get a 'feeling' of punch speed, and of any anomalies which may exist in their boxing style. Then, the fight was notated using the pause function on the video and, at instances when numerous punches were thrown within a very short period, a frame by frame analysis was used. The raw data was then collated by frequency tallies (Figures 8.4, 8.5). Summary totals could then be calculated and represented graphically (see results).

Table 8.2 Example data from the Tyson–Bruno fight (1989) using the data gathering system for boxing

Tyson	Bruno		Tyson	Bruno		Tyson	Bruno
–]				<			<URm
	–]			<UR			<URm
(	)			<UR			<URm
)				<)m			<)m
	.)			<UR			)
	)			<)		–]	
	)			<)m		(	
(				<)			<UR
BUR	<)			)			<UR
	<)			<)			<UR
(			(	<)		(m	
–]				<)			<(
)			–]				)m
(m			)				–]
URm							–]
	V			<>			
(	<			UR		(	
	<			)		)m	
	)			–]			–]
			)			(m	
<)	<)			<)			–]
<)	<)			<)		)m	
	(			<)			)
)			(	<)		(	

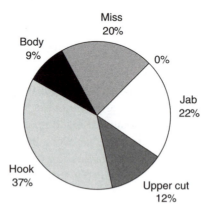

Figure 8.4 Distribution of the types of punches thrown by Tyson in the Bruno–Tyson match (1989)

examples of notation systems

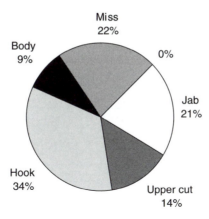

Miss
22%

Body
9%

0%

Jab
21%

Hook
34%

Upper cut
14%

Figure 8.5 Distribution of the types of punches thrown by Bruno in the Bruno–
Tyson match (1989)

From the results, we can see that Bruno threw 55 per cent of the punches,
however if these are broken down round by round, we see that in the first three
rounds he threw more than Tyson, and in Rounds 4 and 5 Tyson threw more
than Bruno (Table 8.3). This suggests that he was tiring and was failing to counter
punch. So the fight was essentially lost in Rounds 4 and 5.

Both boxers had almost identical punch compositions (Table 8.4) with Bruno
missing 1 per cent more than Tyson. However, during the fight Bruno was
cautioned for holding. This is illustrated by Table 8.5 which shows the percentage of punches made while holding. Bruno made 41 per cent of his punches

Table 8.3 Collated data of total punches thrown

	Tyson	**Bruno**
Round 1	38	68
Round 2	36	54
Round 3	27	47
Round 4	32	24
Round 5	48	23
Total	**181**	**216**

Table 8.4 Analysis of the number of types of punches thrown by both boxers

Punch	Tyson		Bruno	
	Number	% of total	Number	% of total
Jab	40	22	45	21
Uppercut	22	12	29	13
Hook	66	37	72	36
Body punch	16	9	19	9
Miss	37	20	46	21

while holding compared with Tyson's 4 per cent. This is probably a reflection of Bruno trying to punch 'inside' Tyson, i.e. by staying close you have less chance of being knocked out with one punch, which is characteristic of Tyson's fights. This was therefore intentional and probably not due to fatigue alone.

Table 8.5 The number of punches thrown while holding

Tyson	Bruno
8	89

Bruno has a reputation for his jabs which intimidate his opponents. In the first three rounds, his jabbing more than doubled those of Tyson (Table 8.6).

Table 8.6 The number of jabs thrown in each round

	Tyson	Bruno
Round 1	5	9
Round 2	8	21
Round 3	8	20
Round 4	15	7
Round 5	6	5
Total	**42**	**62**

examples of notation systems

However, from then on the number of his jabs decreased dramatically and Tyson's increased. The final round contained roughly the same number of jabs thrown by each opponent. This was probably due to Bruno having only the strength to produce jabs and Tyson trying to finish the fight off with hooks and uppercuts, which are more powerful punches. All the statistics tend to suggest that the fight was won in rounds four and five (Figure 8.6).

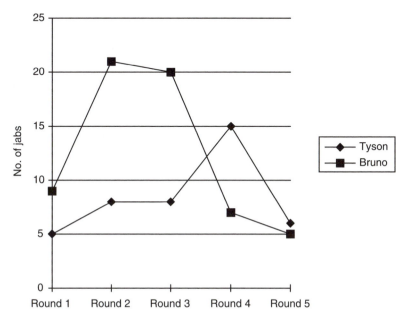

Figure 8.6 Distribution of jabs on a round by round analysis by both fighters (Bruno–Tyson, 1989)

8.2.2.2 Conclusions

1   This simple system does enable the notation of a boxing match by a post-event analysis of video. While acknowledging that the results describe the basic techniques employed by a boxer during a match, one must recognize that the notation in itself was very simplified and somewhat crude, and did not address many essential aspects of a fight, namely positional information, defensive information and subjective measures of power and accuracy (which may require the knowledge of a skilled coach).
2   Considering the speed of boxing matches, it was almost impossible to notate a fight live. The use of video and playback was therefore essential.

However, some very simple and basic information clearly maps the progress of the fight and gives a quantitative analysis of the progress of the two boxers during the bout.

8.3 TEAM SPORTS

8.3.1 A notation system for basketball

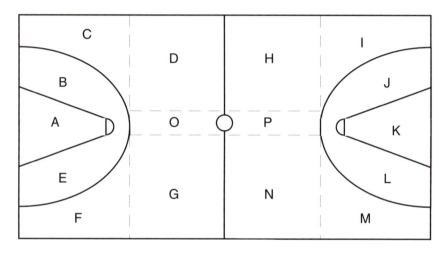

Figure 8.7 Schematic representation of the basketball court in order to define position cells for a data gathering system

The schematic representation of a basketball court, in Figure 8.7, shows the court position used in the notation. In basketball a team squad consists of 10 team members, five on the court at any one time. For the purpose of this notation, the players were assigned numbers in the range 4–14 (1, 2 and 3 were not used to avoid confusion with the letters I, Z and B), although some teams, and all American ones, often use numbers like 33, 42, etc.

The actions under consideration in this hand notation and the symbols used to represent them are listed as follows:

Actions	Symbol
Tip off	TO
Dribble	D
Drive	V

Shot	S (B or M)
Lay-up	L (B or M)
Rebound	R
Pass	P
Fastbreak	F
Foul	FL (Time)
Free throws	FT (Time)
Turnover	T (Time)
Substitution	SB (Time)
Out of court	0 (Time)
Sideline ball	SL
Baseline ball	BL

B, basket good; M, basket missed; Time, the time the action occurred should be recorded.

Table 8.7 A demonstration of how the notation system works

Time	Team A	Team B
TO 6 P		
H 7 D		
I 7 P		
K 13 S M		
		K 4 R
		K 4 D
		L 4 P
	2:20	N 13 FL (5)
		SL-N 13 P
		N 10 P
	2:59	T
C 6 P		
3:01	I 13 L B	
2–0		
		BL-K 4 P
		I 0
	3:05	SB-4/6
		SL-I 6 P
	Etc.	

These symbols, together with the player number and his position on the court, are written down in columns in a table in the following manner:

6   G P

i.e. Player No. 6, in position cell G, passed the ball.

The following is an explanation of the events notated in Table 8.7.

Line	Comments
1	The tip off was won by 6 who passed.
2	No. 7 received the ball in H and dribbled
3	to I where the ball was passed
4	to No. 13 in K who shot and missed.
5	Team B: No. 4 rebounded in K
6	dribbled from K
7	to L where the ball was passed
8	to 13 in N who was fouled by No. 5.
9	No. 13 took a sideline ball in N passing
10	to No. 10 in N who dribbled
11	to O where the ball was passed
12	Turnover – after 2 min 59 s.
13	No. 6 intercepted the ball in C and passed
14	to No. 13 in I who scored a lay-up.
15	The running score is 2–0, time 3 min 01s.
16	Baseline ball in K is passed by No. 4,
17	the ball goes out of court in I.
18	Substitution: No. 6 comes on for No. 4.
19	Sideline ball in I is passed by No. 6.

8.3.1.1 Conclusion and discussion

A coach or analyst can use this very simple notation system to gather performance data of individual players or the whole team. It can be used to analyse from which side of the court the most successful attacks come; what success rate the team and individuals achieve at rebounds (do they win more than they lose); how successful they are in the majority of freethrows; is there any increase in success rate/performance after a time out, etc. The coach can then assess the strengths and weaknesses of the individuals and the team, or their opponents, and be able to make an attempt at correcting them.

126

This type of system is very easily changed to suit any team sport, re-defining the playing surface, the number of players and the actions, and their outcomes, accordingly.

8.3.2 A notation system for soccer

The aim of this notation system was to notate the distribution ability of a right full back in soccer.

8.3.2.1 Method

Notation occurred each time the subject, the right full back of Brook House FC, appeared to play or distribute the ball. The following symbols and meanings were used in order for the system to function.

Passes/Clearances/Shots	Distances	Symbols
By foot	<10 yards	F1
	10–30 yards	F2
	>10–30 yards	F3
By head	<10 yards	H1
	10–30 yards	H2
	>10–30 yards	H3
By hand (i.e. throw-in)	<10 yards	T1
	10–30	T2

- Clearances above symbols preceded by 'C', e.g. CF2 is a clearance by foot of between 10–30 yards (It should be noted that clearances were neither counted as completed or incompleted passes)
- Shots above symbols for feet or head preceded by (i.e. F,!) for a goal and 'X' for a miss
- Completed Pass above symbols for feet, head or hand
- Uncompleted Pass above symbols for feet, head or hand, *circled*
- The time elapsed of the half was also recorded at the end of each piece of information.

Therefore, an example of notated data is as follows:

CH3 12, 37

This refers to a clearance by head of a distance of 30 yards or more, that occurred after 12 min 37 s of the half. These data were then recorded in columns on a prepared data collection sheet.

8.3.2.2 Results

The data was collected over 45 min (one half) of a 'local Sunday football league' match.

> Match Information Date = 29/10/89, Start = 12.09 p.m.
> 1st half of Bow & Arrow FC vs Brook House FC
> (Black & white stripes) vs (Royal blue & navy stripes)
> Half-time score: 1–3

The data were obtained by notating the 1st half of the above match and processing the data in a very simple way. From these results the following analysis was carried out.

8.3.2.3 Analysis

1 Number of touches of the ball = 29
2 Number of touches of the ball by each method
   i   Number of foot contacts = 21
   ii Number of headed contacts = 3
   iii Number of throw-ins = 5
3 Percentage of touches by each method:
   i   Feet = 21/29 = 72.4%
   ii Head = 3/29 = 10.4%
   iii Throw-ins = 5/29 = 17.2%
4 Number of incomplete passes (i.e. errors), signified by circled symbol = 9
5 Number of errors by each method
   i   Feet = 8
   ii Head = 0
   iii Throw-ins = 1
6 Percentage of errors by each method
   i   Feet = 8/9 = 88.9%
   ii Head = 0/9 = 0%
   iii Throw-ins = 11.1%
7 Distribution at the various distances:
   A   Total analysis

128

i   Total < 10 yards = 14
        [By foot = 12, By head = 1, Throw-in = 1]
ii   Total 10–30 yards = 11
        [By foot = 5, By head = 2, Throw-in = 4]
iii   Total > 30 yards = 4
        [By foot = 4, By head = 0, Throw-in = 0]
        Total = 29
Percentages of this total analysis, A, i–iii
        <10 yards = 48.3%
        [By foot = 85.7%, By head = 7.1%, Throw-in = 7.1%]
        10–30 yards = 37.9%
        [By foot = 45.5%, By head = 18.2%, Throw-in = 37.4%]
        >30 yards = 13.8%
        [By foot = 100%]
B   Completed pass analysis (not including clearances)
    i   Total <10 yards = 3
        [By foot = 2, By head = 0, Throw-in = 1]
    ii   Total 10–30 yards = 6
        [By foot = 3, By head = 0, Throw-in = 3]
    iii   Total >30 yards = 2
        [By foot = 2, By head = 0, Throw-in = 0]
        Total = 11 (includes one successful attempt at goal)
    Percentages of completed pass analysis, B (i–iii)
        Total <10 yards = 27.3%
        [By foot = 66.7%, Throw-in = 33.3%]
        Total 10–30 yards = 54.6%
        [By foot = 50%, Throw-in = 50%]
        Total >30 yards = 18.2%
        [By foot = 100%]
C   Uncompleted pass analysis (not including clearances)
    i   Total <10 yards = 6
        [By foot = 6]
    ii   Total 10–30 yards = 2
        [By foot = 1, Throw-in = 1]
    iii   Total >30 yards = 1
        [By foot = 1]
        Total = 9
    Percentages of uncompleted pass analysis, C (i–iii)
        Total <10 yards = 66.7%
        [By foot = 100%]

Total 10–30 yards = 22.2%
    [By foot = 50%, Throw-in = 50%]
Total >30 yards = 11.1%
    [By foot = 100%]

8   Ratio: completed passes to total number of passes =11/20 = 0.55
     Ratio: uncompleted passes to total number of passes =9/20 = 0.45
      [*Note*: does not include clearances]

9   Clearance study:
   A   Total number of clearances = 9
   B   Total number of clearances at each distance
      i   Total <10 yards = 5
         [By foot = 4, By head = 1]
      ii   Total 10–30 yards = 3
         [By foot = 1, By head = 2]
      iii Total >30 yards = 1
         [By foot = 1]
     Percentages of B, (i–iii)
       Total <10 yards = 55.6%
         [By foot = 80%, By head = 20%]
       Total 10–30 yards = 33.3%
         [By foot = 33.3%, By head = 66.7%]
       Total >30 yards = 11.1%
         [By foot = 100%]

10 Outline of the subject's activity:

	Section	No. Touches	Successful	Unsuccessful	Clears
i	0–5 min	2	1	1	0
ii	5–10 min	2	0	1	0
iii	10–15 min	4	1	2	1
iv	15–20 min	4	1	1	2
v	20–25 min	3	3	0	0
vi	25–30 min	3	1	2	0
vii	30–35 min	1	0	0	1
viii	35–40 min	3	1	0	2
ix	40–45 min	4	3*	1	0
x	45–50 min	3	0	1	2

* including one successful attempt at goal. See Figures 8.8–8.11 for visual representation of some of the data.

examples of notation systems

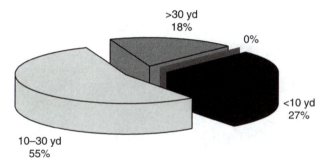

Figure 8.8 Representation of the number of completed passes

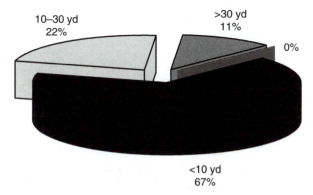

Figure 8.9 Representation of the number of incomplete passes

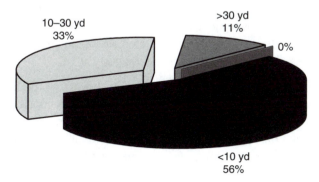

Figure 8.10 Representation of the clearances

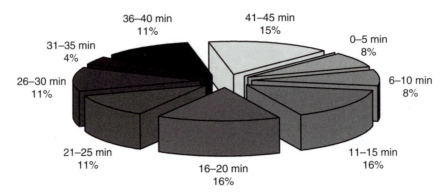

36–40 min
11%

41–45 min
15%

0–5 min
8%

31–35 min
4%

6–10 min
8%

26–30 min
11%

21–25 min
11%

11–15 min
16%

16–20 min
16%

Figure 8.11 Representation of percentage of activities throughout the first half

8.3.2.4 Discussion

Just one half of a soccer match does not produce anything like a significant amount of data about which conclusions can be drawn, but this example does give ideas about analysing and presenting data. A few statements can be made about these interpretations. The majority of the full-back touches, 72.4 per cent, were performed by the foot. But this percentage led to a larger amount of errors, 88.9 per cent, being by foot contact. There was a roughly equal distribution of passes performed over distances of <10 yards and between 10 and 30 yards, 48.3 per cent and 37.9 per cent, respectively. Despite this almost equal distribution, the subject was twice as successful at passing over a distance of between 10 and 30 yards as one of <10 yards. This success over the intermediate distance (10–30 yards) is mirrored by the fact that the subject committed only 1/5 of the total errors committed over the distance. From the analysis it was found that the subject performed 10 per cent more completed passes (not including clearances) that uncompleted passes (not including clearances).

Analysis of the clearances the subject performed shows that the majority were carried out over the short distance of <10 yards. As the 'direction of distribution' was not recorded (see adjustments) this aspect of clearance distance is difficult to interpret, but a part explanation could be that the full back plays near to the touchline and so a safe clearance will be over this touchline, which in many situations will be <10 yards from the point of play. The subject's intense periods of involvement were evenly spread throughout the half, with no one 'five minute section' having no activity. A more general observation is of the small contribution that heading made to the subject's play, but this could be explained by the opposition employing two small forwards and subsequently not playing the ball to them in the air.

examples of notation systems

It would be interesting to see if these statements still held true with 6–8 matches of data. Many of these points are somewhat subjective as they are made on the basis of only one short data collection session. It could be that all of the points made came about due to the context of the game, and a completely different set of remarks could have occurred if a different game had been notated.

The exercise did however produce some recommendations to improve the system.

8.3.2.5 Adjustments to the system

1 Divide foot passes into left foot or right foot passes. Therefore the present symbol would be preceded by a 'L' or a 'R'.
e.g. F1L = a left foot pass of 10 yards or less.
2 Notate fouls and indiscretions (i.e. bookings or 'sendings-off')
3 Notate attempts on goal with a separate symbol = 'S'
e.g. SF1L,! = a successful attempt at goal with the left foot <10 yards from goal.
SH1, X = an unsuccessful attempt at goal with the head <10 yards from goal.
4 Notation of tackles could be introduced; but this is moving away from the aim of notating the 'distribution ability' of a full back.
5 Notation with the aid of a grid. The grid could be designed by measuring the length and width of a pitch and dividing it into nine equal areas (Figure 8.12), and then notation of positional data from where the full back passes, and to where the passes go, becomes possible.

This grid adjustment could lead to two methods of notating:

1 Produce printed sheets of the grid and for each piece of notation draw a line from the origin of the pass (i.e. position of full back) to its destination, and on the same sheet include the appropriate symbol and time as before.
or
2 Similar to the original system notating in columns, the following type of codes could be used:

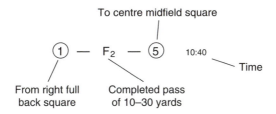

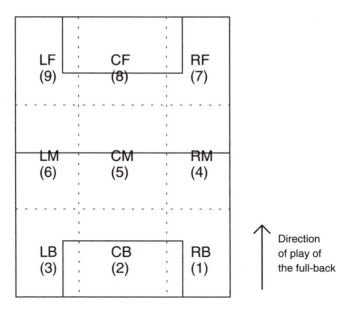

Figure 8.12 Schematic diagram of a soccer pitch showing suggested divisions of the playing area into a grid for notation

Method 1 would be more accurate as the exact position and not just the square would be notated. But it would require one sheet for each piece of information notated. Also learning time would be much longer and 'logging time' for each action would be longer and more complicated.

8.3.3 A notation system for netball

A netball team consists of seven players. Each player has a limited area within which to operate. Every player is allocated a specific role in the game which corresponds to the area in which they operate. The object of the game is to attempt to score as many goals as possible. To achieve this requires team cohesion, co-operation and understanding between all the team members. A skilful game of netball relies on effective passing to maintain possession of the ball.

8.3.3.1 Method

Before outlining the system, it is necessary to ensure that you understand the basic rules of the game.

Essential rules of netball
Like any other team game, netball has its own specific set of rules which must be adhered to throughout the match. Before a system of notational analysis can be designed it is important to be familiar with these rules:

1   There is a 3 s limit on the time it takes a team member to pass the ball or attempt a shot at goal.
2   The ball must be caught or touched in each third of the court during play.
3   The centre pass must be caught or touched by a player allowed in the centre third of the court (Figure 8.13).
4   When a ball goes out of court, it can only be thrown-in by a player allowed in that particular area.
5   Only the goal-shooter or goal-attack can score a goal. The ball must also have been wholly caught within the goal circle.
6   A player must keep within the limits of area prescribed by her position.

8.3.3.2 Notation symbols

The symbols to be used will record the following:

1   The team member in possession of the ball and the position on the court where they received the ball.
2   What happens at the end of the passing sequence before reverting back to the centre pass or change of possession.
3   Out-of-court shots where the ball has been passed outside the side line.

Each player wears a vest with letters representing their roles (each one is self-explanatory):

GK = goal keeper
GD = goal defence
WD = wing defence
C   = centre
WA = wing attack
GA = goal attack
GS = goal shooter

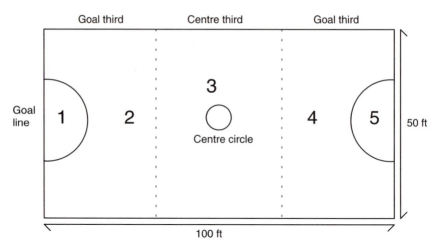

Figure 8.13 Schematic representation of the netball court for divisions of the playing surface

The court was divided into five areas so that a simple view of the path of the ball can be deduced (Figure 8.13):

1 = goal circle
2 = goal third
3 = centre third
4 = goal third
5 = goal circle

Each player has a prescribed playing area – these are designated in Table 8.8.

Table 8.8 Each player has designated areas within which they must play

Player	Areas for team playing from area 1 towards area 5		
GK	1	2	
GD	1	2	3
WD	2	3	
C	2	3	4
WA		3	4
GA	3	4	5
GS		4	5

Actions:

/
\\/ = goal scored (should be followed by a centre pass)
X = goal attempted but missed
O = out-of-court shot (the appropriate team is given a free throw from the side
line where the ball went out)
C = centre pass (no court position number is added since it is always taken from
within the centre circle).

Continued notation within the column implies a successful pass.

8.3.3.3 The record sheet

It is necessary for the recording sheet to contain descriptive details of the match
or practice session so that the information obtained is available for analysis and
for future reference if required.

1   Match or practice session?
2   Venue
3   Date
4   (If possible) names of players.

The recording sheet consists of vertical columns under the headings of red and
blue (referring to the team colours). Play is recorded in the appropriate column
according to the team in possession of the ball. Play is recorded from the top
to the bottom of the column. The score is shown at the left side of each
column.

8.3.3.4 Recording a sequence

Each sequence begins with the centre pass represented by the symbol 'C'. The
centre pass is always taken from within the centre circle. Play continues and
the player and position are notated. The sequence is completed when a goal is
scored and represented by the symbol 'V'. An example of a record sheet is
shown in Table 8.9.

8.3.3.5 Results

The results (Table 8.10) showed that the red team were more successful at
retaining possession once they had got it. The red team averaged three passes

Table 8.9 Example of a record sheet for simple data gathering for notation of netball

Score	Red	Blue	Score	Red	Blue
		C		O	
		WA 3		GD 4	
		GA4		WD 3	
		GS 5		C 3	
		X		O	GK 2
		GS 5			O
0–1		√		WA 3	
	C			C 3	
	WA 3			GA 2	
	C 2			GS 1	
	GS 1		2–1	√	
1–1	√				
	C			Etc.	

Table 8.10 Data processed from a notated netball match (part only)

	Red	Blue
Number of possessions	7	10
Number of passes	21	16
Average sequence	21/7 = 3	16/10 = 1.6
Number of passing errors	2	4

per possession and had only two passing errors. Both passing errors were caused by the red centre player passing the ball out-of-court.

The blue team had more possessions but that did not compensate for their passing errors since they only managed 1.6 passes per possession and incurred more passing errors. From this short example of data, few conclusions can be drawn about the play. Much more data is needed. But the notation exercise enabled an assessment of the notation system. By examining the record sheet there are several factors that can be analysed without a great deal of effort:

1   The number of possessions by each team. A possession is defined as a single player or sequence of players following each other simultaneously in the team's column on the record sheet.
2   Related to the number of possessions is the number of passing errors induced by a team and the frequency of passing errors by a particular player. To obtain a percentage of passing errors it would be necessary to evaluate the

number of touches by that player. It is then also possible for the coach to assess whether the team is making good use of all the players in the team although this is somewhat dependent on their accessibility at the time. The latter information would need to be combined with the coaches own subjective observations.

A passing error would be defined as the ball changing possession or going out-of-court. A touch would be defined as the ball actually being caught and passed or being touched as it travelled through the air.

3   It is possible to calculate the average number of passes in a sequence. This is important when assessing the path of the ball particularly from the centre pass to an attempt at goal. A common strategy outlined in books is a three pass attack down the centre although a two pass attack is possible. The greater the number of passes incurred the greater the opportunity for defenders to break the attack.

4   A percentage success rate of goals by the goal shooter and goal attack can be calculated. It allows the coach to assess which, or if both, players need goal-shooting practice.

5   When analysing who attempted the most shots at goal it could be beneficial to work backwards and see the shots leading to the attempt. With sufficient data it may be possible to outline a common attacking strategy.

Although the record sheet appears 'simplistic', a great deal of information can be gleaned from it. It is possible to assemble a quick summary after the match. Given more time more detailed information may be extracted. Once the notation is sufficiently rehearsed it is easy to modify the system to take into consideration a number of other factors.

Possible improvements

1   The court could be subdivided into smaller sections to outline a more accurate path of the ball which can then be transferred to plans of play. For example, this would be useful when tracing the path of the ball from centre pass – a common strategy advocated in coaching books is an attack down the centre. By recording the team's patterns with their centre-pass, the coach can conclude whether the centre line attacking strategy is successful for them or whether the team tends to play more down one side than the other. On the other hand, having more position cells will mean that more matches will have to be analysed to produce significant amounts of data in all the cells.

2   Players can be penalized for foot-faults, but this is not a common occurrence in experienced players. So it would be only relevant when notating novices.

3   A throw-up is called for when a player of each team gains possession of the ball equally at the same time. A throw-up is then called for and the success of gaining possession by a particular team could be notated.

8.3.4 A motion analysis of work-rate in different positional roles in field hockey

8.3.4.1 Aim

The aim of this investigation is to analyse the overall movement patterns of elite male field hockey players. Furthermore, to compare and contrast the difference in movement patterns with a players position.

8.3.4.2 Hypothesis

Null hypothesis (H_0)
There will be no significant difference in the movement patterns of field hockey players in relation to their position.

Experimental hypothesis (H_1)
There will be a significant difference in the movement patterns of field hockey players in relation to player position.

8.3.4.3 Devising the method

The analysis of team games has tended to be more of a subjective and qualitative nature, and is characterized by observational techniques relying on the coaches' evaluation of the game. An objective and quantitative paradigm should lead to a greater insight into the physiological demands of invasive games.

There are indicators of the physiological demands of different sports, including heart rate response (Carter 1996; Boddington et al. 2001), distance covered and work-rest ratios (Lothian and Farrally 1994; O'Donoghue and Parker 2001). The most interesting time–motion analysis studies have been in the movement patterns of different positional roles (Reilly and Thomas 1976; Herbert and Tong 1996).

According to Hughes and Franks (2004), any statistics being gathered from a dynamic environment, like field hockey, can be difficult to obtain. Therefore, any quantitative analysis must be structured, for example, a flowchart. Franks and

Figure 8.14 Hierarchical structure representing events that take place in team games (Franks and Goodman 1984)

Goodman (1984) produced a hierarchical structure for initiating a notational system (cited in Hughes and Franks 2004), (Figure 8.14).

8.3.4.4 Pilot study

A pilot study was carried out for approximately 10 min. From conducting the pilot study, strengths and weaknesses of the system could be identified. It demonstrated that although the system collected great amounts of data, the system was too complex. The difficult decision is knowing when the limitations of a hand notation are acceptable within the terms of reference of the desired data collection. The hand notation was revised and evaluated, thus allowing a more effective methodology to be utilized.

8.3.4.5 Finalized method

The male hockey match recorded ($n = 1$) was of international standard, between Spain and Germany in the semi-final of the World Cup 2006. The location of the camera is unknown, but assumed its location is approximately the half way line. The game was viewed once for each discipline ($n = 3$; 1 forward, 1 midfield and 1 defence) for a total of three players and for the duration of 20 min.

Due to lack of technological equipment, movement classifications were timed with a stop watch and, by a random sampling method, Spain were selected to be the team of focus. In addition, the recording of data required two operators and movements patterns were operationally defined.

Table 8.11 Short-hand symbols

Movement	Short-hand symbol
Stationary	O
Walking	W
Jogging	J
Shuffling	Λ
Sprinting	*
Game-related activity	G

By adopting both Hughes and Franks (2004) and Frank and Goodman's (1984) theories, a simple flowchart was devised appropriate for this investigation (Figure 8.15).

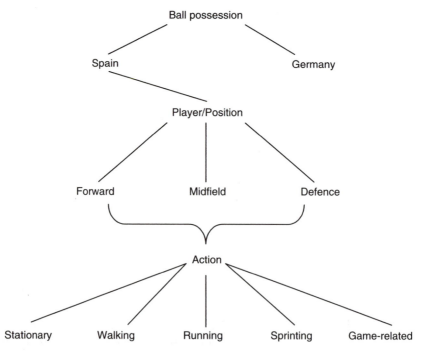

Figure 8.15 Hierarchical model of time–motion analysis in field hockey

examples of notation systems

8.3.4.6 Limitations

There will be limitations placed upon this investigation such as a time and word limit, and lack of technological equipment, which prevents the investigation going into too great a depth.

Former type error occurs when an operator unintentionally enters incorrect data. For example, uses the wrong short-hand symbol. The chance of error possibilities occurring is heightened within this study due to there being two operators.

Due to the continuous nature of running, it is difficult to strictly classify its movement into such discrete categories such as sprinting and jogging. Therefore, the study is subjective, thus affecting the reliability and repeatability of this notation.

8.3.4.7 Operational definitions

Stationary
Standing, sitting, lying or stretching – activity that portrays little exhaustive movement.

Walking (forwards, backwards, lateral)
The back foot does not leave the floor until the front foot makes contact with the ground. This movement is slow in nature.

Running (forwards, backwards)
This is a slow running movement without obvious exhaustive effort.

Sprinting
Explosive movement that involves rapid extension of the hip and knee. There is obvious acceleration.

Game-related activity
This is any time during the game where the player is either in contact with the ball or attempting to become in contact with the ball; hitting, dribbling, tackling, channelling, side line balls, free hits, passing, etc.

8.3.4.8 Reliability

The repeatability and accuracy of a study is a central facet to notational analysis. Hughes *et al.* (2004) found that within analysing 72 research papers, 70 per cent of investigations did not report any reliability study. A simple inter-operator test for reliability was performed using an equation suggested by Hughes et al. (2004):

$$(\Sigma \ (\text{mod} \ [V_1-V_2] \ / \ V_{mean}) \times 100\%$$

V_1 and V_2 are variables, V_{mean} is their mean, mod = modulus, and Σ means 'sum of'. The calculation will give a percentage error for each variable and operator. Significance level was set at 5. If a value is $p>5$ it is assumed that the test is not significant, therefore not reliable.

From the results illustrated in both Table 8.12 and Figure 8.16, it can be identified that the overall reliability of the system was 1.01 per cent, suggesting that the system is reliable. However, when analysing the discrete values, there are large discrepancies within the data. For example, the least significant value is 19 per cent for shuffling. The most significant value was 4.7 per cent for walking. This emphasizes the subjective nature of the investigation. Also, dynamic activities such as shuffling and sprinting are more arduous to identify than walking and stationary movements. This heightens the importance of operational definitions.

Using computerized methods such as the CAPTAIN system (McLaughlin and O'Donoghue 2004) may increase the reliability of future time–motion analysis systems.

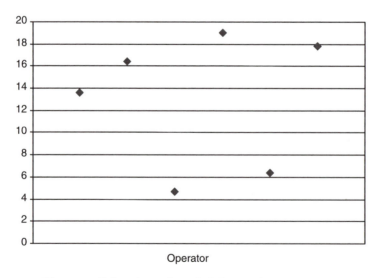

Operator

Figure 8.16 The overall data from the reliability study

Table 8.12 Data from a field hockey game notated once by two operators for 20 min, presented as an inter-reliability analysis

	Operator 1 (V1)	Operator 2 (V2)	Percentage error
Sprinting	4.71	4.11	13.6%
Running	4.55	5.36	16.4%
Walking	4.78	5.01	4.7%
Shuffling	1.85	2.24	19.0%
Stationary	3.5	3.28	6.4%
Game-related activity	2.26	1.89	17.8%
Overall percentage error			12.9%

8.3.4.9 Results

From both Table 8.13 and Figure 8.17, it is illustrated that a forward position in hockey spent 5.57 min (26 per cent) of the 20 min of performance sprinting. This is followed by 5.23 min running and 5.07 min walking.

It can be assumed that a forward may sprint and run more often during a game as it is their short duration bursts of activities into space that create through balls, and therefore attacking opportunities. In contrast, only 1.28 min of the game was spent doing game-related activity. This suggests how the results may be influenced by the state of play. For example, if Spain had less possession, or more defensive play.

Table 8.14 and Figure 8.18 show the results of the movement patterns of a specific midfield hockey player. In comparison, the midfield player spent a longer duration in a wider range of activities than the forward. This may be because of

Table 8.13 Movement patterns of a forward

FORWARD		
Movement		**Time (min)**
Sprinting		5.57
Running		5.23
Walking		5.07
Shuffling		1.05
Stationary		3.08
	Total	**20**
Game-related activity		1.28

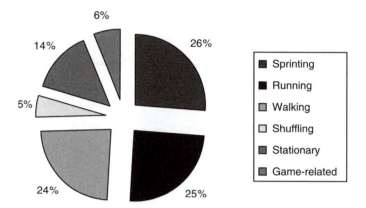

Figure 8.17 Pie chart displaying movement pattern breakdown of a forward

Table 8.14 Movement patterns of a midfielder

MIDFIELD		
Movement		**Time (min)**
Sprinting		5.24
Running		6.41
Walking		3.52
Shuffling		2.01
Stationary		2.82
	Total	**20**
Game-related activity		3.07

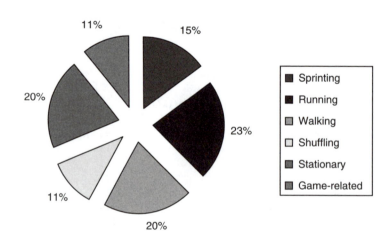

Figure 8.18 Pie chart displaying movement pattern breakdown of a midfield

the specific role of a midfield player: they create links with the defence and forwards, therefore adopt both an attacking role consisting of short duration bursts of activity (23 per cent running), and defending play consisting of shuffling (11 per cent) movements associated with channelling and tackling. Furthermore, this may suggest why the midfield player has more game-related activity, 3.07 minutes.

The movement patterns of a defender, as show in Table 8.15 and Figure 8.19 are similar to that of a midfield player (9 per cent of activity was spent shuffling which is associated with tackling, and channelling movements typical of a defender). This is in complete contrast to a forward who spent only 5 per cent of the game shuffling. Furthermore, the defending and midfield positions spent more time in game-related activity suggesting the team was adopting a defending strategy rather than attacking (Table 8.16 and Figure 8.20).

Table 8.15 Movement patterns of a defender

DEFENCE		
Movement		**Time (min)**
Sprinting		3.37
Running		5.01
Walking		4.55
Shuffling		2.48
Stationary		4.59
	Total	**20**
Game-related activity		2.42

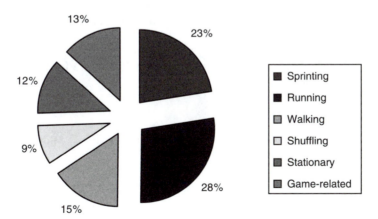

Figure 8.19 Pie chart displaying movement pattern breakdown of a defender

Table 8.16 Movement patterns for an average hockey player

Movement	Mean and SD
Sprinting	4.71 ± 1.18
Running	4.55 ± 0.75
Walking	4.78 ± 0.79
Shuffling	1.85 ± 0.73
Stationary	3.5 ± 0.96
Game-related activity	2.26 ± 0.91

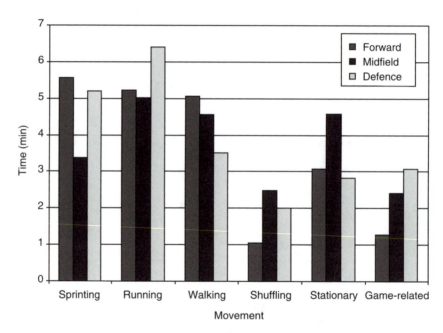

Figure 8.20 Bar chart representing movement patterns of a forward, midfield and defence

Table 8.17 Independent *t*-test results

	Forward/Midfield	Forward/Defence	Midfield/Defence
p value	0.846	0.791	0.903

A simple independent *t*-test was carried out upon three groups of paired data (Table 8.17). The significance level was set at 0.05. The results illustrate that there is no significant difference the movement patterns of field hockey players in relation to their position.

8.3.4.10 Application

Measurement parameters such as heart rate, body temperature and respirometers are impractical during competitive play. Time–motion analysis aids the coach in assessing the physiological demands of a performer: its most important application is to assist the coach in devising an accurate fitness programme that will train the specific physiological systems that are in high demand during competition.

8.3.4.11 Conclusion

From this study it can be concluded that there is no significant difference in the movement patterns of elite male field hockey players in relation to position. Future research must be carried out both reliably and effectively in order to solidify such conclusions as this one.

8.3.4.12 Recommendations for further research

The following are recommendations for future research investigations within the area of time–motion analysis of field hockey:

1   The inclusion of heart rate monitors
2   Blood lactate measurements
3   The effect of the scoreline upon the work-rate
4   Group efficacy beliefs and work-rate.

SUMMARY

As previously stated in other chapters of this notation, systems such as this can provide coaches with reliable, calculated data to provide precise feedback to performers (Hughes and Franks 2004). By evaluating important and effective aspects of competition, the adoption of a rational and systematic approach to improving performance and reduce the unpredictability of a team can be applied to coaching practices (Lyle 2002).

CHAPTER NINE

ANALYSIS OF NOTATION DATA: RELIABILITY

Mike Hughes

In this chapter we:

■ aim to investigate the issues associated with reliability studies and sub-sequent analyses in performance analysis by using practical examples from research.

9.1 INTRODUCTION

The key factor in any research that uses new equipment is the repeatability and accuracy of this equipment. In most performance analysis papers, the researchers are presenting systems that have been specifically designed for that experiment. It was the exception (Hughes *et al.* 1989; Wilson and Barnes 1998), rather than the rule that most papers presenting new systems produce evidence of systematized testing of the reliability of these new systems. In a number of studies, parametric techniques were used with data that were non-parametric, although, in some cases, the means of the data sets appeared ordinal, they were often means of nominal data and therefore the use of a parametric test put the conclusions at risk.

There are many similarities in the nature of the data generated by experiments in performance analysis of sport. Although Atkinson and Nevill (1998) have produced a definitive summary of reliability techniques in sports medicine, no similar attempt has been attempted to make recommendations in the use of techniques in performance analysis for solving some of the common problems associated with these types of data. Since Hughes and colleagues (2002)

150

produced their paper on reliability and statistical processes, the presentation of reliability, and the application of correct statistical techniques, has improved immensely. Some of the issues that were perceived as being causes for uncertainty are explained below.

- It is vital that the reliability of a system is demonstrated clearly and in a way that is compatible with the intended analyses of the data. The data must be tested in the same way and to the same depth in which it will be processed in the subsequent analyses. In some cases, the reliability studies were executed on summary data, and the system was then assumed to be reliable for all of the other types of more detailed data analyses that were produced.
- In general, the work of Bland and Altman (1986) has transformed the attitude of sport scientists to testing reliability; can similar techniques be applied to non-parametric data?
- It is clear that just applying a test of differences about the mean or median (t-test, ANOVA, Mann–Whitney, Kruskal–Wallis, χ^2, etc) is not enough, and a measure of absolute differences of the means or medians should also be applied.
- The most common form of data analysis in notation studies is to record frequencies of actions and their respective positions on the performance area, these are then presented as sums or totals in each respective area. What are the effects of cumulative errors nullifying each other, so that the overall totals appear less incorrect than they actually are?
- The application of parametric statistical techniques is often misused in performance analysis – how does this affect the confidence of the conclusions to say something about the data, with respect to more appropriate non-parametric tests?

9.2 THE NATURE OF THE DATA; THE DEPTH OF ANALYSIS

9.2.1 Sample data

As a test of inter-operator reliability, a squash match was notated in-event, by two experienced analysts. A computerized system was used. The match was analysed live, rather than from videotape. It was a match in the squash team World Cup, played in Holland, July 1999. Both analysts had already gathered data for four matches that day and were therefore tired and errors could be expected. Both recorded the match from similar positions from behind the court, both using similar laptop computers with which they were very familiar. The data input system required the number of shots in each rally, the outcome, which player made the rally ending shot, the type of shot and from which position on the court this shot was struck (the court was divided into 16 position cells, coded by number). The system stored the data of each rally sequentially in the 'Access' database and, as part of the system, there was specifically written software to process the data into graphical output for feedback to coaches and athletes. The 'raw' data in the database were used, rather than the processed output, as this enabled certain questions to be posed that could not otherwise be answered from the processed data, that no longer retained the sequential nature of the data.

Analysing the total shots in each analysis of the match indicates 100 per cent accuracy between the two operators (Table 9.1). The analysis of the different totals of shots in each game demonstrates how adding frequency data from two or more sources can hide differences. The different totals now indicate that there are errors but they are still all <1 per cent. This is a very simple example, and more complex data analyses are demonstrated below; adding data together in this way will lead to masking 'true' error figures. The results will always depend upon the relative depth of analysis that is applied to the sequentiality of the data and also the definition of the terms involved in per cent error. Let us examine different ways of analysing these types of data. Percentage differences are a simple but effective way to measure the absolute difference between sets of data.

Table 9.1 The total shots per game

	Shots per game		
	Analyst 1	Analyst 2	% Difference
Game 1	789	792	0.38
Game 2	439	435	0.91
Game 3	457	458	0.21
Total	1,685	1,685	0

9.2.2 The sequential nature of data

It is becoming more and more clear that the first step in a reliability study should always be to compare the raw data of the study, if this is possible, in their original form. Sometimes, in the case of pre-programmed computer systems, this is not always possible. The raw data sets in this example from squash, two sets of columns, were scanned and it was seen that they were of different lengths. One of the sets of data had a series of null data that occupied a row of data. This could have been a software error, an operator error or a combination of both. This row was deleted and the two sets of data were of equal length. This process was repeated four times until the differences in the data were within the expected range from operator errors. So the data had five errors in non-matching lines of data due to either operator or software error. The two data sets then appeared to match in length and content. The respective shot and/or error totals had not indicated these errors.

9.3 CONSISTENCY OF PERCENTAGE DIFFERENCE CALCULATIONS

Consider now the simple concept of calculating the percentage difference in the repeatability of counting the number of shots in each rally. We have already seen the different values obtained by using the game totals and the match total (Table 9.1). Let us examine some of the different possible interpretations of 'percentage difference'.

- There were 20 lines of data in which there were differences between the data sets, errors made, in counting the lengths of the rallies. There was an (adjusted) total of 105 rallies in the match, so the percentage error, based upon the number of lines with differences in them, and the five mismatches, could be stated as 24.1 per cent of the number of rallies.
- The differences of the 20 error measurements totalled 37 shots, 1.85 shots/line. The average rally length was 16.2 shots, so the average percentage error per average rally length was 1.85/16.2 = 11.4 per cent.
- When each error was calculated as a percentage of the length of that particular rally, then the error on the length of the rally (1.85/9.25) averaged a 20.0 per cent error of the length of the respective rally.
- However, taking into account all the rallies, then by calculating:

$(\Sigma \, (\text{mod} \, (V_1 - V_2)) \, / \, V_{TOTmean}) \times 100\%,$

where 'mod' is the modulus and 'Σ' indicates the 'sum of', the overall percentage error figure for rally length comes out as 2.1 per cent, and $V_{TOTmean}$ is the mean of the total variables measured.

By examining the data at different levels, and using different definitions for the calculations involved, then very different values for the percentage error of the rally length have been obtained. There are no right and/or wrong answers in these scenarios, but it does emphasize the necessity for analysts to be very explicit when presenting these types of data analyses, so that their audience can clearly understand what is meant by the definition of 'percentage error' presented.

9.4 PROCESSING DATA

Let us consider another example from these data. It would be expected, from experience of previous work in performance analysis, that a notation of position would result in the largest source of errors in this process. The positions were defined in a 16-cell distribution across the court (Figure 9.1). Figures 9.2 and 9.3 show the data, a correlation was performed on the two adjusted sets of data ($R = 0.998$; adjusted $R = 0.987$), indicating strong reliability.

Comparing each pair of positions in each data line (Table 9.2) tallied the differences in position. The total number of differences is 34 in 104 measurements, which would seem to support Bland and Altman's (1986) statement that correlation alone is not sufficient to test reliability. The value of the differences was noted to examine how many were perceptual errors and how many were likely to be typographical errors. The data in the shaded areas of the Table 9.2 are attributed to typographical errors, as differences of 1, 3, 4 or 5 can be attributed to perceptual differences of the two analysts. There were 34 differences in 104 rallies in total, i.e. percentage error of 32.7 per cent, of which 31 were perceptual (29.8 per cent) and three were typographical (2.9 per cent).

By summing each column, the number of rally ending shots played in each

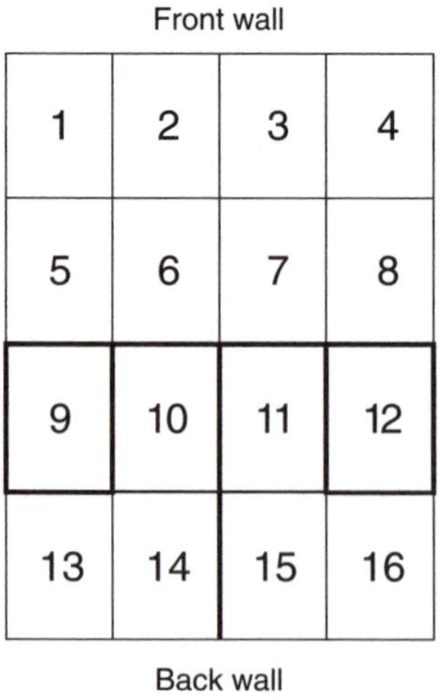

Front wall

1	2	3	4
5	6	7	8
9	10	11	12
13	14	15	16

Back wall

Figure 9.1 The definition of positional cells across the squash court area

analysis of notation data: reliability

Front wall

13	4	3	17
4	5	3	3
21	2	2	9
8	1	1	8

Back wall

(Fig 9.2)

Front wall

16	0	3	17
8	3	2	4
23	2	0	11
6	0	3	7

Back wall

(Fig 9.3)

Figures 9.2 and 9.3 The data added by column to give the positional frequency of rally ending shots in the example squash match data

position in the court, gives the totals shown in Figures 9.2 and 9.3. This is the way an analyst will usually add up the data to present patterns of play across a playing surface. Between these two sets of data, there are 27 (26 percentage error) differences, from the data checked sequentially there were 34 (32.7 percentage error). The seven errors were missed due to the process of adding the data,

155

Table 9.2 The arithmetic differences in the positions recorded by the two analysts

Value of the difference	Frequency
−11	1
−8	1
−4	7
−3	2
−1	4
0	70
1	7
4	10
5	1
11	1
Total	104

effectively eliminating some mistakes from the sum. Adding frequencies masked errors again; this is a very dangerous contaminant of reliability tests of data of this nature, particularly where there are large amounts of data, cf. the percentage errors of the total numbers of shots per game and per match.

A $\chi 2$-test of independence was used and a value of X = 11.16 (df = 15) was obtained.

9.5 VISUAL INTERPRETATION OF THE DATA (A MODIFIED BLAND AND ALTMAN PLOT)

A modified Bland and Altman plot was constructed for the variable – number of shots in a rally (Figure 9.4). But what does this plot mean with this type of data? The range of errors across the mean (16.2) was found to be ±2, i.e. a percentage error of 12 per cent. The normal process is to include on the graph an indication of the range of ±1.96 × SD to demonstrate how the data varied about the mean. The mean of the data is 16.2 shots with a standard deviation (SD) of 12.88 – to plot these data as a Bland and Altman range is meaningless. The range is ±1.96 × SD = ±25.2 shots, but a range of ±25.2 is obviously unacceptable. Confidence levels can be calculated (Bland and Altman 1986), but perhaps, in notation studies with non-parametric data, we have to reconsider the logic behind the idea of these plots. The abscissa, with parametric data such as these, is different. This is not a continuous scale, each of the items (in this case the length of rally) is different, they are not related in any simple way. Better to

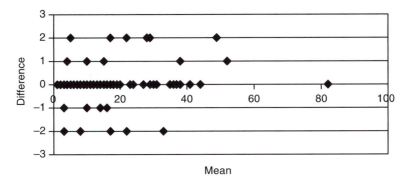

Figure 9.4 A Bland and Altman plot of the differences in rally length plotted against the mean of the rally length from the two tests

modify the graph to meet the same ideas of Bland and Altman – how much of the data falls within the range of accuracy set by the researcher (usually <5 per cent error, but it may be 10 per cent or 15 per cent depending on the nature of the data)?

Instead of plotting the differences in measurements on the same subjects against their means (a continuous scale), let us consider summing the differences found and non-dimensionalizing them with the sum of all the readings taken. Multiplying this by 100 will then, in effect, give a plot of percentage errors. Hence, by calculating and plotting:

$$(\Sigma \ (mod \ (V_1 - V_2)) \ / \ V_{TOTmean}) \times 100\%$$

against each variable reading, then the data should fall within the range of the percentage error already indicated acceptable by the researcher. Let us examine a more complex reliability study.

9.5.1 Sample data

Consider an example from rugby union. Five analysts were to undertake an analysis of the recent World Cup and all five notated the same match twice each, so that data was available for intra- and inter-operator reliability studies. The data for the frequencies of the simple variable actions of tackle, pass, ruck, kick, scrum and line are shown in Table 9.3. An accepted way of testing these operators would be to use χ^2 and percentage differences for the intra-operator tests, and to use Kruskal–Wallis and percentage differences for the inter-operator

157

Table 9.3 Data from a rugby match notated twice by five different operators and presented as an intra-operator reliability analysis

Operators	L		S		I		G		O	
	V_1	V_2	V_1	V_2	V_1	V_2	V_1	V_2	V_1	V_2
Tackle	51	53	53	55	54	49	53	56	53	55
Pass	102	108	97	99	94	97	98	99	99	97
Kick	39	40	38	39	39	38	39	41	37	39
Ruck	49	49	50	51	49	46	51	49	44	49
Scrum	6	6	6	6	6	6	6	6	6	6
Line	14	15	14	14	14	15	14	15	14	15
Σ (mod (V_1–V_2))	10		6		13		9		12	
Σ (V_1+V_2)/2	264.5		261		258.5		263.5		260	
% Error overall	3.8		2.3		5.0		3.4		4.6	

tests. The χ^2 and Kruskal–Wallis tests reflect the shape of the data sets rather than the actual differences and so there is a need for a second simple difference test. However, care must be taken with the percentage difference test, in both its definition and application.

The overall percentage differences in Table 9.3 show a satisfactory analysis, all of the operators scoring 5 per cent or less. They are presented in Figure 9.5 as a plot of (Σ (mod (V_1–V_2)) / V_{mean}) × 100 per cent) for each operator. As the expected limits of agreement in this study were 5 per cent then all the data should fall

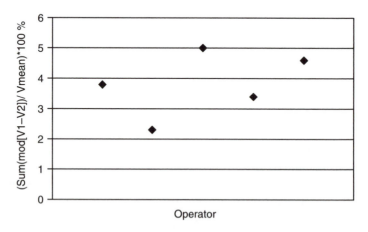

Figure 9.5 The overall data from the reliability study, the intra-operator test, presented as a function of the accuracy of each operator

below this line. There is a similarity in presenting the data in this way with that of the Bland and Altman plot, the visual power of the chart is its ability to immediately identify those measurements that are in danger of transgressing the limits of agreements.

The processed data in Table 9.4 is the intra-operator test for reliability of each of the separate variables with the difference between tests 1 and 2 shown as a percentage of the respective operators' mean for that particular variable. The error percentages for each of the variables vary much more, as would be expected, depending upon the degree of difficulty of recognition of the defined action. This variation may depend upon the accuracy of the operational definition of that action by the operators, the quantity of training of the operators, or it may be that there are accepted difficulties in observation of that particular variable.

Table 9.4 Data from a rugby match notated twice by five different operators and the differences for each operator expressed as a percentage of the respective mean

	L	S	I	G	O
Tackle	3.8	3.7	9.7	5.5	3.7
Pass	5.7	2.0	3.1	1.0	2.0
Kick	2.5	2.6	2.6	2.5	5.3
Ruck	0	2.0	4.0	4.0	10.8
Scrum	0	0	0	0	0
Line	6.9	0	6.9	6.9	6.9

Some observations are more difficult to make than others, for example, in rugby union, deciding when a maul becomes a ruck or, using the previous example, the identification of position in a squash match. It is logical then to have different levels of expected accuracy for different variables. Some research papers have argued for different levels of accuracy to be acceptable, because of the nature of the data they were measuring (Hughes and Franks 1991; Wilson and Barnes 1998).

These data were then plotted as percentages against each of the actions in Figure 9.6a. They can also be plotted against each of the operators (Figure 9.6b) to test which of the operators are more, or least, reliable and by how much. These charts are very useful, highlighting which variables are most contributing to violations of the levels of expected reliability.

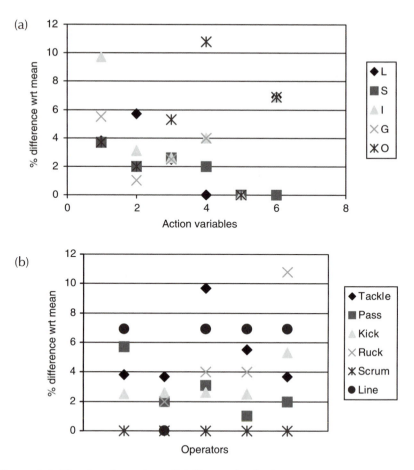

Figure 9.6 The data from the reliability study, the intra-operator test, presented as a function of the action variables and the operators

SUMMARY

It was found that many research papers in performance analysis present no reliability tests whatsoever and, when they do, they apply inappropriate statistical processes for these tests, and the subsequent data processing. Many research papers have used parametric tests in the past – these were found to be slightly less sensitive than the non-parametric tests, and they did not respond to large differences within the data. Further, the generally accepted tests for comparing sets of non-parametric data, χ^2-test analysis and Kruskal–Wallis, were found to be insensitive to relatively large changes within the data. It would seem that a simple percentage calculation gives the best indicator of reliability, but it was demonstrated that these tests can also lead to errors and confusion. The following conditions should be applied.

- The data should initially retain its sequentiality and be cross-checked item against item
- Any data processing should be carefully examined as these processes can mask original observation errors
- The reliability test should be examined to the same depth of analysis as the subsequent data processing, rather than being performed on just some of the summary data
- Careful definition of the variables involved in the percentage calculation is necessary to avoid confusion in the mind of the reader, and also to prevent any compromise of the reliability study
- It is recommended that a calculation based upon:

$$(\Sigma \ (\text{mod} \ (V_1 - V_2)) \ / \ V_{mean}) \times 100\%,$$

where V_1 and V_2 are variables, V_{mean} their mean, mod = modulus and Σ means 'sum of', is used to calculate percentage error for each variable involved in the observation system, and these are plotted against each variable, and each operator. This will give a powerful and immediate visual image of the reliability tests.

It is recommended that further work examine the problems of sufficiency of data, first to ensure that the data for reliability is significant, and also to confirm that the data present in a 'performance profile' have reached stable means.

CHAPTER TEN

QUALITATIVE BIOMECHANICAL ANALYSIS OF TECHNIQUE

Adrian Lees

In this chapter we:

■ aim to provide an essential background into the recommended approaches for identifying and diagnosing faults in performance: through either a *phase analysis model*, which is sequential in nature, and based on the use of movement principles, or through a *performance outcome model* which is hierarchical in nature and based on the mechanical relationships underpinning performance.

10.1 INTRODUCTION

Technique is defined in general terms as the 'way of doing' and the technique used in the performance of a specific sports skill can be defined as the way in which that sports skill is performed. Technique can be analysed using biomechanical methods and the 'biomechanical analysis of technique' is a specific aspect of *performance analysis* and undertaken using qualitative, quantitative and predictive methods. This chapter is concerned with the *qualitative biomechanical analysis of technique* (or *technique analysis* for short) as this is descriptive, based on observation, usually with the aid of video recordings, but with no measurements made. In teaching or coaching, qualitative biomechanical analysis can provide the learner with detailed feedback to improve performance.

Technique analysis is mostly used with reference to specific individual sports

162

skills, which are single or sequential in nature, rather than with the wider aspects of sports and games where tactics and strategy are often influencing factors. The skills which are most amenable to technique analysis are:

- event skills which themselves constitute a sporting event, such as:
  - ☐ the high jump in athletics
  - ☐ a springboard dive
  - ☐ a vault in gymnastics
  - ☐ a shot put in athletics.

- major skills which are dominant in a sport, such as:
  - ☐ the hurdle clearance in sprint hurdles
  - ☐ a move during the floor exercise in gymnastics
  - ☐ a golf swing
  - ☐ bowling in cricket.

- minor skills which are important to the overall performance but do not dominate the sport or game, such as:
  - ☐ a kick in soccer
  - ☐ a serve in tennis
  - ☐ a spike in volleyball
  - ☐ a throw in water polo.

Technique analysis has two-stages: the first is based on observation and its purpose is to *identify and diagnose faults* in performance, i.e. the causes of any discrepancies between the actual and desired performances of a sports skill or its outcome. The second is *remediation*, which is based on instruction and its purpose is to try to eradicate these discrepancies. This chapter will only be concerned with the first of these issues, as the process of feedback is itself a complex area worthy of further study. In practice, teachers and coaches develop their own methods of feedback and remediation, based on their experiences within the teaching and coaching fields and common practice within each sport.

The recommended approaches for identifying and diagnosing faults in performance are through the use of either a *phase analysis model*, which is sequential in nature, and based on the use of movement principles, or through a *performance outcome model*, which is hierarchical in nature and based on the mechanical relationships underpinning performance.

Qualitative analysts need knowledge of these two approaches. In addition, they also need a good grasp of the techniques involved in specific sports, experience of these sports and the ability to relate to coaches and athletes.

10.2 THE PHASE ANALYSIS MODEL AND MOVEMENT PRINCIPLES

10.2.1 The phase analysis model

Phase analysis is the descriptive process of dividing up a movement into relevant parts so that attention can be focused on the performance of each part. Some authors identify three main phases to a skill (*retraction, action and follow-through*), while others identify four main phases (those above but preceded by a *preparation phase*), recognizing that how a movement starts also influences the way a movement is performed (e.g. in a soccer kick the distance away from the ball and angle of approach are relevant factors to performance; in golf, the stance, how the club is held and position of the feet relative to the ball are also relevant factors). Some authors identify more than four phases but these are often sub-phases of the four main phases mentioned above. Most authors acknowledge that the phases can be further broken down into *sub-phases* and that the distinction between one phase or sub-phase and another is arbitrary and determined by the particular skill and the needs of the analyst. Nevertheless, this process of breaking a skill down into its functional parts is an important first analytical step.

The *preparation phase* describes the way in which the performer sets or prepares for the performance of the skill. For example, as noted above, it may relate to the start position and/or the way the ball is placed in a soccer penalty kick, or the way the club is held and/or ball placed on the tee in a golf drive. The *retraction phase* refers to the withdrawal of, typically, the arm or leg prior to beginning the main effort of performance. For example, in kicking the kicking leg is drawn back, and in tennis this is represented by the backswing. The *action phase* is where the main effort of the movement takes place. For example forward motion in executing a tennis serve, or the throwing action when propelling a javelin. The *follow-through phase* allows the movement to be slowed down under control and is thought to be necessary to avoid injury that might occur as a result of rapid limb deceleration. Some examples are given in Table 10.1.

As noted above, the precise start and finish of a phase may be difficult to decide in any given case, and sub-phases may be identified. Nevertheless, the phase analysis model requires the phases and sub-phases, if appropriate, to

qualitative biomechanical analysis of technique

Table 10.1 Examples of the four phases of selected skills

Event/skill	Preparation	Retraction	Action	Follow-through
Long jump	Run up	Body adjustments during penultimate stride to touch-down	Take-off, from the moment of touch-down to take-off	Flight from take-off and landing
Golf swing	Correct grip and stance	Backswing	Downswing	Follow-through
Penalty kick	Run up	Retraction of kicking leg	Forward swing of kicking leg and contact	Follow-through

be identified and each described. Some examples of sub-phases are given in Table 10.2.

The description of phases and sub-phases should identify *key moments* and *critical features*. Key moments are those points in time in which an important action is performed related to the 'way of doing'. One important key moment in striking sports is impact. However, events such as toe-off, foot-strike, maximum knee flexion, or minimum elbow angle, to name a few, would all be actions that define a key part of the technique. Critical features are observable aspects of a movement, and refer to body or limb position (e.g. when catching a ball – crouch with arms and legs flexed; for a tennis serve – the 'back-scratch' position of the racket in the backswing), and motions (e.g. when catching a ball – give or retract the hands retract with the ball). It is worth noting that critical features are

Table 10.2 Examples of the sub-phases for the action phase of selected skills

Event/skill	Action phase	Sub-phase 1	Sub-phase 2	Sub-phase 3
Long jump	Take-off	Compression (knee flexion)	Extension (knee extension)	–
Golf swing	Downswing	Weight shift: initiation of movement with the hips	Wrist locked and arms rotate as single unit	Wrist unlocks and arms rotate as a double unit
Penalty kick	Forward swing of kicking leg	Hips rotate forwards and leg flexes at knee	Knee extends to contact	–

Table 10.3 Schematic template for a phase analysis model

Phase description	Preparation	Retraction	Action	Follow-through
Sub-phase description[1]				
Key moments[2]				
Critical features[3]				
Movement principles[4]				

[1] Each box under each phase should contain a brief description of the phase or (if appropriate) the sub-phase.
[2] Key moments are often related to the start and end of a phase or sub-phase.
[3] Critical features are often related to key coaching points.
[4] Movement principles can be identified by their abbreviated title.

often related to coaching points and often are expressions of selected underlying movement principles (dealt with below).

To complete the phase analysis model, the movement principles associated with the phase or sub-phase, key moments and/or critical features need to be identified. Movement principles are dealt with separately below. The phase analysis model is given schematically in Table 10.3.

10.2.2 Movement principles

The earliest and perhaps the most widely used scientific approach to the evaluation of technique is the application of mechanical principles. As these have been articulated and developed they have tended to be referred to as 'biomechanical principles of movement' or *movement principles* for short. In general, these are a combination of principles based on simple mechanical relationships, multi-segment interactions and biological characteristics of the human musculoskeletal system.

A movement principle is a description of how to achieve a specific movement outcome based on sound mechanical and/or biomechanical principles. A movement principle is applied in general terms to help to understand how sports skills are performed.

Movement principles can be classified according to the general outcomes which they are associated with. These outcomes are speed production, force

166

production and movement coordination. In addition, it is possible to identify principles which are related to specific performances.

There is no general agreement as to the number – or even the names –. of movement principles. Some authors have identified as many as 53 movement principles, while others as few as six. The higher number tends to reflect the specific mechanical principles while the lower number tends to reflect the more general principles. There have been some attempts to reduce the larger number of principles to a manageable form as 'core concepts' which contain a mixture of mechanical, multisegment and biological principles and which provide some use in practical context. Before illustrating how these are applied, it is necessary to identify what they are and give examples of how each can be used. Below is a list of those relevant to most sports and suitable for a qualitative biomechanical analysis of performance. They are classified into speed, force, coordination and specific principles.

10.2.2.1 Speed (S) principles

These are a range of movement principles which relate to the generation of speed in a part or the whole of the body.

(S1) Whole body running speed
Maximum running speed is achieved after about 40–50 m of sprinting. Therefore to reach maximum speed, a person must be able to sprint for at least this distance. Some consequences of this are (a) running speed is often controlled by the performer due to the complexity of the skill and/or the high forces involved. In these cases the speed is kept sub-maximal in order to complete the skill and (b) in field games players are unlikely to reach their top running speed over a 10–15 m sprint, therefore their ability to accelerate is important.

(S2) Whole body rotational speed
Rotational movements of the whole body are completed more rapidly by bringing the limbs closer to the body's axis of rotation. For example, in a tucked somersault the trampolinist rotates more rapidly when tucked; in a pirouette the ice skater rotates more rapidly when the arms are brought close to the body; in a squash backhand stroke the action phase begins with the racket arm close to the body so that the whole body can rotate into the movement before extending the racket arm. Conversely, extending the limbs slows the body down. This is done not only to slow down the rotation but to allow the performer more time to make a good landing. For example, stretching the arms above the head

after a gymnastic vault slows the forward rotation of the gymnast; opening out after a tucked somersault slows the rotation of a trampolinist.

(S3) Limb rotational speed
To rotate a limb (e.g. arms or leg) rapidly requires the limb to be flexed and held close to the body. For example, in sprinting the leg is flexed tightly during the recovery part of the cycle. In a tennis serve the racket arm is flexed to achieve a back scratch position (a critical feature); in golf the arm and club are in a flexed position at the top of the downswing.

(S4) End point speed
A high end point speed requires a large distance from the axis of rotation to the end point. Consequently at impact (or release) the limb is at or close to full extension. For example when striking in sports like tennis, golf, baseball, cricket the action phase begins with the limb and implement held close to the body. As the phase develops the end point (hand, foot, racket head, club head) is allowed to move away from the axis of rotation, thus increasing its distance of rotation.

10.2.2.2 Force (F) principles

These are a range of movement principles which relate to the generation of force used to achieve a specific movement outcome.

(F1) Maximum force production
To produce the maximum effective force, a firm base is required on which to push. For example, in throwing events such as shot put and javelin the action phase occurs when the delivery foot is in firm contact with the ground; in jumping events such as long, triple and high jump a firm surface is always used to push from. Conversely, if the surface moves the effective force produced is reduced. For example, soft surfaces – such as turf and sand – are more difficult to run and jump on due to the deformation of the surface.

In tennis serving, the server is often seen to come off the ground. Is this an exception? Not really. To gain maximum racket head speed the server extends the legs (generating maximal effective force) and it is only after this that the player throws the racket head towards the ball. This combination of vigorous movements directed vertically causes the body to lift off the ground. Other principles are also used in the performance of this skill in order to achieve high end point speed (see C2 and C4 below).

qualitative biomechanical analysis of technique

(F2) Range of motion
Muscle force can be applied for longer, the greater the limb's range of motion. Consequently, there is a possibility of achieving a greater effect by contracting muscle over a greater range of motion. For example, in running, as speed increases, the stride length increases, which occurs due to the greater extension (i.e. range of motion) of the leg during the drive-off.

One implication of this principle, is that if the joint has greater flexibility, it is likely that this will allow a greater force producing range of motion leading to enhanced performance. Consequently there is thought to be a performance aspect to flexibility training.

(F3) Change of running direction
A change in direction of motion when running is produced most effectively by applying a force at right angles (perpendicular) to the current direction of motion. For example, in a side step or swerve made by a player in field games the foot is placed so as to maximize the friction force applied to the surface. This friction force should be directed perpendicular to the current direction of motion and *not* towards the intended direction of motion.

(F4) Impact – stationary ball or object
When hitting a stationary ball or object, the implement making the impact must move in the direction it is intended that the ball or object being hit should to go. For example, when taking a penalty kick, a goal keeper can sometimes guess correctly the direction of the ball by carefully watching the motion of the kicker's foot as it moves to strike the ball.

(F5) Impact – moving ball or object
When hitting a moving ball or object, the striking implement must move in such a direction so as to take into account the motion of the moving object. It will always be the case that the direction of the striking implement at impact will be different from that which the ball or object subsequently goes. This divergence is related to the mass and speed of the two objects respectively (and is another expression of principle F3 above). When heading a moving ball, or making a cricket, baseball or tennis shot if the implement is swung to drive it in the direction of intended motion the ball will *not* travel off in this direction

(F6) Stability
Objects are more stable if they have a wide base and low centre of mass. For example, in wrestling – at the start of a competition wrestlers spread their legs and lower their centre of mass to provide a stable base.

(F7) Resistance to motion in fluids
Resistance to motion when moving through air or water is reduced by reducing the area presented to the on-coming air or water (known as the cross-sectional area) and making a more streamlined shape. For example, in cycling, handle bars which are lowered and extended forward enables the cyclist to adopt a smaller cross-sectional area and more streamlined shape. Conversely, resistance is increased by increasing the cross-sectional area and making the shape less streamlined. For example, in swimming, the area of hand can be increased by the use of a hand paddle.

10.2.2.3 Coordination (C) principles

These are a range of movement principles which relate to the coordination of motion between segments so as to achieve maximal or optimal performance.

(C1) Action–reaction: simultaneous movements of opposing limbs
The movement of one limb or body part helps the movement of the opposite (or contralateral) limb or body part. For example, in walking, running and sprinting, as one leg comes forward the contralateral arm also comes forward; an effective sprint start is one in which the arms drive vigorously to aid the force generation of the opposite leg – a good coaching point is that 'the arms drive the legs'; in hurdling (crossing over the hurdle) the lift of the lead leg is helped by bringing the opposite arm forward as far as possible; in pike movements in gymnastics, trampoline and diving, the performance of the pike is aided if the upper and lower body are brought together at the same time – the movement of one is helped by the movement of another; when heading a soccer ball the same pike movement is produced which increases the speed with which the head makes contact with the ball.

(C2) Proximal-to-distal sequence of movements
This is used when producing high speed movements. Many skills require a coordinated sequence of rotational movements to achieve a high end point velocity. This is achieved by rotating the large segments close (proximal) to the body first and terminating in the rotation of the segment farthest (distal) from the body. For example, in most throwing/striking/kicking skills – the action often starts with a step forward with the leg contralateral to the throwing/striking/kicking arm or leg, which has the effect of opening the hips. It continues with the hips rotating forward and is then followed by the trunk, shoulders and finally the elbow, hand and implement. The speed of the rotation of the earlier segment is built upon by the next segment, so as to build-up the speed of the end point

qualitative biomechanical analysis of technique

sequentially. Rotation of the distal segments cause the end point to move away from the axis of rotation, thus increasing the distance of rotation (see speed principle S4).

(C3) Simultaneous joint movements for force/power production
Simultaneous joint movements are used when producing forceful or powerful actions for a linked body segment chain that includes several of the major joints of the body. To ensure that this link system provides a firm base (see force principle F1) it is important that the muscle groups operate simultaneously. Therefore, forceful/powerful movements require muscles about joints to act synchronously. For example, when jumping for height, the hip and knee muscles act simultaneously to generate high force; in the shot put the drive from the trunk and legs occur simultaneously; in the bench press the muscles activating the shoulder and elbow joint act together; in the sprint start – the hip, knee and ankle joint extend together.

Detailed biomechanical analysis has shown that in some cases, even though the muscles act synchronously, the joints do not extend synchronously. Typically in the vertical jump, the ankle joint extends after the hip and knee joints generate their main effort. As the ankle joint is weaker than these other two joints, its role is to maintain a firm base for the other stronger joints as they produce their effort. Once this diminishes the ankle, which is kept in a position of flexion, extends making its contribution to the movement. The sequence of joint motion is a reflection of the relative strength and function of the joints rather than a violation of the principle.

(C4) Stretch–shorten cycle
Many actions involve a pre-stretching of the muscles and tendons which aids performance by enabling the highest muscle forces to be built up at the beginning of the movement.

Consider a throw (or jump) in which the starting position is in the squat position. When the muscles begin to shorten, their force develops gradually. As this force develops, the movement velocity increases as does the speed of shortening of the muscles, which are now less capable of generating force (as determined by the force-velocity relationship for muscle). The net effect is that the movement is less effective.

If the muscles are pre-stretched by a counter-movement, the muscles are fully active at the beginning of the upward movement. This means that as they begin the upward movement, they are generating their maximum effort. The muscle and tendon 'stretch' should be quickly followed by the 'shorten' in order to maximize this effect.

10.2.2.4 Specific performance (P) principles

These are a range of movement principles, which identify the underlying factors relevant to specific aspects of performance.

(P1) Flight and projectile motion
An object which moves through the air under the influence of gravity is called a projectile. The outcome of projectile motion is often the range, but sometimes the height reached and time of flight are important performance measures. The mechanical factors determining projectile motion are the height, angle and speed of release, with the speed of release being the most important.

The effects of air resistance can be important in many situations, particularly those where the ball is light, the relative velocity of the wind is high, or the object is shaped so as to have aerodynamic properties. The flight path of the projectile is modified accordingly and more complex effects need to be taken into account.

(P2) Speed–accuracy trade off
In the performance of many skills, the outcome is determined by both speed and accuracy. It is generally found that as the demands for accuracy increase, the speed of the movement decreases. For example, when kicking a football for accuracy (i.e. a penalty kick), a very hard hit shot is less accurately placed than one hit less hard; in a basket ball shot, the greater the distance of the throw the less chance the ball will go into the basket; in the long jump approach jumpers need to hit the take-off board accurately so there is a tendency to reduce their speed close to touch-down.

10.3 AN APPLICATION OF THE PHASE ANALYSIS MODEL AND MOVEMENT PRINCIPLES

A soccer penalty kick is used to illustrate how the phase analysis model and movement principles are used. The kick would typically be recorded on video and be available for repeat viewing, and inspection of individual frames. A series of still images have been extracted from such a video and presented in Figure 10.1, which cover the kick from take-off kicking leg on the last stride to follow-through.

qualitative biomechanical analysis of technique

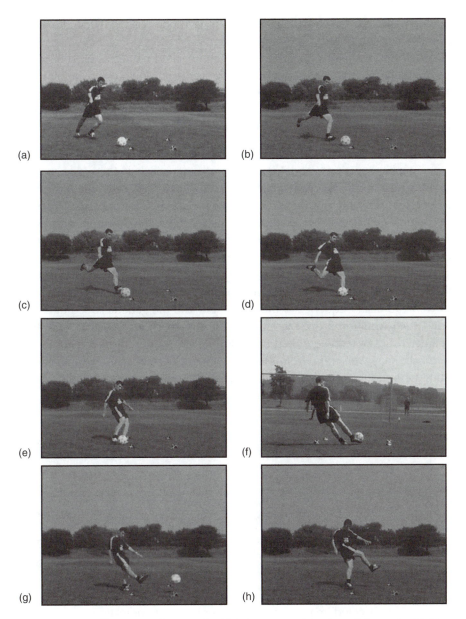

Figure 10.1 Still images of a penalty kick in soccer. (a) take-off from the kicking leg, (b) last stride, (c) touch-down support leg, (d) maximum knee flexion of kicking leg, (e) contact, (f) contact rear view, (g) post-impact, (h) follow-through

In the phase analysis template (Table 10.4), each phase is identified along with the relevant sub-phases, key moments, critical features and movement principles. The movement principles are the abbreviated names as used above. It can be seen from this analysis that several movement principles may apply at the same time. Some of these movement principles can be more easily appreciated by drawing appropriate indications on the images. For example, in Figure 10.2 the stretch shorten cycle, range of motion and action-reaction principles are easily appreciated from annotations to the images.

Once a phase analysis model is completed, the coach is then able to view performances of the skill with a knowledge of what to look for in the movement (critical features) and how these relate to the mechanical performance of the skill (movement principles). For example, if a player needed to improve kick speed, then the coach would reasonably look at the range of motion achieved as indicated by the length of last stride, the degree of retraction of the hips and the use of the contralateral arm. Once these aspects of technique had been improved, the coach may then focus on the coordination of the movement, specifically the proximal-to-distal sequence of the movement and the general speed of execution which would improve the effect of the stretch–shorten cycle. Once these characteristics of technique had been developed, further improvement in performance may well come from the development of muscle strength characteristics. One should note that as strength changes so too may the technique, so a continual monitoring of technique used should always be made.

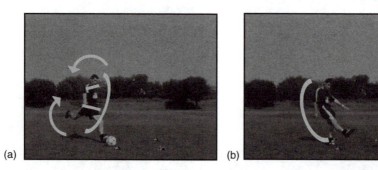

(a) (b)

Figure 10.2 Selected images from the soccer kick with indications of important movement principles. A. Illustration of the stretch arc (stretch shorten cycle principle), retraction of the hips and the hip-shoulder separation (both range of motion principle) and the simultaneous retraction of the kicking leg and opposite arm (action reaction-principle). B. Illustration of the shorten arc (stretch shorten cycle principle) in the follow-through

Table 10.4 Phase analysis model template for the soccer kick

Phase description	Preparation (run up)			Retraction (retraction of kicking leg)	Action (forward swing of kicking leg)		Follow-through	
Sub-phase description	Place ball. Withdraw to start position	Approach strides	Last stride	Forward placement of support leg (Fig. 1b) and hip extension of kicking leg (Fig. 1c)	Hips rotate forwards; leg flexes at knee (Fig. 1d)	Knee extends to contact (Fig. 1e)	Knee extends from contact to full extension (Fig. 1g)	Knee flexes to complete movement (Fig. 1h)
Key moments			Take-off kicking leg (Fig. 1a)	Maximum hip extension of kicking leg (Fig. 1c)	Maximum knee flexion (Fig. 1d)	Impact with ball (Fig. 1e)	Fully extended kicking leg knee (Fig. 1g)	Flexed knee (Fig. 1h)
Critical features			Last stride length	Kicking leg hip extension (Fig. 1c) and opposite arm backwards	Maximum flexion of kicking leg knee (Fig. 1d)	Body posture at impact (Fig. 1e)	Fully extended kicking leg knee (Fig. 1g) and opposite arm forwards	Flexed knee (Fig. 1h)
Movement principles			ROM	ROM SSC (stretch) AR	PDS	PDS SSC (shorten) EPS	AR	

Refer to Figure 10.1 for descriptions.
Movement principles: ROM, range of motion; SSC, stretch shorten cycle; AR, action–reaction; PDS, proximal-distal sequence; EPS, end point speed.

10.4 THE PERFORMANCE OUTCOME MODEL

An alternative approach to the analysis of performance is through the analysis of the factors that influence performance. By focusing on those factors, it is claimed that faults and limiting factors in performance can be identified. The most influential of these is the Hay and Reid model. The model was first developed for use in qualitative analysis but has also found widespread use in quantitative analysis to assist biomechanists to identify important variables for quantification. As the model focuses on performance outcome it is more suited for use as a 'performance' model, hence has value outside of the field of technique analysis. The model does not address aspects of technique (the way of doing) directly, but the mechanical relationships that govern performance. In that sense, the model is more closely linked with the movement principles noted above, and one may view the model as a more direct and systematic approach to the identification of the mechanical principles that govern performance.

The model is constructed as a hierarchy of factors on which the result (outcome) of the performance is dependent (Figure 10.3).

The rules that govern the constructing of a model for a particular skill is that each of the factors in the model should be completely determined by those factors that appear immediately below it either (1) by addition or (2) known mechanical relationships.

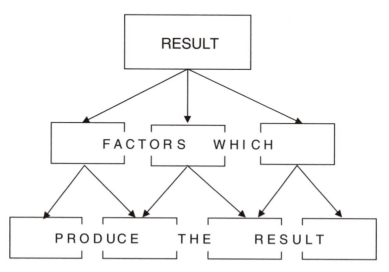

Figure 10.3 The Hay and Reid performance outcome model

As noted above, the performance outcome model does not address issues of technique directly. For example, in a golf drive, the model will tell us that the speed of the clubhead must be high at impact but not how to achieve it. Information on how to use the arms and club as a two lever system, weight shift and hip-shoulder rotation are beyond the scope of the model. In other words, the model is able to identify factors relevant to performance but not aspects of technique relevant to these factors. Nevertheless, the Hay and Reid model would appear to be valuable for identifying a range of factors influencing performance and providing a framework from which technique can be discussed. To do this requires the use of one or more of the methods described earlier. In this sense, it is not an alternative model for technique analysis but is complementary to these other methods.

10.5 AN APPLICATION OF THE HAY AND REID PERFORMANCE OUTCOME MODEL

The long jump is used to illustrate how the performance outcome model can be used. The measure of performance in the long jump is the official distance jumped. As that athlete must take-off in front of the take-off foul line, athletes often give themselves a margin of safety by taking off a few centimetres in front of the foul line. This distance is known as the toe-to-board distance. Thus, the actual distance jumped is almost always greater than the official distance. In fact, by simple addition, the actual distance jumped = the official distance + toe-to-board distance. This is an example of rule 1 above for the construction of the model. The actual distance can then be divided into the take-off distance (the distance that the centre of mass is in front of the toes at take-off), flight distance (the distance the centre of mass moves through the air) and the landing distance (the distance that the centre of mass is behind the heels at landing). This is also an example of rule 1. Of these three distances, the most important is the flight distance. In flight, the body is a projectile and so the flight distance is governed by the mechanical relationships that determine projectile flight. These mechanical relationships are the height, velocity and angle of projection at release (see performance principle P1). For practical reasons, is more convenient to combine the velocity and angle together and to use their components in the vertical and horizontal directions. Thus, in this example the three projectile parameters used are height, horizontal velocity and vertical velocity of the centre of mass at release. This is an example of rule 2, which is based on mechanical relationships.

A full hierarchical analysis for the long jump is given in Figure 10.4. Note that

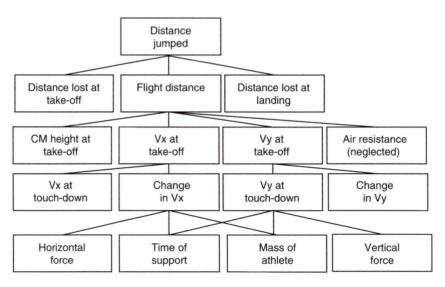

Figure 10.4 Performance outcome model for the long jump. (See text for further explanation.) CM, centre of mass; Vx, horizontal velocity; Vy, vertical velocity

only the main factors are followed through. Nevertheless, the model is quite comprehensive and has been used by the author to provide scientific support for international long jumpers. The model clearly identifies what needs to be measured through biomechanical analysis. For example, the horizontal velocity of the centre of mass at touch-down and take-off are key factors. These factors can be measured from motion analysis during competition. This provides a strong rationale for the provision of biomechanical services during competitive events. If one wants to measure factors deeper into the hierarchy, such as force, then the model implies that a force platform needs to be used. So far, this has not been done in high level competition and it may never be done. This type of information is therefore only gained in a training environment. The implication is that suitably instrumented training environments need to be available to provide comprehensive support to high level athletes.

Finally, we need to return to the issue of how this model can be used to analyse technique. Implicit in the model is the need to quantify the factors identified. This is the role of biomechanists but once this is done then the results of their analyses can be used with the model to provide advice on aspects of technique. For example, it is clear in the model that performance is dependant on the horizontal velocity. Thus, it is also apparent that maximizing this will be advantageous. It is also apparent from the model that vertical velocity is important, but

qualitative biomechanical analysis of technique

the only place that vertical velocity can be generated is at take-off. Thus, attention should be focussed on the actions of take-off and the actions leading up to take-off. This then implies that a more detailed investigation of the technique during this phase is warranted, and that may be approached using the phase analysis model described in detail above.

SUMMARY

This chapter has sought to introduce the methods relevant to the qualitative biomechanical analysis of sports skills. Qualitative biomechanical analysis is appropriate to the analysis of sports technique and two major approaches have been identified for the identification and diagnosis of faults. The phase analysis model is appealing in that it is based on a sequential breakdown of performance, performed from visual images gained, typically, from video analysis. By identifying phases and sub-phases of movement, the key moments and critical features it is possible to identify the principles that govern performance. Using these principles, faults can be diagnosed from which it is hoped that performance can be improved. In order to use this model effectively, a sound knowledge of movement principles is needed. These are not readily available in the literature so the opportunity has been taken to outline them in this chapter. In contrast, the second approach is based on performance outcome. This leads to a hierarchical model of performance which identifies the relationships and mechanical factors that govern performance. It is implicit in this model that many of these factors need to be measured quantitatively. This is something that we have to rely on others to do, but based on their information it is possible to gain an insight into the key factors that influence performance and attend to these directly (such as the importance of approach speed in the long jump) or to use this information to guide a more 'technique' orientated analysis using the previous phase analysis model.

The tools provided in this chapter should enable the enthusiastic student of sports science to undertake an effective analysis of sports technique using qualitative methods.

CHAPTER ELEVEN

TIME–MOTION ANALYSIS

Peter G. O'Donoghue

In this chapter we:

- describe the main performance indicators involved in time–motion analysis and the data gathering processes.
- discuss approaches to investigating reliability of time–motion data as well as statistical analysis procedures that can be used within time–motion investigations.

11.1 INTRODUCTION

Performance analysis involves the investigation of actual sports performance or training. Performance analysis can be undertaken as part of academic investigations into sports performance or as part of applied activities in coaching, media or judging contexts. There is considerable overlap between performance analysis and other disciplines, as most performance analysis exercises are concerned with investigating aspects of performance such as technique, energy systems or tactical aspects. What distinguishes performance analysis from other disciplines is that it is concerned with actual sports performance rather than activity undertaken in laboratory settings or data gathered from self reports such as questionnaires or interviews. There are a variety of methods that can be used to gather data for performance analysis exercises, ranging from highly quantitative biomechanical analysis to qualitative analysis. There are cases where laboratory based biomechanics exercises can count as performance analysis. If the technique under investigation is an important skill within the sport of interest, then there is an argument that detailed biomechanical analysis of the technique is performance analysis. This is an especially strong argument where a skill such as running stride, golf swing or tennis serve is critically important to success in the sport and where the detailed data required cannot be gathered during actual competition. Notational analysis is a method of recording and analysing dynamic and complex situations such as field games. It allows the data to be gathered in an efficient and abstract way that focuses on relevant detail. In early manual notational systems, short-hand symbols and tallies allowed data to be recorded efficiently. More recently, computerized notational analysis systems have followed advances in data entry technology and allowed flexible and highly efficient processing of match data. Qualitative analysis has been used in observational studies in sociocultural areas of sport and has potential for obser- vational analysis of sports performance. The strength of qualitative analysis is that the data is not restricted to a predefined set of events. Physiological and other variables such as heart rate response and blood lactate accumulation can be gathered in many situations including sports competition where the nature of the sport allows such measurement to be made in a relatively non-invasive manner. The fact that the measurements relate to sports performance rather than a fitness test or laboratory-based test or exercise is enough to permit such method to be used within performance analysis investigations. The use of questionnaire instruments within performance analysis is possible where such instruments have been validated against other gold standard measurements. The profile of mood states (POMS) inventory or the rate of perceived exertion (RPE) scale are examples of self reports that can be used periodically during sports performance to record useful information about the performance.

Hughes (1998) described five purposes of notational analysis; tactical evalu- ation, technical evaluation, analysis of movement, coach and player education and performance modelling using match analysis databases. These five purposes are not just five purposes of notational analysis but are also five purposes of performance analysis in general. This chapter is concerned with one of these purposes in particular which is the analysis of movement. Analysis of movement or time–motion analysis is the investigation of the activity of players during competition and is not restricted to on-the-ball activity. This type of performance analysis seeks to develop an understanding of the physical and physiological requirements of participation in given sporting activities. Such information may not be directly applicable to weekly coaching cycles, but indirectly supports coaching by better informing those who develop conditioning elements of play- ers' training programmes. There are many good sources of information about time–motion analysis. These include Reilly's (2003) chapter on work-rate and physical demands within Williams and Reilly's (2003) textbook on *Science and*

Soccer. Bangsbo's (1993) book on physiology of intermittent high intensity activity in soccer contains two excellent chapters describing how performance analysis techniques have been used to develop an understanding of the physiological demands of soccer match play. Interested readers are encouraged to read these and other material on time–motion analysis. However, like all other areas of performance analysis, the nature of time–motion analysis has changed dramatically in recent years. Therefore, the purpose of the current chapter is to provide an up to date survey of time–motion analysis techniques and their applications. In particular, the use of automatic player tracking technology has provided a more efficient and accurate means of summarizing the movement patterns of players in sport. Another recent area of interest has been speed agility quickness requirements of sports. These need to be understood by those developing speed agility quickness training programmes.

This chapter is broken down into four parts which relate to different types of sports. First, there is a part on cyclic sports such as running, swimming and cycling. Time–motion analysis can be used to analyse tactical, technical and physical aspects of these activities. The second part is concerned with the analysis of racket sports. Movement in racket sports is often difficult to classify into locomotive movements such as running because of the restricted court areas used. The different methods of analysing rallies and the activity that occurs within rallies are discussed in this part of the chapter. The third part of the chapter describes the range of methods that can be used to analyse movement in field games including automatic player tracking. The fourth part of the chapter describes the Bloomfield Movement Classification (Bloomfield *et al.* 2004), which can be used to analyse the speed agility quickness requirements of games. Each of these sections describes the main performance indicators involved, the data gathering processes, discusses approached to investigating reliability of time–motion data as well as statistical analysis procedures that can be used within time–motion investigations.

11.2 TIME–MOTION ANALYSIS OF RUNNING EVENTS

Time–motion analyses of running events should have a clear purpose rather than merely determining and presenting split times. An example of a clear research purpose is characterizing the nature of elite sprinting (Bruggerman *et al.* 1999; Korhonen *et al.* 2003). Bruggerman *et al.* (1999) analysed sprint events from the World Athletics Championships in 1997 in Athens. The variables determined for each 100 m, for example, performance included reaction time, various parameters derived from kinematic analysis of the video recorded races as well as split times every 10 m. Mean velocity during each 10 m section can be computed together with mean acceleration between successive 10 m sections. This provides knowledge of how elite athletes run the 100 m. This allowed Bruggerman *et al.* (1999) to characterize the 100 m as comprising of an 'acceleration phase' and 'peak velocity phase'. Korhonen *et al.* (2003) analysed the 100 m using similar methods but this analysis identified a 'final phase' in addition to the two phases identified by Bruggerman *et al.* (1999).

The purpose of Brown's (2005) analysis of the 2004 Olympic Games women's 800 m and 1,500 m was to compare the tactics of athletes attempting the 800 m and 1,500 m double with those of athletes who were attempting a single event. Split times determined during the various rounds of the competition gave an indication of the tactics of the different types of athlete. Nominal variables for the athlete's position within the field of athletes during a race also gave an insight into the similarities and differences of the tactics used. The positioning of an athlete with respect to the leading athlete was classified using the following terms:

■ Leading – at the front of the leading pack
■ Sitting – sitting on the shoulder of the leaders
■ Trailing – in the leading pack but not in a prominent position
■ Back – at the back of the leading pack but still in contention.

Lateral positioning was also indicated by the position of the athlete as follows:

■ Outside – on the outside of other athletes within one pace distance away or in lane two or above
■ Boxed in – either having other athletes within one pace distance away on the outside or having athletes to the front and side making it harder to move to a better position in the field
■ Alone – having no athletes within one pace distance away.

The marathon is an event where pace needs to consider the profile of the course as well as the need to conserve energy. Figure 11.1 is a type of graph used by Brown and O'Donoghue (2006) to describe the running strategy of world class female athletes. This form of presentation deliberately shows how far inside or outside an even paced schedule for some target time (in this case, an even paced 2 h 18 min 47 s world record pace is used). Where the gradient of the graph is 0, the athlete is running at the target pace; where the gradient is <0, the athlete is running faster than the target pace and where the gradient is >0, the athlete is

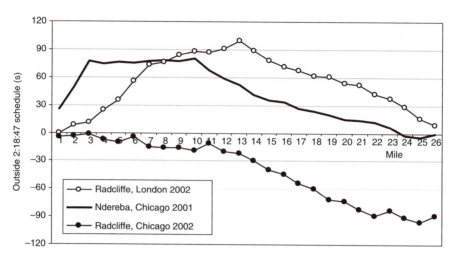

Figure 11.1 Marathon performances of Catherine Ndereba and Paula Radcliffe (2001 and 2002)

running slower than the target pace. As we can see, when Catherine Ndereba's set this world record in Chicago in 2001, the performance was not even paced. In London, Paula Radcliffe was making her debut at the marathon distance and may have been running cautiously until 13 miles, where she may have considered her lead in the race to be sufficient to risk trying for a fast time. The evidence supporting this from Figure 11.1, is the distinction between the first 13 miles, where she was running slower than world record pace, and the remaining 13 miles 365 yards, where she was running faster than world record pace, missing the world record by just 9 s. In the 2002 Chicago marathon, Paula Radcliffe broke the world record. She was between 0 s and 20 s inside an even paced world record schedule, until she reached 11 miles, where she started to run 5 s per mile faster. From 11 miles to the end of the race, Figure 11.1 shows that Paula Radcliffe ran at a similar pace to Catherine Ndereba a year earlier on the same course. The profile of the course may have been responsible for this parallel pattern between the performances of the two athletes at Chicago. Alternatively, Paula Radcliffe and her advisers may have considered the split times of Catherine Ndereba a year earlier and they may have viewed the first 11 miles as an area where Paula Radcliffe could run 1 min faster than Catherine Ndereba did, without running faster than an even paced world record schedule.

As with all performance analysis methods, it is essential to demonstrate the reliability of the data gathering system. Split times are measured on a ratio scale and their reliability can be assessed using change of the mean and standard error of measurement (Hopkins 2000) or 95 per cent limits of agreement (Atkinson and Nevill 1998). The use of percentage error is not advised as the magnitude of error is expressed as a percentage of the mean split value, making methods appear more reliable than they actually are. Brown and O'Donoghue (2007) describe how percentage error should express absolute error as a percentage of a more meaningful interval, recognizing minimum possible split values that an athlete would not run faster than. Mean absolute error has been used (Brown and O'Donoghue 2006) with the advantage that error is expressed in terms of the units of measurement of the split times. This allows measurement error to be related to the analytical goals of investigations as recommended by Atkinson and Nevill (1998). The reliability of nominal positioning variables can be expressed as the percentage of recordings where two independent observers agreed on the athlete's position.

Split times can be compared between different groups of athletes or between different samples of data related to the same group of athletes. Where the assumptions of parametric statistics are satisfied, independent and paired *t*-tests can be used to compare independent and related samples respectively. Future studies may consider expressing split times in relation to athletes' seasons best times so as strategy can be investigated in away that controls for running speed. Nominal positioning variables have been compared between samples of performances using chi squared tests of independence (Brown 2005). The tactics of athletes are often dependent on the tactics of opponents they are competing against. Therefore, further research into running tactics, no matter whether using nominal positioning variables and/or ratio scale split times, should explore ways of showing the dynamic interrelationships between the tactics adopted by different types of athlete within the same race. Some of the methods described here can also be used for the analysis of walking, swimming and cycling events as well as the triathlon.

11.3 TIME–MOTION ANALYSIS OF RACKET SPORTS

Rally times and the recovery times in between rallies give an indication of the demands of different levels of competition within the different racket sports. Rally times have been analysed for table tennis (Drianovski and Otcheva 2002), badminton (Liddle and O'Donoghue 1998), tennis (Collinson and Hughes 2002) and squash (Docherty 1982). O'Donoghue and Ingram (2001) determined mean rally lengths for men's and women's singles as shown in Figure 11.2. This study revealed that rallies were significantly longer in women's singles than

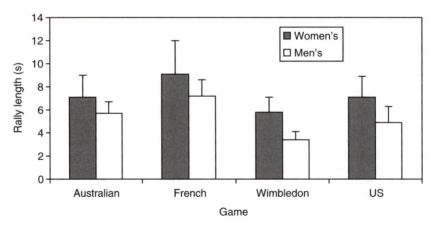

Figure 11.2 Rally length for different singles games

men's singles. Furthermore, there were significant differences between the rally lengths at different tournaments indicating a surface effect on rally length. The rallies at the French Open, which is played on clay courts, was significantly longer than at other tournaments. Rally lengths at Wimbledon, which is played on grass courts, were significantly shorter than those played at other tournaments.

Table 11.1 shows other relevant timings that should be considered along with rally durations when undertaking time–motion analyses of tennis (O'Donoghue and Ingram 2001). Rally times and inter-point times can give an indication of work to rest ratios in racket sports such as squash, badminton and table tennis. In tennis the inter-serve, where players serve faults or lets are required, also needs to be considered when determining work to rest ratios. O'Donoghue and Liddle (1998) showed the distribution of tennis matches among playing rallies, time between serves, inter-point times within games, inter-game times where players

Table 11.1 Inter-serve and inter-point times (mean±SD) in Grand Slam singles tennis (O'Donoghue and Ingram 2001).

Timing factor	Gender	Tournament			
		Australian	French	Wimbledon	US
Inter-serve (s)	Women	9.8 ± 0.9	10.4 ± 1.4	10.3 ± 0.9	10.6 ± 1.3
	Men	9.3 ± 1.5	9.2 ± 1.3	11.0 ± 1.3	10.0 ± 1.4
Inter-point (s)	Women	17.1 ± 2.0	18.2 ± 1.6	18.1 ± 1.6	18.1 ± 2.0
	Men	18.7 ± 1.9	19.5 ± 2.1	19.4 ± 1.6	18.3 ± 2.0

time–motion analysis

remain at the same end of the court and inter-game times where players change ends. The approach used by O'Donoghue and Liddle (1998) and O'Donoghue and Ingram (2001) can be criticized as it assumes that serves are instantaneous events occurring at the instant where the racket strikes the ball. This can lead to an under-estimation of high intensity activity performed within tennis matches. A further limitation arises from the objective definition of a point which is based on the rules of lawn tennis. A point is deemed to have ended when the tennis ball strikes the net, lands out of court or bounces for a second time before a player is able to reach it with the racket. There are many occasions where players will cease high intensity activity before the point has officially ended. For example, where a player miss-hits the ball, it may be obvious from the point of impact that the ball is going out and so both players will cease high intensity activity. However, the end of the point will not be recorded by the methods used by O'Donoghue and Liddle (1998) and O'Donoghue and Ingram (2001) until the ball has landed out of court.

Further criticisms of the use of rally lengths to indicate the intensity of play within rallies comes from the nature of the court surfaces resulting indirectly in different durations of rallies. The coefficient of friction affects the horizontal component of a tennis ball's velocity. A surface with a low coefficient of friction will cause the ball to bounce faster than a surface with a high coefficient of friction. The coefficient of restitution is the ratio of the vertical component of the tennis ball's velocity before it strikes the surface to after it strikes the surface. Therefore, a surface with a high coefficient of restitution will cause the tennis ball to bounce higher than a surface with a low coefficient of restitution. Cement and grass courts are faster than clay surfaces. Clay has a higher coefficient of friction and higher coefficient of restitution than the other surfaces, resulting in a high and relatively gentle bounce. This leads to players being reluctant to adopt a serve volley strategy as they wish to avoid being at the net when the opponent has more time to play a lob or passing shot. The longer rallies that occur on clay result in prolonged matches that induce fatigue increasing error rates (Vergauwen et al. 1998). Grass surfaces have lower coefficients of friction and restitution causing the ball to bounce lower losing little speed as it does so. This places additional time pressure on the player making a shot encouraging the opponent to advance to the net more often which in turn results in shorter rallies.

The rally duration alone does not give a complete indication of the nature of work within rallies. Figure 11.3 shows that more shots are played per second (s) in Wimbledon than other tournaments and fewer shots are played/s in the French Open than in other tournaments (O'Donoghue and Ingram 2001). Therefore, rallies at Wimbledon could be considered to be played at a higher

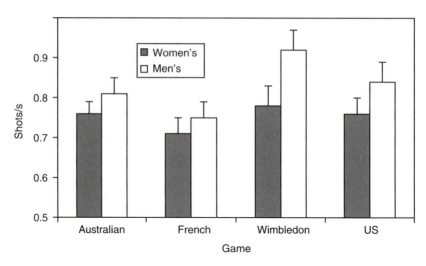

Figure 11.3 Shots played per second of rally time (O'Donoghue and Ingram 2001)

intensity than those the other tournaments, while rallies at the French Open might be considered to be played at a lower intensity than those at the other three tournaments. Significantly more shots are played in men's singles than in women's singles. Revisiting the data used by O'Donoghue and Ingram (2001) reveals a strong association between the number of shots played/s and rally duration (r^2 = 0.750). Therefore, a higher intensity of play within rallies could be leading to rallies breaking down earlier. Liddle and O'Donoghue (1998) analysed rally lengths, inter-rally times and shots played/s within rallies in badminton and also found that rallies in the games with the most shots played/s were shorter than the rallies in other games. A criticism of using shots played/s as an indication of intensity of play is that higher shot rates may merely indicate that the ball is travelling a shorter distance between shots. For example, singles tennis at Wimbledon has a significantly greater proportion of net points than is observed at other tournaments (O'Donoghue and Ingram 2001). Much of the difference in shot rate between Wimbledon and the French Open may result from the greater use of a serve volley strategy on grass courts than on clay surfaces.

There are other means of investigating the nature of activity within rallies besides shot rates. For example, Liddle et al. (1996) counted shots of different types and determined the distance travelled during men's singles and men's double rallies played in badminton. To measure the distance covered by the subject, the path travelled during each rally was entered onto a court diagram, during post-match

time–motion analysis

video analysis. This was done, pausing the video tape each time the subject changed direction and drawing a line representing the current phase of the movement. A ruler was used to measure the path travelled. The court diagram used was drawn to scale and the grid represented the 0.5 m × 0.5 m divisions that were marked on the actual court. Distance covered was also recognized as an important indicator of work-rate in rally sports by Underwood and McHeath (1977) who devised a manual notation method for estimating distance covered. Since Underwood and McHeath (1997) and Liddle et al. (1996) described their manual methods of estimating distance covered during tennis and badminton rallies respectively, automatic player tracking systems have been developed based on image processing technology. These have been used in the analysis of distance covered in squash rallies (Vučković et al. 2004).

Time–motion analysis studies in field games typically determine the distribution of match time among different stationary and locomotive movements such as standing, walking, jogging, running and sprinting. It is very difficult to classify movement in racket sports into such movements due to the smaller playing area that results in much more shuffling and rotation movement. Therefore, Richers (1995) analysed footsteps made by players within rallies. She defined a continuous footstep movement as being a series of steps without changing direction. The number of periods of continuous footstep movements and the number of footsteps made within such periods were counted for rallies on different surfaces, revealing that the number of footsteps within continuous footstep movements was similar between surfaces (5.4 on hard courts compared with 5.7 on clay and grass courts). However, there were fewer continuous footstep movements made within rallies on grass than on the other surfaces leading to shorter rallies being played on grass.

Reliability of timing factors has been described using 95 per cent limits of agreement (O'Donoghue and Ingram 2001). Alternative methods of describing reliability can also be used with such ratio scale variables; these include mean absolute error and a combination of change of mean and standard error of measurement. These reliability statistics can also be applied to distance covered during rallies. A criticism of mean absolute error is that it does not separate the systematic bias and random error components of total error. The importance of understanding these different components of error is that if there is a known general tendency for one observer to record higher values on average than another observer, then recorded values within main studies can be adjusted to account for this. Techniques such as 95 per cent limits of agreement, standard error of measurement and mean absolute error rely on the same number of rallies being recorded within independent observations. Hughes et al. (2004)

show an example of the effect of mismatches between two observations of squash rally lengths (shots within the rally) on the association between the data sets. Therefore, corresponding rallies should be identified during the process of preparing data for reliability testing. The number of shots played/s is measured on a discrete scale rather than a continuous scale. Therefore, Liddle and O'Donoghue (1998) described the reliability of the number of shots recorded within badminton rallies as the percentage of rallies where the observers agreed on the number of shots played. The number of continuous footstep movements within rallies (Richers 1995) can be assessed for reliability using a similar technique. However, where observers disagree on the number of continuous footstep movements within a rally, they will also disagree on the number of footsteps within continuous footstep movements. Therefore, special care must be taken to relate corresponding continuous footstep movements recorded within independent observations when describing the reliability of footsteps recorded within continuous footstep movements. Shot type, as recorded by Liddle et al. (1996) is a nominal variable whose reliability can be described using the kappa statistic.

The analysis of time–motion variables in racket sports typically involves the use of non-parametric statistics. O'Donoghue and Liddle (1998) showed the number of rallies of different duration sub-ranges in men's and women's singles tennis at Wimbledon and the French Open. In all four cases, the rally durations were positively skewed. The number of shots played per rally is measured on a discrete scale rather than a continuous scale and would also typically be positively skewed. Liddle and O'Donoghue (1998) provided evidence that in badminton, the duration of recovery periods was related to the duration of the rallies that preceded them. Therefore, recovery periods could be positively skewed as well as rally durations. O'Donoghue and Ingram (2001) used non-parametric tests to compare independent samples of tennis matches in terms of timing factors and shots played per rally. Mann–Whitney U tests were used to compare genders in terms of ordinal and ratio scale variables while Kruskal–Wallis H tests were used to compare the four different tournaments. Where a Kruskal–Wallis H test revealed a significant tournament effect, Bonferroni adjusted Mann–Whitney U tests were used to compare individual pairs of tournaments. The Bonferroni adjustment deliberately chooses an alpha level that leads to an overall alpha level of 0.05 for the chance of a Type I error anywhere in the pairwise comparisons being done. Vincent (2000: 238) describes how the standard error derived from numbers of values in each sample can be used as an alternative means of performing pairwise comparisons in the event of the Kruskal–Wallis H test revealing a difference between three or more independent samples. There may be occasions where timing variables need to be compared between samples relating to the same set of players. For example, one may wish to compare rally lengths played by the same set of players when playing on different surfaces. This would require the use of a Wilcoxon Signed Ranks test if two surfaces were being compared or a Friedman test if performances on three or more surfaces were being compared for the set of players. Some performance analysis studies explore associations between performance indicators. Where the assumptions of Pearson's r are not satisfied by timing factors, non-parametric alternatives such as Kendall's τ or Spearman's ρ should be used instead. The analysis of nominal variables or ordinal variables with a small number of values (such as number of continuous footstep movements per rally) can be done using chi square tests of independence to compare frequency profiles between samples.

11.4 TEAM GAMES

Time–motion analysis is an area of performance analysis that has the purpose of determining movement profiles of players during competition or training. Time–motion analysis studies have determined the frequency, duration and distribution of match time among different classes of stationary and locomotive movement in many team sports including netball (Steele and Chad 1991), soccer (O'Donoghue et al. 2001), field hockey (Robinson et al. 1996a), Gaelic football (McErlean et al. 2000), rugby league (Beck and O'Donoghue 2004) and rugby union (Treadwell 1987). Each class of movement must be clearly defined and operators of time–motion systems need to be trained to operate such systems for data to be objective. The CAPTAIN system (O'Donoghue 1998) is a time–motion analysis system that permits users to define a classification of movements for the sport or activity they are studying. The user will classify some of the activities as being of a high intensity and the others as being of low intensity. Activities such as standing, walking and jogging have been deemed as low intensity movement while activities such as running, sprinting, shuffling, on-the-ball activity and challenging for the ball would typically be defined as being of a high intensity. Function keys are used to enter instances of each movement. The CAPTAIN system is then able to determine the frequency, mean duration and percentage of match time for each movement class. The system also strings together all consecutively performed high intensity activity instances into high intensity bursts and all consecutively performed low intensity activity instances into low intensity bursts. This permits the system to output the frequency of high intensity bursts, the mean duration of high intensity bursts, the mean duration of recovery periods between high intensity bursts and the percentage of match time spent performing high intensity activity. The number of bursts of under 6 s, 6 s to under 10 s and 10 s or longer are output to give an indication of the energy systems that are utilized during high intensity movement. Figure 11.4 shows an example of the distribution of match time among different activities that can be produced using the CAPTAIN system. The shaded sectors represent high intensity activity.

Time–motion analysis produces information about activity profile and work-rate during competitive sport. Pioneering work on soccer used hand notation to analyse player movements that had been verbally described using a learned map and recorded on audio-tape (Reilly and Thomas 1976). Advances in technology have been exploited by time–motion analysis with automatic player tracking systems being available today (Liebermann et al. 2002). However, at this time such systems remain too expensive for many academic researchers. Therefore, time–motion analysis research continues using methods that involve human observation of player movement. Given that such methods have limited objectivity and reliability, there is a need to train system operators and evaluate the level of inter-observer agreement. Time–motion analysis studies of soccer have provided valuable information about player activity during the match in terms of work to rest ratios, the percentage of match time spent performing high intensity activity and the duration of the average high intensity burst (Bangsbo et al. 1991; Withers et al. 1982).

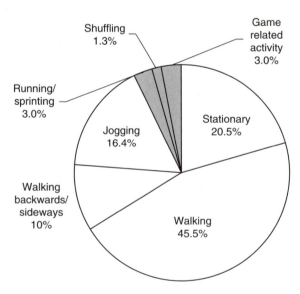

Figure 11.4 Distribution of match time in hurling (O'Donoghue et al. 2004)

The intensity of exercise during team games can be indicated by the distance covered during competition and the proportion of that distance covered when performing each class of non-stationary movement. Distance measurements have been made by time–motion analysis studies of soccer (Reilly and Thomas 1976; Withers *et al.* 1982; Bangsbo *et al.* 1991). Figure 11.5 shows an example of the movement data entered for an individual netball player during a time–motion study (O'Donoghue and Loughran 1998).

Figure 11.6 shows how individual subjects' data is combined to allow the mean player within each positional group to be represented. In this example of netball activity, we cannot only see that the centre covers the greatest distance during a match quarter with the goal keeper and goal shooter covering the least distance, but we can also that a larger proportion of the distance covered by goal keepers and goal shooters is taken up with shuffling movements.

The use of the CAPTAIN system to determine the distribution of match time among different activities has limited reliability due to the choice reaction time when classifying movement together with the subjective nature of classifying movement. A further consideration of this type of analysis is that most discussions of these kinds of results focus on the proportion of match time spent performing high intensity activity, the duration of high intensity bursts and the recovery periods that follow them. Therefore, the POWER system (O'Donoghue *et al.*

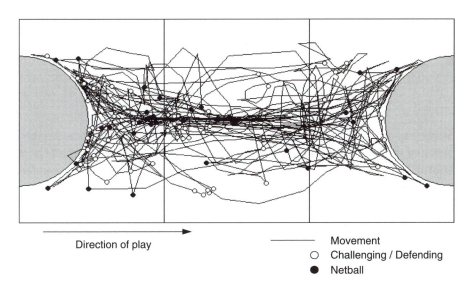

Direction of play

——— Movement
○ Challenging / Defending
● Netball

Figure 11.5 Example of data entered for an individual netball player (O'Donoghue and Loughran 1998)

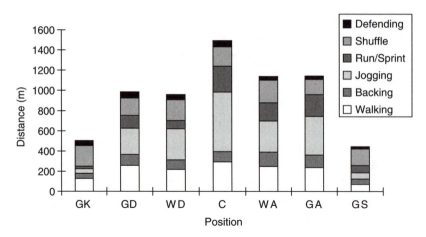

Figure 11.6 Distance covered by different positions during a match quarter

2005a) was developed to allow 'work' and 'rest' periods to be entered directly without recording any individual types of low intensity recovery activity or any individual type of high intensity activity. The system is subjective in that 'work' represents any activity perceived by the observer to require a high intensity effort to perform. Therefore, reliability assessment would be essential for any scientific investigation where the POWER system was to be used. The two movement classification of the POWER system reduces choice reaction time and, therefore, improves reliability of data collection. Despite only considering two types of activity, there are a variety of different outputs that are produced by the POWER system to give an indication of the intermittent nature of activity performed by players in team games. These include frequencies of bursts of different duration classes, recoveries of different duration classes as well as analysis of repeated work bouts.

Spencer et al. (2004) introduced the concept of repeated sprint bouts when they analysed the activity of 14 field hockey players. They defined a repeated sprint bout as a period of three or more sprints where the sprints were separated by non-sprint periods averaging <21 s. This value of 21 s was based on the 25th percentile of recoveries in the data collected. When developing the POWER system, O'Donoghue et al. (2005a) decided to use repeated work bouts based on the repeated sprint bouts introduced by Spencer et al. (2004). The repeated work bouts recognized that high intensity activity did not only include sprinting. A further development was that O'Donoghue et al. (2005a) wanted the definition of the repeated work bouts to be independent of individual data sets. Repeated work bouts are defined as periods of two or more periods of work

time–motion analysis

separated by recoveries of <20 s. The rationale for this was based on a labora-tory study by Hughes *et al.* (2005) that revealed that a set of 6 s sprints were performed with a significantly lower power output when performed every 25 s than when performed every 45 s or every 55 s.

To illustrate the activity profile produced by the POWER system, the activity of an international netball player was analysed during a league match of four 12.5 min quarters, for the purpose of the current chapter. The player, a wing attack, spent 24.8 per cent of the match performing high intensity activity with 275 bursts of high intensity activity of a mean duration of 2.8 s separated by recoveries with a mean duration of 8.5 s. However, not all bursts of high intensity activity are of the mean duration and not all recovery periods are of the mean duration. There were 262 of the high intensity bursts that were of durations of under 6 s, 125 of these with durations of under 6 s. The player was required to perform 11 bursts of between 6 s and 8 s, nine bursts of between 8 s and 10 s, two bursts of 10–12 s and one burst of >12 s during the match. There was a full range of recovery durations with only 79 of the 275 recovery periods being in the range 4–12 s that included the mean recovery of 8.5 s. There were 124 recoveries of under 4 s, 45 recoveries of between 12 s and 20 s, 25 recoveries of between 20 s and 45 s, two recoveries of 45 s to 90 s and no recovery periods of >90 s. Table 11.2 shows that there was an association between the duration of bursts performed and the duration of the recoveries that followed them with all 27 recoveries of 20 s or longer following bursts of 6 s or longer ($\chi^2_1 = 31.8$, $p < 0.001$). This is in contrast to findings for Gaelic football (King and O'Donoghue 2003) and soccer activity (O'Donoghue *et al.* 2005b).

There were only 27 recovery periods of 20 s or longer and there were no individual bursts of activity with such recoveries preceding and following them. Therefore all high intensity activity bursts were performed within the 28 repeated work bouts that were separated by these 28 recovery periods. The shortest repeated work bout consisted of 2 bursts while the longest consisted of

Table 11.2 Duration of bursts and following recoveries performed by a netball player.

Burst duration	Duration of the following recovery		
	Under 20 s	20 s or longer	All
Under 6 s	144	0	144
6 s or longer	104	27	131
All	248	27	275

33 bursts. The mean repeated work bout consisted of 9.8 bursts of high intensity activity lasting 2.8 s on average with a mean recovery of 6.2 s. The short recoveries experienced by netball players may mean that the energy used for short high intensity bursts may not be solely derived from the ATP-PC system. This is because laboratory based investigations have shown that the duration of recovery periods has an influence on physiological responses to performing repeated 6 s bursts of high intensity exercise (Balsom et al. 1992; Wootton and Williams 1983; Hughes et al. 2005). The prolonged repeated work bouts might also explain the higher mean heart rate response of 88 per cent HR max found in netball (Keating and O'Donoghue 1999) than the 75 per cent HR max found in women's field hockey (Robinson et al. 1996b).

The POWER system determines a variety of outputs based on the periods of work and rest entered during observation. These outputs can be combined with ball-in-play time to give a better indication of the work to rest ratios experienced during match play. For example, in soccer 55.3 per cent of match time involves the ball being in play (O'Donoghue and Parker 2001) with players not required to perform high intensity effort during the remaining stoppage time. Therefore a work to rest ratio of 1:10 during the entire 90 min (8.2 min of work and 81.8 min of rest) is equivalent to a work to rest ratio 1:5 during the 49.8 min of ball-in-play time (8.2 min of work and 41.6 min of rest).

Those undertaking time–motion investigations of team games need to be able to discuss and explain their findings with reference to the physiology of intermittent high intensity activity. Typically, work to rest ratios, duration of work periods and rest periods are discovered through time–motion analysis research. There are laboratory based studies where the physiological aspects of intermittent high intensity activity have been investigated under controlled conditions. Variables such as oxygen cost of activity, heart rate response, onset of blood lactate and power output during laboratory based tests all provide evidence of the energy systems utilized during intermittent high intensity activity. Reasoning about the findings of time–motion investigations using the published findings of relevant laboratory based studies allows inferences to be made about the energy systems utilized during team games. Most time–motion researchers will assume that low intensity recovery periods are performed using aerobic sources of energy. The duration of the high intensity bursts performed gives an indication of the energy systems utilized. During a Wingate test, there is evidence that the energy used for the first 6 s of intense exercise is predominantly derived from the ATP-PC system (Smith and Hill 1991) with glycolytic sources being introduced as the intense exercise burst continues beyond 6 s and aerobic sources being introduced when the intense exercise continues

196

beyond 10 s. It was for this reason, that the CAPTAIN system reported the bursts of high intensity activity that were <6 s, 6–10 s and 10 s. Most of the energy used for short high intensity bursts in soccer is derived from the breakdown of CP-ATP and glycolysis (Bangsbo 1997). Experimental research has also shown that 6 s bursts of high intensity activity derive 50 per cent of the energy required from the breakdown of CP-ATP and 50 per cent from glycolysis with the contribution from glycolytic sources increasing as the duration of high intensity activity increases (Boobis 1987; Gaitanos et al. 1993). During high intensity bursts performed in soccer, the glycolytic system involves the production of lactate which is considered to be associated with fatigue (Bangsbo 1993). During low intensity recovery periods, lactate is metabolized within active muscles (Brooks 1987). The energy sources utilized for work periods may not be exclusively anaerobic. A laboratory experiment has shown that the reduction in mean power output as a 30 s sprint progresses was not as great as the reduction in anaerobic ATP utilization (Nevill et al. 1994). This suggests that aerobic sources of energy make an increasing contribution to the energy required as the sprint continues.

A major criticism of the CAPTAIN system is that recovery periods were not classified in the same way as the high intensity bursts were. The POWER system determines the number of recovery periods of eight different duration classes ranging from under 2 s to 90 s or longer. This allows the effect of recovery duration to be considered when discussing time motion findings. Laboratory-based research has shown that blood lactate accumulation and performance decrements over five 6 s maximal sprint bouts performed on cycle-ergometer equipment were greater when a recovery of 30 s was taken between sprint bouts than when the recovery was 60 s (Wootton and Williams 1983). Furthermore, muscle CP may not be sufficiently replenished after recovery periods of under 45 s (Balsom et al. 1992; Bogdanis et al. 1995). Therefore, the number of recoveries of different durations determined using the POWER system has implications for the sources of energy utilized in team games. There is a decline in sprint performance after only seven 6 s sprints out of a series of ten when recoveries of 30 s are taken (Balsom et al. 1992). Hughes et al. (2005) demonstrated that short recovery durations of 19 s decreased repeated 6 s sprint performance compared with when 34 s or 49 s recoveries were taken. The analysis of repeated work bouts (O'Donoghue et al. 2005a, b) as well as repeated sprint bouts (Spencer et al. 2004) should be explained with reference to the physiology of intermittent high intensity activity. In particular, laboratory based investigations showing the additional cost of performing high intensity bursts when recovery is restricted should be consulted.

The Prozone® system is an automatic player tracking system that allows the movement of players, officials and the ball to be tracked automatically. The data capture component of the system uses image processing algorithms to identify players on the playing surface. A set of typically six cameras are configured to cover the entire playing area. The location of each player and object of interest is determined every 0.1 s. The time–motion data recorded is fully integrated with match event information and the match video. The fact that the movement data is gathered automatically for all players, officials and the ball makes Prozone far more efficient than the other methods surveyed in this part of the chapter.

O'Donoghue (1998) spent a soccer season going to 24 soccer matches, recording the activity of one player at a time using audio equipment. This required an extra 90 min for each player so as the audio recording could be played back and the times sequence of movement entered into a computerized time–motion analysis system. O'Donoghue's (1998) method only allowed the distribution of match time among different activities to be recorded; distance covered was not recorded. With Prozone, the activity of 22 players can be analysed during a single match in a way that allows results for distribution of match time, distance covered, velocity profiles and accelerations to be produced. Activity is classified by the speed at which a player moves. The speed zones representing jogging, running and sprinting can be adjusted to be specific to individual players where necessary. The distribution of match time and the distribution of the total distance covered can be determined in terms of these different speeds of movement. This can be done for the whole match or for identified periods of the match that are of interest to the user. The path of movement can also be shown on a diagram of the playing surface for the whole match or different sub periods, colour coded to identify different speeds of movement during the path travelled. The location of accelerations can be presented on a diagram of the playing area. In addition to these static outputs, Prozone allows the movement of players to be animated on a bird's-eye view of the playing surface. This can be done for all players involved or for an individual player or individual unit within a team. Direct manipulation of the symbols used to represent player locations gives access to further information about the player or the play being represented. This includes video sequences from the point of the match corresponding to the time in the match where the player was at the location depicted on the playing surface animation. There are other methods of automatic player tracking which use GPS technology. These have been used to investigate the work-rate of referees in Gaelic football (Gamble et al. 2007).

There are many issues in evaluating the reliability of time–motion analysis systems such as the POWER system and the CAPTAIN system. A version of the kappa statistic has been developed allowing continuous time data to be used (O'Donoghue 2004). The algorithm computes the proportion of observation time where two independent observations of the same performance agree on the movement class being performed, adjusting this for the proportion where they could be expected to agree by chance. This has been used with the CAPTAIN system (McLaughlin and O'Donoghue 2002a, b) and the POWER system (O'Donoghue et al. 2005b).

One issue with the kappa statistic is the interpretation of the kappa values produced. Altman (1991) classified kappa values of between 0.6 and 0.8 as indicating a good strength of agreement and values of over 0.8 as representing a very good strength of agreement. O'Donoghue (2007) deliberately created two synthetic activity profiles based on two movement classes (work and rest) that would use different energy systems based on the laboratory based study of Hughes et al. (2005). The kappa value of 0.603 found for these two synthetic profiles indicates that 0.6 is not a good kappa value for time–motion data. Therefore, O'Donoghue (2007) recommended that kappa values of >0.8 should be interpreted as good and values <0.5 should be interpreted as poor. Another issue with the use of the kappa statistic is that it gives a value for the strength of agreement between two independent observations but it does not report on the reliability of any time–motion performance indicator. This concise expression of reliability may be seen as a strength of the kappa statistic, particularly where a multitude of time–motion outputs produced.

However, others would insist on some indication of the reliability of key performance indicators produced. The main performance indicators to summarize the intermittent nature of high intensity activity in team games are the percentage of time spent performing high intensity activity and the duration of the mean high intensity burst. The work to rest ratio and the duration of the mean low intensity recovery period are functionally dependent on these two variables (McLaughlin and O'Donoghue 2002a, b). Therefore, the reliability of the percentage of time spent performing high intensity activity and the duration of the mean high intensity burst have been determined using 95 per cent limits of agreement (McLaughlin and O'Donoghue 2002a, b). Such reliability studies involving multiple subjects (>40 for 95 per cent limits of agreement to be used validly) may require more data collection effort than can be made in an undergraduate student research project, especially if reliability is being assessed before the student continues to progress with the main purpose of the study. There is a trade-off between precision of measurement and reliability in time–motion analysis (O'Donoghue 2007). McLaughlin and O'Donoghue found that they could not reliably measure the mean duration of high intensity burst to the nearest 0.1 s. However, by classifying values as being under 6 s or not, they were able to use a less precise but more reliable indicator of reliability. The importance of doing this is that despite the poor reliability of the original continuous scale version of duration of mean high intensity burst, the reliability is not so poor that one cannot even state that the nature of activity is intermittent. Those faced with poor reliability of such variables should decrease precision of measurement in attempt to obtain a categorical version of the variable that can be used. The fact that Prozone involves automatic player tracking does not mean that reliability testing is unnecessary. Indeed Di Salvo et al. (2006) report on the results of a reliability test of the Prozone system.

Statistical analysis of time motion data for team games depends on the purpose of the study and the performance indicators being investigated. Performance indicators such as the percentage of time spent performing high intensity activity, the mean duration of high intensity bursts and the mean duration of recovery periods are measured on a ratio scale and could be investigated using parametric statistics where the relevant assumptions are satisfied or more typically alternative non-parametric tests. The percentage of match time spent performing movement classes (such as jogging, standing, running, etc.) and the mean durations of instances of individual movement classes can be analysed in the same way. Chi square should not be used to compare the distribution of match time between different samples because the percentages for each sample may be the means determined from many different players. Frequency variables are not measured on a continuous scale and should be analysed using non-parametric techniques. A variable such as the frequency of standing instances is a mean frequency for the sample under investigation rather than a frequency of independent cases. Therefore, chi square is not recommended for the comparison of the frequency variables between samples. Even when the frequency of high intensity bursts (or low intensity recoveries) of different duration classes is being compared between samples, χ^2 should not be used. Consider O'Donoghue et al.'s (2005b) analysis of FA Premier League soccer players. There were 277 players observed in this study with two of the three positional groups containing over 100 players. Therefore, a series of Kruskal–Wallis H tests were used with follow-up Bonferroni adjusted Mann–Whitney U tests employed for pairwise comparisons. Other independent factors that can be used in time–motion investigations are level of player (O'Donoghue et al. 2001), the particular game (O'Donoghue et al. 2004b) and gender (McErlean et al. 2000). There are also within subjects effects such as score-line within matches (Shaw and O'Donoghue 2004) that can be compared.

11.5 THE BLOOMFIELD MOVEMENT CLASSIFICATION

The time–motion analysis techniques traditionally used to describe the distribution of match time or distance covered use a small set of movement classes to help manage the complexity of the movement performed in team games. A two movement classification as used in the POWER system or a movement classification of up to nine different movements as used in the CAPTAIN system will not include every type of movement that is of interest to a conditioning coach. In recent years, the development of specific movement abilities has become important in the training of players in team games. Speed agility quickness training programmes with associated equipment are being used in an attempt to make conditioning training more specific to the demands of the games. If we wished to investigate the agility requirements of games, the CAPTAIN and POWER systems would not provide the necessary information about turns, swerves, lunges, jumps, leaps, breaking movements or direction of movement. Given the importance of such movements, Bloomfield embarked on a programme of research to investigate the speed agility quickness demands of activity performed during professional soccer competition. This required the development of a very detailed time–motion analysis technique that would allow the movement class, direction of movement, intensity of movement, turning and game related skills to be entered. The method produced was the Bloomfield Movement Classification (Bloomfield et al. 2004), which has since been used to investigate the speed agility quickness demands of team games (Bloomfield et al. 2007) and injury risk in netball (Williams and O'Donoghue 2005). The method used by Williams and O'Donoghue (2005) was actually a modified version of the Bloomfield Movement Classification that considered turning to be an attribute of other movement that occurred over a measurable duration, where as Bloomfield et al. (2004) considered turning to be an instantaneous event performed in between other movements which would occur over a measurable duration.

Williams and O'Donoghue's (2005) modified version of the Bloomfield Movement Classification was tailored for analysis with the sport of netball. There were 12 movement classes which are defined as follows:

- Stationary – staying in one spot
- Stepping – raising and replanting of foot
- Walking – moving slowly by stepping
- Jogging – moving at a slow monotonous pace (slower than running, quicker than walking)

- Running – manifest purpose and effort, usually when gaining distance
- Shuffling – moving with a very short stride length, for example readjusting footwork or stumbling
- Skipping – moving with small bound-like movements
- Hop – taking off and landing on the same foot
- Jump – propulsion from one/both feet onto one/both feet with definite landing position that differs to running/jogging movements
- Leap – jumping with greater effort, to achieve maximal height or distance
- Lunge – a sudden thrust to an outstretched position
- Braking – sudden deceleration from high intensity movement.

These movements could be performed in a number of different directions with respect to the direction faced by the player at the start of the movement. The directions recorded included forward, backward, left, right, vertical, the four diagonal directions, eight arced directions or not applicable. Players could move in any direction within and so forward represented the 45° sector the player was facing. There were eight such 45° sectors including forward, backward, left, right and the four diagonal directions. Turning during movement was classified into turns to the left or right, up to 90° or >90°, or no turning occurring. This is illustrated in Figure 11.7.

The biggest difference between the original Bloomfield Movement Classification (Bloomfield *et al.* 2004) and Williams and O'Donoghue's (2005) classification was that Williams and O'Donoghue made turning an attribute of other movement classes. For example, a player might turn while jumping or skipping. The

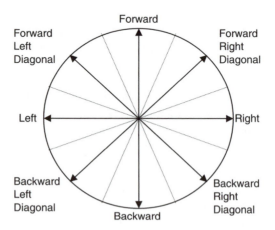

Figure 11.7 Direction of movement

Bloomfield Movement Classification cannot be used during live observation and has had to be implemented on commercial performance analysis software to allow frame-by-frame inspection of subject movement, tagging the video with the start of movements identifying turning, direction and intensity attributes of those movements. Williams and O'Donoghue (2005) used Focus X2 while Bloomfield et al. (2007) used Observer Pro.

Both Bloomfield et al. (2007) and Williams and O'Donoghue (2005) investigated the reliability of the Bloomfield Movement Class using kappa. This is because kappa can be used with instantaneously performed events, such as the on-the-ball skills or turns recorded by Bloomfield et al. (2007), or events that require a measurable period of time to perform such as locomotive movements. The weighted version of kappa might be better to give some credit where recorded values for movement type, direction or turning recorded by one independent observer are adjacent to those recorded by the other observer within a reliability study.

Figure 11.8 shows how a disagreement for direction of movement and a disagreement for turning during movement can occur but with the subject being seemed to start movement in the same place by both observers and finish movement in the same place according to both observers. However, two errors will be deemed to have occurred by kappa. For example one observer might record a forward left arc movement with no turning as the forward left arc movement results in the player making an aspect change anyway. The other observer may record the same movement as being in a forward left diagonal direction without an obvious arc in the path taken. However, because movement in a diagonal direction does not automatically result in an aspect change for the player, this observer will also record a left quarter turn during the movement. Hence a slight disagreement about such a movement can lead to disagreements in relation to the direction of movement and turning during the movement. Such disagreements are given no credit by the kappa statistic, which makes the moderate levels of agreement achieved for direction of movement and turning, reassuring to the author. However, by merging some directions we will actually improve reliability while losing precision.

The Bloomfield Movement Classification is very time consuming and can require 30 min to tag 1 min of player video with time–motion events. Therefore, subject numbers within studies are restricted. Williams and O'Donoghue (2005) only used 7–8 min of video recorded movement for seven netball subjects during their study. This has implications for the statistical analyses that can be performed on the data. The frequency and percentage of observation time for

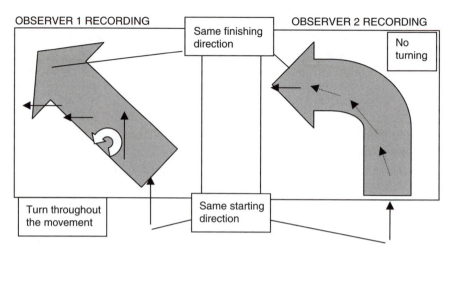

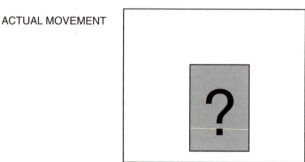

Figure 11.8 Disagreement concerning movement direction and turning

each movement class, direction and turning class as well as combinations of movement, direction and turn are computed. A series of χ^2-tests of independence can be applied to these summary results to investigate associations between movement class, direction of movement and turning during movement. To validly perform χ^2-tests of independence on this type of data, movement directions may have to be combined due to low percentage times for some directions. For example William and O'Donoghue (2005) had to collapse their 12 movement classes into five broader movement classes and their 18 directions of movement into six broad categories of direction in order to meet the assumptions of the χ^2-test of independence; these are shown in Table 11.3.

Table 11.3 Differences between directions for different movements (netball players)

Direction	Movement type				
	Walking	**Jog/Run**	**Skip/Shuffle**	**Jump/Leap**	**Other**
Forward	33.3	61.2	12.4	26.9	60.8
Backward	22.2	0.5	9.2	4.6	2.8
Sideways	10.9	0.5	24.1	13.9	15.8
Diagonal	14.2	12.6	22.3	14.3	15.4
Arced	17.1	24.5	23.7	0.0	0.0
Other	2.5	0.7	8.3	40.2	5.2
Total	100.0	100.0	100.0	100.0	100.0

SUMMARY

There are a range of time–motion analysis methods ranging from the manual notation methods used by Reilly and Thomas (1976) and Liddle et al. (1996) to automatic player tracking systems such as Prozone. The decision as to which method to use depends on performance indicators of interest, permission for filming, cost of systems and time constraints for the time–motion studies being done. Prozone provides efficient and accurate time–motion results within a fully integrated match analysis and video feedback system. However, the classification of movement according to speed has its limitations. High intensity shuffling movement can be performed at low speeds and the direction of movement will influence the energy cost of movement. Laboratory studies have shown that moving with the ball increases the energy cost of movement at the full range of movement speeds (Reilly and Ball 1984). Therefore, there is still a role for non-automated data gathering where human input allows movements to be classified in a subjective manner but based on observer expertise.

CHAPTER TWELVE

PROBABILITY ANALYSIS OF NOTATED EVENTS IN SPORT CONTESTS: SKILL AND CHANCE

Tim McGarry

In this chapter we:

- present some examples to introduce the idea that the behaviours and outcomes in sports contests can usefully be analysed on the basis of chance (or probability).
- demonstrate that considerations of sports contests from the perspective of chance, using probability analysis, is a useful way of analysing and informing on sports behaviours.

12.1 INTRODUCTION

On first consideration from sports experience, the viewpoint that sports actions and sports outcomes might be thought of, and even explained, with reference to chance might seem questionable and, for some perhaps, objectionable. Nonetheless, in the following sections we demonstrate that considerations of sports contests from the perspective of chance, using probability analysis, is a useful way of analysing and informing on sports behaviours and to do this, we first consider some definitions.

12.1.1 Sports contests

For exactness, we use the term 'sports contests' to mean a contest between two opponents – singles (e.g. squash, tennis, or badminton), doubles (same example

206

as for singles, except with two players on each side), or teams (e.g. baseball, volleyball, or soccer). Other types of sports, such as track and field, gymnastics and golf are excluded from this definition of sports contests, even though the outcome for these types of sports may likewise be viewed on the basis of chance.

12.1.2 Skill and chance

The words skill and chance may seem a contradiction in terms when combined in the same phrase. They are not. The word chance refers to uncertainty, so chance may be defined, or at least quantified, as the probability, or percentage likelihood of a future occurrence. (Probability and percentage are the same thing except that probability is measured and reported between values of 0 and 1, and percentage is measured and reported between values of 0 and 100.) Incidentally, chance should not be taken for fortune (good luck) or misfortune (bad luck), terms of common usage when interpreting the outcomes of chance. In contrast, the word skill implies an ability to obtain a desired future occurrence. Thus, the definition of skilled actions often makes reference to the ability (or probability) of the willed action to attain its intended outcome. To illustrate this concept, imagine two basketball players, A and B. Imagine too that A and B score free throws with probabilities of 0.9 and 0.6, respectively. The player with the higher scoring probability (A) is more skilful at taking free throws than the one with the lower scoring probability (B), by definition (i.e. A is more likely to score on a given free throw than B). Similarly, A would be expected to score more free throws than B should both players be awarded an equal number of free throws. In fact, the chances of A outperforming B increases as the number of free throws increases for reasons that we will consider shortly. Put simply, skill wins out more often than not, and with increasing likelihood over the long run, as might be expected. This conclusion with regard to skilled action, however, does not deny the presence, or the contribution, of chance on determining the final outcome.

12.1.3 Probability: stationarity and independence

In later sections, we report on some investigations of sports behaviour using probability analysis. For now, however, we must consider two important concepts, or assumptions, for probability analysis: *stationarity* and *independence*. Stationarity refers to the assumption that the probability of an event, or occurrence, does not change from one instant to the next. Thus, if one were to consider a sequence of coin tosses then stationarity would assume that the same probability of a 'heads' (or 'tails') is the same from one coin toss to the next. Independence refers to the assumption that the outcome of a given event, or occurrence, does not affect the outcome of a next event, or occurrence. For example, if the result of the first coin toss was heads, the result of the second coin toss is just as likely to be heads or tails as it was on the first coin toss. The second coin toss is not affected by the result of the first coin toss. Similarly, the outcome of the third coin toss in the sequence is unaffected by the second outcome, and so on. While it might seem from the example presented that stationarity and independence speak to the same properties, suffice to say that, while complementary, the properties of stationarity and independence are not the same thing.

12.1.4 Taking a random walk in a field of probabilities

The combining of probabilities by addition and/or multiplication is known as combinatorial probability. To illustrate this concept, we consider a sequence of three coin tosses, assuming stationarity and independence, with the probability (p) of heads and the probability (q) of tails on any coin toss being equal, as expected (i.e. $p = q = 0.5$). (Since the probabilities of all possible outcomes must sum to 1, it follows that if p or q is known, then the other is known also, i.e. $p = 1 - q$ and $q = 1 - p$). Each of the possible outcomes from a sequence of three coin tosses, together with the paths, or probability sequences, that lead to these outcomes are presented in Figure 12.1.

Taking what is known as a random walk through Figure 12.1, we start at the beginning of the sequence of coin tosses. Tossing the coin on the first trial yields a heads with probability p_1 or a tails with probability q_1. (The integer subscript following the probability notation indicates the trial number in the trial sequence simply for purposes of tracking convenience). Should the random walk proceed on the first trial on the upper path then the outcome of the first coin toss is heads (p_1), otherwise a tails is the result if the lower path is followed (q_1). Whether the upper or lower path is followed in this instance is determined by chance (or probability) hence the notion of a random walk. Whatever the result of the first coin toss in our example, the random walk depicts the new 'state' of the system. The new state is determined from the outcome of the first coin toss and is expressed in one of the two second nodes of Figure 12.1 (counting nodes from left to right there are four nodes in Figure 12.1, representing zero through three coin tosses, respectively). The random walk then continues from its present

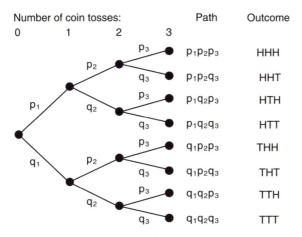

Number of coin tosses:				Path	Outcome

$p_1 p_2 p_3$ HHH
$p_1 p_2 q_3$ HHT
$p_1 q_2 p_3$ HTH
$p_1 q_2 q_3$ HTT
$q_1 p_2 p_3$ THH
$q_1 p_2 q_3$ THT
$q_1 q_2 p_3$ TTH
$q_1 q_2 q_3$ TTT

Figure 12.1 Probability structure depicting a sequence of three coin tosses. p and q denote the probability of heads and tails, respectively. The subscripts 1, 2 and 3 denote the first, second and third trial in the probability sequence, respectively. H, heads; T, tails. The outcome list details the outcome of the three trials, and the path list denotes the path, or probability sequence, that produced that particular outcome

location (one of the two second nodes) in similar fashion and follows the upper or lower path, determined once again by probability, from its present node to its new destination (one of the four third nodes). The process continues in like fashion until the sequence of events, three coin tosses in our example, are completed.

From Figure 12.1, we see eight possible outcomes for a three coin toss sequence ($2^3 = 8$), as expected, but we also see the paths, or the random walk sequences, that produce each of the eight distinct outcomes. For example, if the upper path is followed on all three trials then the outcome of the three coin toss sequence is three heads (HHH), and since the probability of the outcome is expressed in the random walk that produced it, the probability of getting three heads from three coin tosses is $p^3 = 0.5^3 = 0.125$. (Since $p_1 = p_2 = p_3$ the '$p_1 p_2 p_3$' term in Figure 12.1 may be simplified to p^3.) To re-state, if we want to know the probability of obtaining three heads from three trials, we can determine the random walk that produces this particular outcome and use that information to find our answer. For example, the probability of getting the same result from three coin tosses (i.e. three heads or three tails) is obtained from Figure 12.1 by taking one of two possible random walks, p^3 or q^3. To obtain both outcomes we must take two random walks. Since $p^3 = 0.125$ and $q^3 = 0.125$, the probability of getting three heads or three tails from three coin tosses is therefore 0.25 (i.e. $p^3 + q^3$). Similarly, the probability of getting two tails from three coin tosses is $3pq^2 = 3(0.5^3)$ = 0.375. This information is obtained from taking all possible random walks that lead to the outcome of two tails ($p_1q_2q_3 + q_1p_2q_3 + q_1q_2p_3 = 3pq^2$). In this way, the information contained in Figure 12.1 is sufficient to answer whatever questions posed regarding the combination of possible outcomes from three coin tosses.

The point of the above commentary is to demonstrate that the probability of a given outcome can be obtained by accounting for all of the different random walks possible to achieve that outcome. We presented a simple example by which the random walks could each be identified quite easily by enumeration though longer sequences of probability chains quickly render this approach impractical (not to mention increasingly subject to error on the part of the enumerator). Imagine, trying to find the probability of getting eight heads from a sequence of ten coin tosses using enumeration, for example (2^{10} = 1,024 probability sequences). Of course, mathematical formulae may be used in many instances as a shortcut for enumeration though, importantly, both methods achieve the same result in the same way. For instance, in a system comprising of two-states as per the coin toss example used, the probability of getting eight heads from ten coin tosses is obtained quite readily from the binomial theorem (or binomial series), assuming familiarity with the binomial series that is.[a] For example, the binomial series for the three coin tosses is $(p + q)^3 = p^3 + 3p^2q + 3pq^2 + q^3$. (In Figure 12.1, if we enumerate each possible outcome from a three coin toss sequence we get $p_1p_2p_3$, $p_1p_2q_3$, $p_1q_2p_3$, $p_1q_2q_3$, $q_1p_2p_3$, $q_1p_2q_3$, $q_1q_2p_3$ and $q_1q_2q_3$, which when expressed as a sum of all possible outcomes is $p^3 + 3p^2q + 3pq^2 + q^3$ as described in the binomial series.) To re-visit the question of the probability of obtaining two tails from three coin tosses, we simply obtain the q^2 term from the binomial series (i.e., $3pq^2$) and compute accordingly.[b] Similar computational principles apply to the probability of obtaining eight heads from ten coin tosses, if desired. So much for coin tosses. Our interest is in sports contests.

12.2 TAKING A RANDOM WALK IN SPORTS CONTESTS: INVESTIGATION OF SCORING STRUCTURE

There are quite a few examples of authors using probability analysis to investigate sports behaviour, most notably for analysing the scoring structures on the basis of probability, as well as identifying optimal decision-making strategies based on these scoring structures in some instances. For reasons of focus, however, we will skip the details of the authors and their contributions of probability analysis as applied to sport behaviour, and instead present a simplified example of investigating the scoring structure of tennis using probability analysis.

The scoring for a game in tennis consists of the first player to score four points. For simplicity, we ignore the tied situation at three points apiece whereupon the game must be won by a two point margin. We define the probability that the server wins the point as p, and the probability that the receiver wins the point as q (where $p + q = 1$). Since the tennis game must be won within seven rallies, ignoring the tied condition, we get the following expression from the binomial theorem: $(p + q)^7 = p^7 + 7p^6q + 21p^5q^2 + 35p^4q^3 + 35p^3q^4 + 21p^2q^5 + 7pq^6 + q^7$. Since the winner of the game must win four points without the opponent getting four (or more) points, only the paths that contain the winning probability to the power of four (or higher) will be included in the probability of winning the game. Powers higher than four must be included in the calculation since the player will necessarily reach four points following these probability sequences. Thus, the probability that the server will win the game is contained in the expression $p^7 + 7p^6q + 21p^5q^2 + 35p^4q^3$ and, similarly, the probability that the receiver will win the game is the remainder of the expression, i.e. $35p^3q^4 + 21p^2q^5 + 7pq^6 + q^7$ (or, re-arranged, $q^7 + 7q^6p + 21q^5p^2 + 35q^4p^3$).

Figure 12.2 presents the probabilities that the server will win the game for different probabilities of winning a given point from service. The point winning probabilities range from 0.05 to 0.95 in 0.05 increments. (The same results for the same probabilities of winning a given point from receipt of service are found for the receiver too.) For example, if $p = 0.50$, then the probability that the server wins the game is 0.500. If the server increases the probability of winning a service point from p = 0.50 to p = 0.55, say, perhaps as a result of specific practice, then the game winning probability increases from 0.500 to 0.608. Interestingly, then, a 10 per cent increase in the point winning probability (from 0.50 to 0.55) results in a 21.6 per cent increase in the game winning probability (from 0.500 to 0.608). The important point is that because of combinatorial probability small gains in point winning probability lead to larger gains in the game winning probability, at least when the point winning probabilities are within the mid-ranges. Towards the limits this pattern of small gains in point winning probabilities leading to larger gains in game winning probabilities is reversed as the gains won in the mid-ranges must be given back as losses at the extremes.

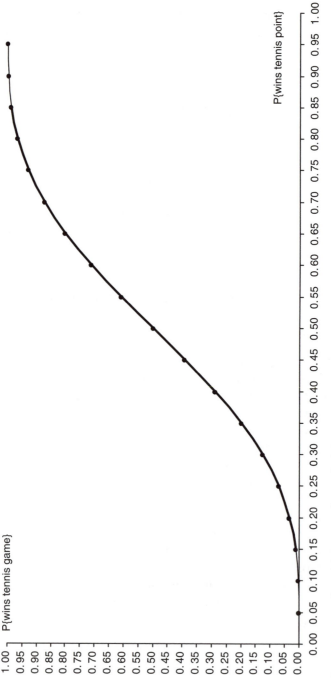

P{wins tennis game}

P{wins tennis point}

Figure 12.2 Relation between the probability of winning a point in tennis and winning the game in tennis (i.e. first to 4 points; ignoring the condition at 3 points apiece, whereupon the game must be won by a 2-point margin)

12.3 TAKING A RANDOM WALK IN SPORTS CONTESTS: INVESTIGATION OF BEHAVIOURS (SHOTS) AND OUTCOMES IN SQUASH CONTESTS

The above example, as with all of the investigations on scoring structures not reported in this article, uses the outcome – the winning of a point – as the unit for probability analysis. Following on from this type of earlier work, we undertook a series of investigations using probability analysis to inform on the shot selection behaviours, and their outcomes, of players in squash contests. There are two important distinctions of this type of research from the previous work using probability analysis to investigate scoring structures and optimization of decision-making strategies. First, the unit of probability of analysis is changed from the outcome (i.e. the winning of a point) to the behaviour (i.e. the type of shots produced that lead to the outcome). Second, the probabilities to be used in the analysis are obtained from data collected from observation using the principles of scientific notation outlined elsewhere in this book.

To investigate squash behaviour, we first recorded in sequence the types of shots produced in a number of squash rallies from a number of squash contests. The outcomes of the rallies – winner, error, or let, the latter being a neutral outcome – were also recorded. These shot sequences were subsequently analysed to obtain their frequencies of occurrence within a given squash contest. The probabilities of occurrence were then obtained from the frequencies of occurrence simply by expressing the frequency values as a proportion of their total frequencies. The probability data were then used in a probability model (similar to Figure 12.1) that described the sequence of shot behaviours and outcomes as a probability structure to investigate squash behaviours using computer simulation.

12.3.1 Stochastic processes, shot selections and outcomes in squash contests

Imagine a system of many states, (e.g. A, B, C, D, etc.) whose behaviour is characterized by random switching within and between states (e.g. A → C → D → D → A → B, etc.). If the probabilities of switching between the various states are known, then the probabilities of any sequence of switches within the system is also known using appropriate calculations. The behaviour of the system can therefore be thought of and analysed as a stochastic process. (The term stochastic means random and thus subject to the laws of probability.) In addition, if the switching from one state to the next depends only on where the system is at present (i.e. in which state the system currently resides), then the stochastic process is said to possess Markov properties. In other words, there is sufficient information in the present state to predict the next state without regard for the past. Thus, the path that the system took to get to the present state is of no consequence as to where the system will switch to next since the information necessary is contained within, and only within, the present state. For example, in a system whose behaviour switches from A → C → D → A → B, the system is characterized as a Markov process if the switch from state D to state A is dependent only on state D, and independent of the sequence of steps that the system took to get to state D (i.e., A → C → D). The same condition applies for any of the other states in which the system may reside (e.g. A, B, C, D, etc.) We analysed the shot selection behaviours and outcomes of squash contests as a stochastic (Markov) process. For all of the preceding comments, the analysis of squash behaviours just described is very similar in principle to the probability analysis of coin tosses described previously.

The shot data, including the player, the type of shot selected, where on court the shot was played from, and the outcome of the shot, if any, were recorded from observation of video records of international squash contests (see McGarry and Franks 1996c, d, for further details). Subsequent analysis of these data yielded a playing matrix for each individual. The playing matrix contained two distinct sets of data, a *shot–response* matrix (for an example, see Table 12.1) and a *winner–error* matrix (for an example, see Table 12.2). The shot–response matrix contained the frequency distribution of shots selected by a player in reply to each type of previous shot produced by the opponent. The winner–error matrix contained the frequency distribution of the outcomes that were associated with each type of shot produced by the player, as yielded from the shot–response matrix.

Table 12.1 contains the frequencies of the various shots selected (and produced) by a player in response to the previous shot type selected (and produced) by the opponent. The frequency distribution of a given shot by the player is presented in rows, and the array of shot responses to each previous shot type by the opponent are presented in columns. The shot code that references each column is found in parentheses in the shot listings that reference each row. The data in Table 12.1 can therefore be read by row or by column, as required. For example, in reply to the serve (S) from the opponent, the player produced one drive (A), two cross-court boasts (D), nine long volleys and 12 long cross-court volleys (see column S, Table 12.1). Thus, the shot probabilities in reply to the serve obtained from these data are 0.042, 0.083, 0.375, and 0.500, respectively. Similarly, Table 12.2 contains the frequencies of the various outcomes that were

Table 12.1 Frequency shot–response profile for an individual player

	Previous Shot (Opponent)															
Shot-Response (Player)	**S**	**A**	**B**	**C**	**D**	**E**	**F**	**G**	**H**	**I**	**J**	**K**	**L**	**M**	**N**	**Total**
Drive (A)	1	56	24	1	6	2	3	1	1	17	7	—	—	1	6	126
XC-Drive (B)	—	34	11	2	5	—	4	—	—	13	4	1	—	—	3	77
Boast (C)	—	—	—	—	2	1	—	—	—	2	2	—	—	—	1	6
XC-Boast (D)	2	19	9	—	4	—	1	1	—	4	4	—	—	1	2	46
Drop (E)	—	6	2	1	18	11	6	3	2	—	—	—	—	—	2	50
XC-Drop (F)	—	2	—	1	4	1	1	1	1	1	1	—	—	—	—	13
Volley[Short] (G)	—	14	7	—	—	—	—	—	—	1	4	—	—	—	5	31
XC-Volley[Short] (H)	—	6	—	—	—	—	—	—	—	1	1	—	—	—	—	8
Volley[Long] (I)	9	1	2	—	—	—	—	—	—	—	—	—	—	2	12	26
XC-Volley[Long] (J)	12	10	2	—	—	—	—	—	—	2	3	—	—	—	2	31
Volley-Boast (K)	—	—	1	—	—	—	—	—	—	—	—	—	—	—	—	1
XC-Volley-Boast (L)	—	5	—	—	—	1	—	—	—	—	—	—	—	—	—	5
Lob (M)	—	—	—	—	1	1	3	1	—	—	—	1	—	—	—	1
XC-Lob (N)	—	—	—	1	1	2	3	1	—	—	—	1	—	—	—	9
Total	24	153	58	5	40	18	17	7	4	39	26	2	—	4	33	430

Note: The shot codes for the opponent are found in parentheses in the list of shots for the player.

Table 12.2 Frequency winner–error profile for an individual player

Outcome	Current shot (player)															Total
	S	A	B	C	D	E	F	G	H	I	J	K	L	M	N	
Unconditional winner	–	1	1	–	–	4	4	3	–	–	–	–	–	–	–	13
Conditional winner	–	4	–	3	1	10	1	2	2	2	1	–	–	–	–	26
Unforced error	–	2	1	–	2	4	–	2	–	–	–	–	1	–	–	12
Forced error	–	–	–	1	1	1	–	–	–	–	–	–	–	–	–	3
Let	–	3	1	–	–	2	–	1	–	4	–	–	–	–	–	11
Total	–	10	3	4	4	21	5	8	2	6	1	–	1	–	–	65

Note: See Table 12.1 for a list of shot codes.

associated with the shots produced by the player. The column data indicated that the serve (S) yielded no outcomes whatsoever, as expected. In contrast, the drive (A) produced one unconditional winner, four conditional winners, two unforced errors, zero forced errors and three lets (see column 'A', Table 12.2). In other words, the drive shot for this player won five points (winners), lost two points (errors) and produced three neutral (let) outcomes. The outcome frequencies for the other shot types from the same player are listed in their respective columns. Once again, the outcome probabilities for each shot type are easily obtained from the frequency data, as required.

The sequence of shots in a squash rally were analysed as a stochastic (Markov) process. To describe this process we present a specific example in Figure 12.3, which is necessarily simplified for reasons of space limitations, and a general example in Figure 12.4. Figure 12.3 is used to depict a short rally of fixed length whereas Figure 12.4 is used to depict a squash contest that comprises of an unspecified number of rallies each of unspecified length. In both instances, the switching between states within the system is random and based on the probabilities obtained from the shot–response profiles and winner–error profiles of the two players as appropriate. Since a squash rally is comprised of two players

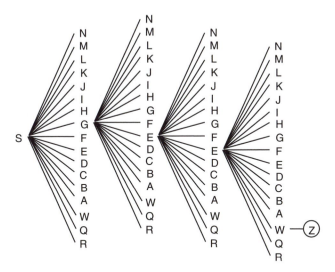

Figure 12.3 Probability structure for a squash rally with a specific example used (see text for details). A to N and S denote certain shot types (see Table 12.1 for a listing of the shot type associated with each shot code). W to R denote the outcomes for the rally: W, winner; Q, error; and R, let. Z denotes the final, or absorbing, state of the probability structure

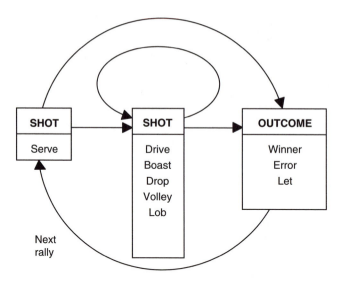

Figure 12.4 Stochastic (Markov) processes for the sequence of shots and outcomes produced in a squash rally and, by extension, for all the rallies in a squash contest

of course, the transition between states within any squash rally is informed on an alternating basis by the respective probabilities of the two players as obtained previously from game analysis.

In any rally, the system begins in an initial state S (serve) before switching in random fashion to the next state (shot or outcome). In the example presented in Figure 12.3, the system from state S (serve) switches to state G (short volley) though a switch to any other state is likewise possible, including the outcomes. This transition means that the server makes a serve and the receiver in this instance responds with a short volley. The system thereafter switches at random to the next state, E (drop) in our example, and so on, until the end state (outcome) is reached. Thus, the server responds to the short volley from the receiver with a drop shot. Similarly, the receiver follows the drop shot from the server with a drop shot of his (her) own (Figure 12.3) from which the system switches to state W (winner), meaning that the receiver wins that rally with the drop shot. The state W (and Q and R too) is known as a final, or absorbing, state since it denotes the end of the process (i.e. the end of the rally). This example of a random walk through the system describes how the stochastic (Markov) process uses random processes and empirical probabilities to construct a sequence of squash shots and a subsequent outcome in the generation of a squash rally. This process can be repeated in iterative fashion to likewise generate a squash contest between two players based upon their empirical profiles, be they obtained from playing against each other, or from playing against other opponents.

In Figure 12.4, the initial state for the system is once again the serve as this type of shot is used to begin each rally. From there, the system passes to the next state in the sequence on the basis of probability. The probabilities for switching between states when analysing a sports contest is obtained from the recorded data of two players as mentioned previously. The probabilities of shot selection for a player (the server of the first rally in our example) are represented in the shot–response profile (see Table 12.1) and the probabilities of outcome attached to a given shot by that player are represented in the winner–error profile (see Table 12.2). The opponent would likewise be assigned a shot–response and winner–error profile as determined from past observations. From the serve, the first decision to be made on the basis of probability is to decide which state the system is to switch to next, an outcome state or a shot state. First, the winner–error profile is inspected for the player that made the serve, and an outcome is assigned, or not, based upon probability. From the winner–error profile (Table 12.2) we see that zero outcomes were assigned to 24 serves, indicating that, unsurprisingly, the serve did not result in an outcome for this player on any instance. The system state therefore switches from the serve to the next to-be-determined shot in the sequence. (For convenience, the listing of shot types in Figure 12.4 are represented in a more generic form. The more specific listings of shot types are identified in Figure 12.3 and also in the shot–response profile presented in Table 12.1.) The next shot will be decided on a random basis as informed from the shot–response profile of the opponent (not shown). We therefore suppose that the next shot by the opponent is a short volley. From this state an outcome is assigned, or not, as indicated earlier from the winner–error profile of the opponent (again, not shown). In this example, we imagine that the system once more switches to the next shot in the sequence. From Table 12.1, we see that the player responded to a short volley from the opponent with probabilities of 1/7, 1/7, 3/7, 1/7 and 1/7, for the drive, cross-court boast, drop, cross-court drop and cross-court lob, respectively. On this occasion, we suppose on the basis of probability that the player responds with a drop shot, and furthermore that an outcome is assigned to it. Of 50 drop shots played by the player (row E, Table 12.1), 21 shots resulted in an outcome (column E, Table 12.2). Furthermore, of the 21 drop shots that produced an outcome, 14 shots yielded some type of winner, five shots resulted in some type of error, and two shots finished in a let (neutral outcome). In this example, we assign a winner to the drop shot played by the player and the rally ends. On instruction, the system is then switched from its final absorbing state and placed into a new transient state, namely the state of serve so that the next rally may begin.

12.3.2 Computer simulation

Once more, we have just taken a random walk through the system for a single squash rally. Of course the system can take many different paths, of many different lengths, with various outcomes, as determined on the basis of chance in each instance. This random (Markov) process repeats for each rally within a contest. Since the outcome of each rally is known, a score is kept and the contest ends when one player reaches a winning score. Indeed, since the outcome of a squash contest as predicted from a Markov process will itself vary, the squash contest is repeated a number of times using simulation procedures until a predicted outcome is settled upon. In simulation procedures the stability of the final prediction is an important consideration. In our studies of squash contests, we selected to contest the playing profiles 1,000 times. We reasoned that this number of contests provided an acceptable degree of stability in the final prediction (standard error ~ 0.016 for $p = q = 0.5$).

12.3.3 Identification of optimal decision-making strategies

The above section details how a squash contest might be described in terms of a stochastic process. The same type of description might be applied equally well to other types of sports contests. In this section, we address some of the possible benefits of using this type of approach for sports analysis.

The valid construction of a stochastic model for sports contests has a two-fold application, first, as a descriptor of sports behaviours and, second, as a predictor of future sports performance. The ability to predict the future on the basis of the past, if possible, gives the sports practitioner, not to mention the sports gambler, an immense advantage. If sports performances can be predicted with accuracy, then those strategies that maximize or minimize the desired behaviours and outcomes can be identified and planned for in advance. For example, a player's shot–response and/or winner–error profile might be changed in systematic fashion and the predicted effects on the final outcome analysed. In this way a shot-response profile might be 'tweaked' towards maximizing a predicted winning outcome. In principle, this information could be used in future practice settings by the coach and/or athlete to help influence decision-making with regard to the

probability analysis of notated events in sport contests

shot-selection responses so as to shape behaviour towards a winning profile. We present an example as to how such a strategy might be identified from the recorded data.

Inspection of Table 12.2 indicates that the player's winner–error profile is influenced strongly by that player's short game (shots C–H). In particular, we see that the drop shot yielded 21 of 65 outcomes (32.3%), including 14 winners (66.7%), five errors (23.8%) and two lets (9.5%). In other words, the player benefited from playing a strong short game against his (her) opponent with high usage of the drop shot. On this information, a subsequent opponent might determine it a good strategy to stay away from, when possible, getting drawn into a short game against this player. To effect this strategy would require the opponent to minimize those conditions from which the player might instigate a short game in order to make use of the drop shot. On viewing the shot–response profile of the player in question, we find that of the 50 drop shots selected, 18 (36%) were made in response to the cross-court boast (D) and 11 (22%) were produced in response to the drop shot (E) (see row E, Table 12.1). One strategy for the future opponent therefore might be to minimize his (her) frequency of cross-court boasts and drop shots, on the supposition that this tactic might be expected to reduce the frequency of drop shots that the player will select to reply with. In general terms, this would mean the opponent using a percentage strategy that is aimed towards a long-game, and refusing when possible to get drawn into a short-game. If necessary, this type of strategy could be developed in practice sessions when preparing for specific future matches. The use of gaming simulations, where the shot selection patterns, and strategies, for a future contest can be practiced using video-like type of games (or virtual reality) offers a striking example of this type of possible application for sports practice.

12.3.4 Interactions between the winner–error profiles

Unfortunately, there are some important limitations on the types of optimal-decision making strategies outlined above. One such limitation is found in the interactions that exist between the two players. For example, the game profiles for one player are influenced somewhat by the game profiles of the other player, and vice versa, and these profiles cannot seemingly be untwined in a meaningful way. For example, a strong playing profile might be attributed to a player after competing against a weak opponent and, similarly, a weak playing profile might be assigned to the same player when competing against a strong opponent. This issue becomes important when, as desired, the profile of a player obtained against one opponent is to be used to predict to future behaviours when competing against other opponents. Somehow the stochastic model described previously must therefore account for the interactions between the players on which the playing profiles were obtained. For example, if a winner–error profile indicates a strong pattern of winners for a given player then a couple of questions present themselves: For example, were the many winners in the winner–error profile obtained against a strong or a weak opponent; and does the present opponent permit many winners against him (her) as indicated from their own profile (as indicated in the few winners that their previous opponent managed against them, somehow keeping in mind the context in which that profile itself was obtained). Similarly, if a winner–error profile contains a strong presence of errors for a given player, the questions to be asked concern whether the opponent induces many errors in his (her) opponents and against whom were these data obtained. We tried to account for these types of considerations by distinguishing unconditional winners from conditional winners, and forced errors from unforced errors, in order to introduce to the stochastic process some type of interaction between the winner–error profiles of the two squash players. The interested reader is referred to McGarry and Franks (1996c) for further specifics on the interactions between the winner–error profiles beyond those details provided below.

In brief, unconditional winners and unforced errors were defined as winners and errors that were awarded without regard for the opponent, whereas conditional winners and forced errors were defined and subsequently interpreted as arising as a direct result of the interaction with that opponent. The aim of this distinction was to document in some way the dependency of the conditional winners and forced errors on the player–opponent interaction, a dependency that changes as the player–opponent interaction changes (i.e. as the player and/or opponent changes). The idea, then, is that a conditional winner, or a forced error, assigned to a player when competing against a given opponent, might be rejected in some instances when competing against a different opponent. While these attempts go some way to recognising the interactions among the assignments of winners and errors, the complexities of these interactions are not well understood at present.

One other limitation on the winner–error interactions described above is found in the strong dependency of the predicted winners and errors on the existing data. This dependency means that more winners or errors (in terms of probabilities not frequencies) cannot be awarded for a player beyond those that occurred in the contest from which the profiles were obtained. The stochastic model reported above, for example, generates a winner for a player from his (her) winner–error profile which, if it is a conditional winner, is then analysed further by looking at the opponent's profile and determining whether or not a conditional winner will be awarded on that instance. For further details on the mechanism of this player–opponent interaction in the awarding of conditional winners and forced errors, see McGarry and Franks (1996c). However, the winner for the player, if awarded, is always generated from his (her) profile and not from his (her) opponent's profile. This arrangement poses a problem when the player competes against a weaker opponent as compared against when his (her) profile was first obtained. The essence of the problem is that it is reasonable to expect the player to make more winners, and conditional winners in particular, when playing against a weaker opponent. For example, if Player-A produces conditional winners against Player-B with a probability of 0.25, and Player-A is simulated to play against Player-C, then the stochastic model will award conditional winners to Player-A against Player-C with a probability of 0.25 as determined from the existing data obtained against Player B. These probabilities might furthermore be reduced depending on the characteristics contained in the winner–error profile of Player-C. On the other hand, if Player-C should have a weaker profile than Player-B, then it would not be unreasonable to suppose an increased probability of conditional winners for Player-A when playing against Player-C as opposed to when playing against Player-B. The stochastic model, as developed, does not contain this feature. Similar considerations for the awarding of forced errors likewise applies when competing against stronger or weaker opponents. The fact that an outcome is initiated on the existing data contained in the profile of the player, and not perhaps also from the profile of the opponent, is considered a limitation of the present model. Specifically, some accounting of the previous outcomes of the opponent when generating outcomes for a given player might yield better predictions of the contest outcome. Further research on this difficult, and maybe impossible, problem is required.

12.3.5 Interactions between shot–response profiles

We reported above that the interactions of the winner–error profiles are important considerations when trying to predict future outcomes. In turn, the interaction of the shot–response profiles is similarly an important consideration for predicting the shot selection behaviours that lead to the outcomes described in the winner–error profiles. We reported mixed findings from a series of statistical analyses designed to investigate whether the shot selection patterns for a given player varied as a function of the particular opponent (see McGarry and Franks 1996d, for further details). Speaking generally, the patterns of shot-selections contained in the shot–response profiles varied between contests sufficiently enough for us to question the validity of the stochastic model for predicting future shot selections from past behaviours. This said, the shot selection patterns of a player became more reliable when the context of the previous shot selected by the opponent was further specified, for example, where on court a selected type of shot was played from. Even so, the specific contexts that yielded the most stable patterns varied between players. These results were taken to suggest that the context of the previous shot is an important consideration when analysing the shot selection patterns of squash players.

The general findings of inconsistent shot selection patterns when a player competes against different opponents might be attributed to a number of reasons. First, there might be too few data that are produced from a single contest on which to generalize to a shot–response profile. This consideration of too few data is analogous to sampling error in a random sample. (Subsequent to these findings are a few research articles that confirm that, as expected, the frequency counts that document the actions of players become more invariant as the sample size increases.) Second, it is possible that the previous shot is not a good predictor of the next shot to be selected. For example, important qualifiers of the preceding shot such as pace, proximity of the ball to a wall, as well as the court location of the player and opponent, would each be expected to have an influence on the shot response. Thirdly, the memory-limiting nature of stochastic (Markov) processes, where the future is predicted only from the present, might be an insufficient descriptor of sports behaviours. For instance, a common idea is that a player will look to create openings in a rally on which to base an attack, using approach shots to displace an opponent on which to force an attack, or to capitalize on a weak shot by the opponent. The use of shot sequences may therefore be a better predictor of shot selections than only the previous shot. Finally, the most likely reason is simply that there might be more inconsistency (or variability) in the selection of shot behaviours on a shot-by-shot basis than first thought. Further research is ongoing in efforts to discriminate between these alternative and competing possibilities.

SUMMARY

In this chapter, we considered the investigation of sports contests on the basis of chance, as described in formal terms using probability analysis. The analysis of sports behaviours using probability analysis, or stochastic processes, is reasonably widespread and represents the most complete basis for explaining the behaviors and outcomes of sports contests to date. This observation is perhaps unsurprising given the widespread uses of statistics based on probabilities in many different fields (e.g. actuarial tables, insurance statistics, health statistics, stock market forecasts, sports betting, etc.). Indeed, the behaviours in sports contests would seem to be good candidates for this type of analysis, not least since the strategies for sports contests are often designed on the basis of future expectations (e.g. the use of strategies based on 'percentage play'). This said, some limitations of this type of analysis for squash contests were reported, indicating that any such type of system description on the basis of probability, at least at the level of game-to-game behaviour, is not as straightforward as might otherwise be imagined. Given the transient, contextual and unique conditions in which sports behaviours are produced, it is perhaps unfortunate that the usefulness of statistics and probabilities for informing on sports performances at a formal level of understanding would seem better suited to the long term rather than the short term, as well as to generalities rather than specifics.

NOTES

a   The other alternative to mathematical computation when enumeration is impractical for performing probability analysis is computer simulation, a popular method given the vast possibilities this technique offers (think of computer chess, for example) coupled with its relative ease of construction.
b   The sceptical reader may verify for himself (herself) the examples presented above, as well as others of their own making for that matter, using experimentation and/or computer simulation. The latter technique may be performed using the random function generator in some type of spreadsheet software or, alternatively, by a computer program should one possess the necessary software (programming) skill set.
c   The sequence of coin tosses considered previously is an example of a system of two states (H and T) whose behaviour is likewise characterized by random switching within and between states (e.g. T $\rightarrow$ H $\rightarrow$ H).

CHAPTER THIRTEEN

RULE CHANGES IN SPORT AND THE ROLE OF NOTATION

Jason Williams

In this chapter we:

- review literature regarding rule changes in sport.
- identify and categorize why rules change in sport.
- investigate the use of notation in tracking the changes.

13.1 INTRODUCTION

Any sporting event is defined and played within a pre-determined framework of rules and the number and complexity of these rules may differ significantly. The process for changing them occur within the environment of a governing body of administrators, but little is known about why they occur. Traditional sport that is played today is the product of many years of evolution and development, but little is known as to why these rules change.

Cooper (1994) found that over a period of years, rules for various games evolved following certain guidelines, just as rules of conduct evolved in society. The reasons for rule change presented by Cooper were specific to American football and were based on his analysis of the history of rule changes. His work did not take into consideration the different types of sports and the types of stresses that those sports are placed under. However, his work did present some clear indications as to why rules change within sport. Research conducted by Kew (1986) highlighted the way that rules change within game-playing in invasive games. He defined three 'Moments' within the development of a sport. The first he defined as the *'Basic challenge'*, whereby the basic theory or aim of the game was introduced. The second moment or *'Establishment'* was deciding on rules to prescribe actions and make the challenge difficult and interesting. Finally, the third moment, the *'Consolidation'* phase corresponded to preserving or enabling rules that were designed to ensure the continuous possibility for the realization of 'Depth' features, and therefore sustain credibility.

Kew (1987) continued his research on rule changes within sport using basketball, hockey and different codes of football. He found that sports change their rules frequently, but little is known of the processes through which such changes are impelled. In his paper, he categorized two types of rule change; the first was the definitive rule – a concern to re-establish and re-emphasize the key characteristics of that specific sport. An example of this may be illustrated with basketball as a variety of ball-handling skills should be displayed in this game. In order to ensure the continuity of the variety of ball-handling skills, changes in the rules need to be made to neutralize the advantage of the taller player and ensure that ball handling skills remain an important aspect of the game. The second category he defined as a shared concern about what must be preserved enhanced or enabled in order to sustain the viability of the sport.

Gardiner *et al.* (1998) had a more controversial viewpoint with regards to rule changes. They stated rule changes are merely tinkered with and are often carried out with the aim of short-term expediency, often to placate external pressures such as sponsors and television. They also put forward the argument that rule changes are needed to secure the integrity of modern sport in the context of making it a commodity. The argument was made that sport was becoming more like a product that can be bought or sold in order to generate income in order to ensure the survival of that particular sport. Their work further stated that rule changes are required to try and re-establish the vitality and balance in a particular sport, introduce new skills and strategies to confront these new rules, creating the continual need for change. They continued by stating that changes to the rules of a sport commonly emerge from a desire to increase the appeal of the sport for players and spectators and to ensure its survival.

Hammond *et al.* (1999) stated that the rules of a game commonly emerge from a desire to increase the appeal of a sport for players and spectators and to ensure its survival. Their work on netball, attributed rule changes to three main factors. The first of these was defined as 'Player performance', which meant that players become bigger, faster and stronger with time. Second, 'Technological advancement' was defined as the development of sporting accessories, scientific tools and aids. They also noted that 'Commercial pressures' played a role in the development of rules. The results of their study highlighted the importance of systematically analysing the effect of rule changes, they also demonstrated that even relatively minor changes to rules have an effect on play.

13.2 SAFETY

The safety and well-being of participants in any given sport may be considered as an important factor in the formation of a new rule, whether the changes have a direct or indirect effect on players safety. The addition or amendment of any rule can have an impact on different levels with regards to safety. In order to investigate the importance of safety and rule changes, the discussion will be categorized into two parts. The first part is defined as contextual, a direct intervention to the rules that is introduced to combat technical offences, such as foul or dangerous play and safety equipment. The second is defined as environmental, a set of rules that address less specific issues such as participation level, environment and fluid intake.

Contextual rule changes or rule changes that are specific to player safety are documented in a few publications. The NCAA magazine (1982) identified the extent of rule changes with regards to safety in American football. They stated that between 1969 and 1982, the NCAA Football Rules Committee made a total of 64 injury prevention rule changes involving personal fouls, penalty enforcement un-sportsmanlike conduct, equipment, the field and signals. Green (1985) also documented rule changes that were introduced specifically for safety. He examined Canadian amateur gridiron football and noted why the rule was introduced alongside the rule itself. These two pieces of work illustrated how much sport has developed over the last forty years and that basic safety issues, such as the high tackle, although seeming very obvious now, had to go through the process of being introduced. Their work also recognized that as the chronological order of the introduction of rule changes were documented, the changes became less radical and more specific. Their work recognized that rule changes with regards to safety are not as radical as when the sport was first introduced as the majority of 'serious' injuries have been reduced.

Sports such as American football, lacrosse and cricket have undergone changes regarding safety equipment. When safety equipment was introduced, great stress was placed on reducing the number of injuries that occurred within the game, but at the same time ensuring that the changes did not have a detrimental effect. Rugby union has recently seen much discussion with regards to safety equipment in the form of padded protection. Gerrard (1998) has showed that

228

some items of padding can be of some benefit to the individual, depending on where the padding is. In addition, Wilson et al. (1999) discussed protection with regards to protective headgear in rugby union and compared it with other sports. Their work recognized that the introduction any item of padding needs careful consideration by the administrators as there is always a chance of the individual relying on padding or testing rules through this new protection. This in turn may then create problems within the game by introducing new types of injuries or introducing new problems to a sport.

Hackney (1994) highlighted issues relating to player safety and discussed how to prevent and manage injuries in sport through adhering to the rules. The compliance of a rule in a sport was also stressed in the study made by Kujala et al. (1995) on acute injuries in soccer, ice hockey, volleyball, basketball, judo and karate. Their research found that each sport had a specific injury profile and that the best way to deal with this was to introduce preventative measures such as improving the rules, supported by careful refereeing. The problems associated with introducing new rules to ensure safety were discussed by Kirkendall (1995). He documented the type of injuries in American football and found that changes in rules led to reductions in one type of injury and increases in others. One example he gave was that neck injuries decreased dramatically since spearing (using the head as a battering ram when tackling) was outlawed, but shoulder tears increased when the blocking rules were changed. His work recognized that sometimes, rules introduced to ensure safety create other problems.

Many problems associated with injuries are connected to the lack of rules or poor implementation of rules. Parkkari et al. (2001) undertook an extensive literature review of a range of sports and their associated injuries to try and find out whether sports injuries could be prevented. They stated that in every sport they examined, rule changes were imperative to player safety and should be continually examined to ensure their safety. The theory of testing a new rule on a group of players was also advised by Burry and Calcinai (1988), with their research on spinal injuries in rugby union. Their work stressed the effect of rule changes in reducing injuries, highlighting the dramatic drop in cervical injuries after changes to the scrum and 'tackled ball' rules in New Zealand rugby union (Figure 13.1).

The above discussion recognized the importance of rule changes that directly influence safety in sport. In addition to rules that are implemented to counter specific areas of dangerous areas of play, rule makers must also consider participatory and environmental factors of a sport. There are issues with the level that the sport is played, such as at the professional and amateur level, for

229

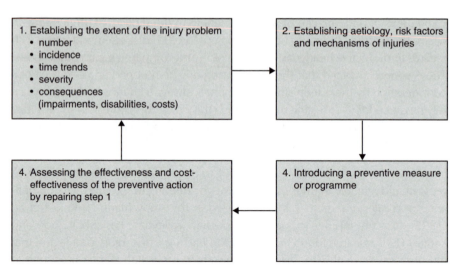

Figure 13.1 The sequence of the prevention of sports injuries (Parkkari *et al.* 2001)

men and women and problems with the differences in the game for children and adults.

The weather conditions that a sport is played is difficult to control which causes a number of problems with regard to safety. In sports such as basketball or ice hockey, these problems are of less significance because the conditions are generally always the same, i.e. played indoors. A controlled environment such as this rarely occurs in outdoor sports, which may have a major impact on the way the sport is played and the safety of the players. The environmental effect on the athlete competing in sport is discussed in detail by Thein (1995), who stated that the environment can facilitate or inhibit performance, or it can cause serious illness or death. Research conducted in rugby league (Hodgson-Phillips *et al.* 1998; Gissane *et al.* 1998) found a direct correlation between conditions and injury and argued that when the rules of a sport are changed administrators must be aware that the sport, if played on a global scale, can be played in different conditions.

Sport administrators continually work to ensure that players' safety is ensured on the sporting arena. Specific problems with regards to foul play or injuries can be dealt with directly through implementing changes within the game using rule changes. However, there are also many safety issues that are not as obvious, but should also be considered. These changes may be more difficult to standardize because of the indirect nature of the safety concerns. The direct or indirect safety implications of changes within the game may also conflict with the spec-tacle, speed or enjoyment of the game both by participant and spectator. The issue of ensuring the safety and at the same time ensuring that participants enjoy the sport is a problem that the administrators of the game constantly need to address.

13.3 NATURAL DEVELOPMENT AND PROGRESSION

The issue of safety is only one of the influences that change the rules of a sport. Another reason that may be considered is that of natural development and progression. Over time, areas of a sport change due to physical changes of the participants or the pushing and testing of the rules by the coaches or the indi-viduals who take part. Training regimes have improved, scientific analysis has grown and there has been a general increase in support for sportsmen and women. Other changes involve areas such as cheating, player size and speed of the sport or improvements in equipment. The stress placed on the rules by such changes may mean that certain rules need updating or rewriting in order to keep the game competitive and fair. This section will discuss these areas of change and will investigate the effect that each has on changing the rules of a game.

It may be considered that rules are introduced to a sport to maintain some form of order and ensure that it is played in a fair manner. It is argued that cheating or testing the boundaries of a rule is an action that takes place in a majority of sporting activities. When a rule is broken, then some form of penalty is awarded against the offending person, such as a free kick in football or a false throw in the javelin event in athletics. There are different ways in which cheating occurs and different reasons as to why rules are broken. The constant pushing and testing of a set of rules creates pressures to create new rules to combat them thorough examinations by players and coaches. Thus, a continual cycle is created where established and new rules are constantly being tested (Leaman 2001).

Prior to any further discussion it is important at this stage to distinguish between the intentional and the unintentional breaking of rules in sport. Loland (1998) defined intentional cheating as breaking the rules to get an unfair advantage and trying to get away with the offence without getting penalized. Unintentional cheating is defined by rule violations where the offender breaks the rules by accident. For example, in football this may be an accidental 'handball' or late tackle. This theory can be developed further with respect to the pressure that is placed on the rules. If a rule is consistently broken, whether the break is intended or not, stress is still being placed on that specific rule. The effect that this has on the sport is the same and there is no distinction between the devious cheat and the accidental cheat. For the purpose of this study, both types of rule breaking shall be referred to as cheating.

Leaman (2001) discussed cheating in more detail and questioned what is morally wrong with it. He argued that cheating may add a new dimension to the sport and that the sport may become more interesting if the rules are stretched in some way. He suggested that cheating in sport is part of its structure and is taken into consideration in its rules. He further argued that if cheating is recognized as an option that both sides may morally take up and then in general, the principles of equality and justice are not affected. This argument leads on to a set of rules that exist below the surface of the intended rules, thus creating a subset that players adhere to. Leaman also suggested that athletes in certain sports simply come to expect and engage in a certain amount of on-field rule violations. The basis for his argument was that cheating should be accepted as a part of the sport and therefore should be accepted as part of the sports progression and change.

Lumpkin et al. (1999) argued that there has been an increase in rule breaking at the elite level because of the pressures placed on athletes to win for financial gain. Emphasis has been placed on winning rather than developing skill and having fun. Athletes realize early in their sporting experiences that only winners receive multi-million pound contracts, endorsements and clothing. When such importance is placed on winning, athletes may turn to drugs to enhance their performance to gain an advantage over the opposition. Drugs in sport are a problem that undermines the very ethos of competing on a level playing field. When such pressure is placed on a sportsperson to win they may try any means possible in order to do so, which then moves cheating from on the field to off it. It may be said that the guile and deviancy that some sports people introduce on the field through pushing the rules to their full extent is far removed from the clinical cheating that may go off the field (Coakley 2001).

The act of breaking a rule of any sport, whether the action is intended or not has an effect on the way a sport is played and commentators may argue whether its effect is of benefit or detriment to the sport. However, it is difficult to ignore its effect on the way a sport changes over time. As with any set of rules, some will be strained or broken to try and gain some form of advantage over the opposition, such as binding in the scrum in rugby union or the offside law in football, but these are part of the make up of the game. The motivation for breaking a rule may vary from simple bad sportsmanship to the need to win for financial gain. With such a driving force behind the need to cheat it may be considered difficult to accept the argument that breaking the rules of a sport is good for the sport's development.

Another area that places stress on the rules of a sport in a less confrontational manner is the size and the speed of the sports men and women that take part. A common contention is that a sport played 30 or 40 years ago is considerably different to the level it is practiced today because of the size and the speed of the participants. Norton *et al.* (1999) conducted work into the changes that have occurred within Australian Rules football investigating the changes in game speed and player size over a 30-year period. They used height and mass data on players that were obtained from official records of registered players. These data showed a significant increase in both areas and in combination with this they found that the speed of the game had approximately doubled over the same time period.

Alongside bigger players, there are also pressures on the rules from the speed of the sport. This may encompass areas such as the speed of athletes running; techniques employed with individual actions and increased endurance. Potter and Carter (1995) noted that the time that the ball in play time in rugby union had increased between world cups. In parallel to the increase in the ball-in-play time they also noted that there had been an increase in the number of actions that occurred within a game. The same was also found with the women's world cup with an increase in ball-in-play time (Thomas *et al.* 2003). Giatsis (2003) and his work on volleyball has also recognized the game becoming faster and more intense. His research recognized that match duration increased and that new rule changes introduced a more exciting game. Norton *et al.* (2001) investigated Australian football and again found that the game was getting faster, which they attributed to improved ground conditions. They concluded that the game speed at the top level of Australian football had approximately doubled over the last 40 years. From these studies, it would be possible to argue that sport has become faster, which would suggest that the same sport, with the same rules, is being played at a quicker pace.

Pressures such as these may be more prevalent in some sports than others. Sports such as rugby union have seen problems due to an increase of player speed and size. In comparison, sports such as football have seen fewer changes to the rules. It is unclear whether this applies to the non-elite participants of the sport, as there is very little research in this area. However, it should be recognized that in many sports, players are getting faster, fitter and bigger and they must play within rules that were written for a sport that was played with a different type of player. Therefore, rules need to change to ensure that it is kept exciting and challenging and caters for the modern athlete.

Technology has also had its part in the development of sport with the equipment used. Perhaps this can be best illustrated with the comparison of the association football ball that was used at the turn of the last century and today's ball. The ball used then was untreated leather, which meant that when it got wet, it would double or triple in weight. This differs greatly from the scientific design of the football that is kicked on today's modern football pitches. Haake *et al.* (2000) explored changing the size of a ball in tennis and by 6 per cent in order to reduce its speed. They found that the introduction of a larger ball slowed down the game of tennis for all strokes and increased the time available for the receiver to return the ball. Baseball bat manufacturers, through modern technology, have been able to create aluminium bats that are lighter in weight than wooden bats, but still meet the required standards (Kelly and Pedersen 2001). This meant that the batsman could hit the ball much further and harder than usual. Other consequences of this are that scoring increased and the sport had become more dangerous. Examples such as these illustrate the effect of changing the equipment used by the participants of the sport. It is argued that these changes are made to improve the game in order to increase speed, power or simply to make the game more competitive, but attention should also be paid to how much the game changes.

In summary, a sport may change over time within its own boundaries without external pressures. Athletes may get bigger, stronger, and fitter and faster which in turn may mean that the sport may have to change the rules to accommodate such developments. At the same time, participants will always want to stretch the rules in some way by intentionally or unintentionally cheating. The development and improvements in equipment has also meant that changes are introduced into the way a game is played. Changes such as these illustrate the constant testing of rules and exemplify that the rules of a game, when pressured, need to be changed in order to keep the game competitive and enjoyable to play and watch.

13.4 ENTERTAINMENT, COMMERCIALIZATION AND THE MEDIA

Professional sports have emerged as global businesses and have become a lucrative product that can be bought and sold. There has also been much discussion as to the ethical issues involved in the use of money within the sport. Many commentators have argued that the commercialization of a sport may be of equal benefit and detriment to the sport. It is suggested that most changes within sport are introduced through changes to its rules, which are often made to try

234

and make the sport more entertaining and exciting for its participants and spectators. However, it may be argued that the growing influence of commercialization and the media may be having more of an effect on the sport than people realize. Indeed, it is only in the last 20–30 years that sports have seen the majority of changes to their rules (Coakley 2001), which may well have occurred because of pressures from the media to make the sport more exciting.

Mason (1999) examined sport as a product and stated that sport, while initially produced to provide entertainment for spectators, is also produced for four distinct groups. He categorized these groups first into: fans who support teams and buy the associated merchandise; second, television and media companies who purchase rights to show sports as television programmes; third, the clubs that build facilities and support lower clubs; and finally corporations that purchase teams outright and provide sponsorship. Many changes within the sport have been to make the sport more entertaining, but the question then needs to be asked as for whom the sport is being made entertaining.

Many commentators fear that sport is being alienated from spectators and is developing more into a media product. Cousens (1997) documented the explosion in revenue gained from television contracts with American sports. She gave the example of American football and the escalation of the revenue gained from television rights. From 1961, when individual NFL teams sold their rights for an average of US$332,000 the revenue, by 1994, had grown to US$1.6 billion. Examples such as this illustrate that there has been a massive increase in the amount of money that enters a sport and this has been met with much criticism. Fennell et al. (1990) stated, 'contracts have been so lucrative that they have changed the very nature of professional sports'. For the sports purist, the power given to the media has become a worrying development, with the sport alienating them and moving more towards corporate organizations and private ownership. Hope (2002) discussed this in his work on the New Zealand All Blacks rugby team. He argued that global media and corporate sponsorship were threatening the nationally constituted heritage of All Black rugby. He believed that there had been a move from the All Black team representing the New Zealand people. Research such as this suggests that many professional sports are developing into a product that may be bought or sold as a commodity.

The undertaking by Tyrrell (1980) developed this argument and he documented the changes that occurred within baseball with its transition from the amateur to professional code. He argued that once large sums of money had been invested, the demands for a quicker and a more exciting game intensified, with significant changes in the techniques of play facilitated by changes in equipment, in the rules of pitching and in the increased competition brought about by professionalism itself. There was a need to make the game more exciting, and one of the methods of doing this was to change the rules of that game. The question then arises as to whether these improvements are for the participants of the sport, or the people watching it. Davies (1999) discussed this problem with rugby union and the problems with the changes to its rules. He argued that the changes to the game used to occur for reasons of simplicity and of clarity, or to remove dangerous play. He stated that television was now the primary motivating force in changing rules. Boyle and Haynes (2000) also discussed this point with their work on the power of the media within sport. They noted that sport had to adapt to the needs of television, and not necessarily the other way round. They listed sports that had developed into a more television friendly format, like rugby league, rugby union and cricket.

Sport in America generates a huge amount of revenue through television and advertising. American football is one of the most popular sports there and thus generates a huge amount of income. In 1970, when the game was being reformed, teams and leagues were not decided by stadium capacities, attendance records or by the calibre of quarterbacks, but by market researchers. The standard by which professional football's new leagues were formed was based on the comparative quality of their respective television markets (Johnson 1971). Chandler (1988) argued that sport has been developed, through a series of rule changes to ensure that it generated as much interest and excitement as possible for the spectator, as well as generating money for the media and advertisers. In 1970–80 the rules in American football were changed to increase unpredictability and tension, which led to high scoring games, which the American audiences preferred. It was considered that high scoring games were a good indication of action and result. At the same time, the number of timeouts was increased to ensure more space for television advertising. Rule changes with regards to making the game more exciting for television have continued over the years in order to make the sport more entertaining for the television viewer. Many American sports have been especially tailored to appeal to millions of potential viewers who were not devoted followers of the games themselves. Sport was transformed to compete more successfully with other forms of entertainment. Football and baseball, through introducing new rules, cheerleaders, men dressed in chicken uniforms dancing on dugouts, exploding scoreboards, artificial grass and tight-fitting uniforms, tinkered with the fundamental nature of their sports (Rader 1984). A look at the rule books of sporting organizations clearly shows that there are literally thousands of rules today that did not exist 20 years ago, in sport (Coakley 2001).

Coakley stated that rule development and rule change associated with commercialization are usually intended to do a combination of five things: (1) speed up the action, so that fans will not get bored; (2) increase scoring to generate excitement; (3) balance competition, so that events will have uncertain outcomes; (4) maximize the dramatic moments in the competition; and (5) provide commercial breaks in the action, so that sponsors can advertise products. Arguably, these changes are improving sport, making it more exciting and enjoyable. Some commentators consider these points, as a worrying development within sport and that the changes are being forced on sport, undermining the natural progression that sports undergo and introduce artificial changes that may be causing irreversible damage to its very ethos.

As shown in Table 13.1, the increasing need to promote sport to a larger audience has seen many rule changes in recent years. A quest has been undertaken to develop sport into an exciting and marketable product that will generate revenue for itself, which in theory, will improve it with better facilities and support for both players and spectators. It may also be argued that this cycle may appear to be one that will be impossible to break out of. A particular sport requires money to compete with other sports, so it must be more exciting to play and watch. There are many sports with little spectator interest, very exciting to play, but are struggling to survive as they have very little revenue. This then creates the cycle of the rich sports getting richer and the smaller, poorer sports decreasing in popularity and losing revenue. It may also be considered that poorer sports are under constant pressure to change their sport to try and compete with their richer counterparts. Of course, this also applies to richer sports, which are under pressure to maintain the interest in their sport. It is impossible to ignore these issues, so developments within a sport must be carefully audited, to ensure that it does not become too product focussed, alienating itself from the people who follow it.

Table 13.1 Milestone deals between TV companies and English football bodies 1983–1997 (Booth and Doyle 1997)

	1983	1985	1986	1988	1992	1997
Length of contract (years)	2	0.5	2	4	5	4
Broadcaster	BBC/ITV	BBC	BBC/ITV	ITV	BSkyB	BSkyB
Rights fee (£m)	5.2	1.3	6.3	44	191.5	670
Annual rights fee (£m)	2.6	2.6	3.1	11	38.3	167.5
Number of live matches per season	10	6	14	18	60	60
Fees per live match (£m)	0.26	0.43	0.22	0.61	0.64	2.79

13.5 THE ROLE OF NOTATIONAL ANALYSIS IN TRACKING THE EFFECT OF RULES CHANGES

It may be considered that the effect of rule changes on traditional sports cannot be objectively determined unless there is some form of measure associated with it. Notational analysis may be used to objectively gauge the effect of any rule change within any particular sport, but very little formal use is made of it. However, there have been some academic studies using notation to examine the effect of changes on game play. Examples of this work have measured explicit changes such as rules that were introduced to increase ball in play time, or to increase the amount of action in a game through measuring the number of passes. Research also indicates that there are many other areas of a sport that may be unintentionally affected with a new rule. Rule changes may introduce both positive and negative aspects to a game and many problems associated with rules that are not properly analysed and discussed can result in turning a sport in chaos (Longmore 1994). The following section will detail the role of notation in tracking the effect of rule changes in a sport through examining research that has been undertaken in the area.

The importance of making the sport more entertaining was the driving force behind changes introduced within Gaelic football in 1990. They were introduced to increase the game's ball-in-play time in order to make the game more attractive. The changes related to sideline kicks such as free kicks and goal kicks, which under the new rules were to be taken from the hand, as opposed to the ball being placed on the floor. Doggart et al. (1993) used a hand notation system to notate and analyse the time saved by the rule changes and the specific aspects of play that contributed to the changes in playing time. Their work discovered that the time that the ball in play time increased by 2 per cent. Other findings showed that there was a noticeable increase in the number of possessions gained and tackles made. The intended increase in the ball-in-play time also introduced other changes within the game that the authorities may or may not have perceived would happen. Their work highlighted some important issues that authorities need to be aware of when changing the rules of their sport.

The desired and actual outcome of new rules on a sport was highlighted with analysis by Hughes and Sykes (1994). They used a computerized notation system to analyse the effects of the 1992 back-pass rule in soccer. Their analysis found that there were significantly fewer back-passes to the goalkeeper as a form of time wasting and thus the goalkeeper had less possession of the ball. Their work also found that the game was made more frantic due to less time and space in the middle of the pitch. The research concluded that although there was an increase in defensive errors, there was no increase in either the number of shots or goals as expected. It was also concluded that time-wasting due to back-passes to the goal keeper was significantly reduced but at the cost of a more congested midfield playing area. The intended outcome of reducing time wasting due to back passes was achieved, but at the same time other unforeseen areas of the game were being affected.

Hughes and Knight (1994) examined a new scoring system that was introduced by the Squash Rackets Association in an attempt to make the game more attract- ive to viewing audiences. It was perceived that the new scoring system would make the players attack more, thus removing 'boring play' from the game. Their work on 500 rallies involving the top 30 players in the world concluded that there was no significant difference between the two scoring systems. It was also found that there was no significant difference in the length of rallies, even though the original belief was that the rallies would be shorter and therefore more interesting to the general public. The rule makers perceived theory on how the game would be played and their desired outcomes from the new scoring system differed considerably.

Watts (2005) continued this work and investigated a new scoring system in professional men's squash, which was introduced in order to make the game more appealing to television audiences. The aim of the study was to analyse any changes in the game structure or differences in the patterns of play occurring amongst men's elite squash whilst playing in competition under the old (point per rally to 15) and new (point per rally to 11) scoring systems. He concluded that the results showed that the new scoring system produced a significant increase in number of winners, and the number of unforced errors per match decreased. It was also concluded that the new method of scoring had no signifi- cant change in patterns of play, but produced shorter games and increased the number of critical points compared with the old method.

Football was again the subject of analysis with an experimental rule change introduced by FIFA in 1994 within semi-professional football in order to make the game more attractive to spectators and to improve specific aspects of play. The aim of this rule change was to provide more continuous entertaining football, more play in the attacking third and more goals through attacking opportunities. Odetoyinbo et al. (1997) analysed a selection of games to test these objectives. The work showed that the ball spent more time in play and significantly less throw-ins and kick-ins were conceded in the defending third. When inter- viewed, the managers felt that fragmentation of play had resulted because play- ers paused over their choice of a throw-in or kick-in. In addition, they believed

239

that the need for attacking creativity when gaining entry into the scoring area was lessened to the detriment of the game. They also felt that the time that the ball-in-play time was less than before the new rules were introduced, where in fact the opposite of this was true.

The idea of making a sport more marketable was one of the reasons for changes to clothing and ball colour in the one-day game in cricket. Scott *et al.* (1999) and their work on the effect of the change in ball colour, found that there was no significant difference with regards to catching and concluded that the change had no detrimental effect on the game. Scott noted that this was considered as a positive move by the authorities, but it must be noted that the work was carried out after the change had been implemented. The results may have been more controversial if there had been significant differences in changing the colour of the ball. A good idea to promote the game and increase the marketing potential of the game may have been an embarrassing introduction.

Rule changes were introduced in cricket in an attempt to make the game more popular and to attract more sponsorship and media coverage. Howells (2000) investigated the one-day game and the effect of introducing a 30-yard circle that all except two fielders were positioned. This new rule was enforced for the first 15 overs of each innings for each team. The research concluded that this led to the tactics in this period of play becoming more important and varied. New strokes previously redundant were once more introduced to the game with the result of a more exciting opening to the innings.

Pritchard *et al.* (2001) assessed the impact of an experimental scoring system upon elite men's badminton. The changes were introduced in order to make the game more exciting to watch, raising its appeal to the mass media and increasing interest from television companies. Previous changes to the game included modernization of the presentation at the Sydney Olympics changes in setting procedure and now saw the introduction of a new scoring format. Rally, game and match lengths were examined, as were work-to-rest ratios. Their work concluded that the changes were a positive step for elite men's badminton and the new structure was better suited to television. Games were shorter and there were more breaks during which commercials and analysis could occur.

In 1997, the IRB (IRB 1997) devised a charter that documented the principles on which the game of rugby union is based. It was suggested that the charter should act as a checklist for judging the mode of play and that the game would maintain its unique character. The IRB believed that this charter would benefit the game because a standard would exist against which the game could be judged. It was

rule changes in sport and the role of notation

believed that it would help prevent anecdotal changes and that any changes would be within the game's unique character. In addition, the IRB set up a game analysis centre to determine the effect of any rule change and highlight any areas of concern within the game (Thomas and Williams 2001). This work involved the general notation of the game in different areas, such as the scrum, lineout and penalties. This enabled the IRB to analyse in detail the state of the game in any one area over any time period. Objective and impartial information such as this permitted a clearer snapshot of the game to be taken, removing subjective analysis from the argument for rule changes.

As discussed, the benefit of using notational analysis within the context of changing the rules of a sport has been recognized by research. The strength of documenting changes that occur within a sport enable administrators to recognize if a rule has had a positive, negative or unforeseen effect, or if areas of the sport need changing. It enables the administrators to measure the effect that the new rule had on any problem areas and empowers them to objectively view perceived problems in a game. It has been recognized that unforeseen areas of the game may change by altering its rules and a change in one area of a sport may lead to other changes that were not perceived. It was also noted that the objective qualities of notational analysis permitted the administrators of a sport to observe any changes, enabling them to objectively view the effect that changes may or may not have.

13.6 CONCLUSION

It is suggested that rules change within a sport for one of three reasons. First and ethically, the most important cause for changing rules is with regards to safety. The player's well-being should always be of paramount importance when any changes are made. Second, changes of sporting rules come from the natural development of the sport and from the people that take part in it. In addition, the speed of the sport, the size of the players, the quality of ground conditions all put stress on the way the rules try and order the sport. Finally, there is also pressure outside the sport from the media and commercial organizations that view the sport as a product that they sell to the public. This area has recently become more influential with an increase in the amount of money paid to the different sporting organizations from the media, marketing companies and sponsors.

SUMMARY

The benefits of using notational analysis within the context of changing the rules of a sport has been recognized by research. The strength of documenting changes that occur within a sport enable administrators to recognize if a rule has had a positive, negative or unforeseen effect, or if areas of the sport need changing. It enables the administrators to measure the effect that the new rule had on any problem areas and empowers them to objectively view perceived problems in a game. It has been recognized that unforeseen areas of the game may change by altering its rules and a change in one area of a sport may lead to other changes that were not perceived. It was also noted that the objective qualities of notational analysis permitted the administrators of a sport to observe any changes, enabling them to objectively view the effect that changes may or may not have.

CHAPTER FOURTEEN

PERFORMANCE ANALYSIS IN THE MEDIA

Nic James

In this chapter we:

- will review the type of information portrayed in the various forms of media and discuss the extent to which they achieve their aim of describing the events of the sport in question.
- will discuss the potential limitations of these methods, giving suggestions for how performance analysts working for sports teams or undertaking research might amend or apply these methods.

14.1 INTRODUCTION

Performance analysis is usually thought of in terms of providing feedback for players and coaches to enable improvement in sports performance. This is not necessarily so, as media coverage of sport often adds statistical detail to their reporting of events for the purpose of informing the sports fan. Consequently, two separate explanations for carrying out performance analysis can be seen to exist, i.e. by those involved in a sport for performance improvement and by media groups for the enlightenment of sports fans. Identifying this distinction also raises the interesting question as to what extent these two performance analysis tasks differ or indeed are similar. This chapter will focus on presenting performance analysis as commonly depicted in the media. Some reference will be made to academic and professional sports teams' use of similar information; although this will not be exhaustive, since other publications offer more of this type of information. For example, students of sport have been well served by previous books edited by Hughes and Franks (1997, 2004), as well as original research published in scientific journals, e.g. electronic *International Journal of Performance Analysis in Sport*. Soccer players and coaches have also had a book written for them (Carling *et al.* 2005) detailing the types of analysis performed at elite clubs. There have also been books aimed at the general public, one which achieved bestseller status in the USA (Lewis 2003), told the account of how Billy Beane, a highly talented but low achieving baseball player became general manager of the Oakland Athletics and transformed the team's fortunes by picking new players solely on the analysis of their playing statistics rather than trusting his scouts' reports and recommendations.

Newspaper, television and internet coverage of sporting events usually presents performance analysis in the form of summary statistics or 'performance indicators' to use the terminology of Hughes and Bartlett (2002). These statistical insights are often debated over in the television studio by the assembled pundits or form the basis of in depth analysis in the newspapers. However, they may also be used as the basis of the topic of conversation in school playgrounds, university cafeterias and business meeting rooms all over the world. Indeed, these statistics are now so common that it would be surprising if anyone with an interest in sport was not familiar with this form of performance analysis, although they might not recognize it as such.

14.2 CLASSIFYING GAMES

The characteristics of a sport determine how the media present both the play itself and the performance analysis results, mainly in an attempt to maximize the enjoyment and interest of the readers/viewers. The sports selected in this chapter are the most watched and read about; at least in relation to the media coverage afforded them. However, while the techniques for performance analysis illustrated here are related to the sports that receive more media coverage than others, they are often transferable to other related sports. For example, calculating the ratio of forced compared with unforced errors in tennis is applicable to squash, badminton, table tennis, etc. Indeed, the extent to which the statistics portrayed for one sport are applicable to another is largely determined by the degree of similarity between sports. Consequently, this chapter will present the media's portrayal of performance analysis in three different sections: invasion, net and wall and striking and fielding sports. This classification scheme for sports is based on the objectives and structure of the games (Read and Edwards 1992) and relates well to the different performance analysis techniques portrayed in the media.

14.3 INVASION GAMES

Invasion games are characterized by playing areas which can be split into two halves, where the objective is for one team to defend its half and attack the opponent's half. Invasion games tend to be amongst the most popular spectator sports, although different ones are popular depending on the part of the world. The common characteristics of these sports include passing, shooting and tackling and performance analysis interest tends to centre on aspects of play such as set pieces, field position, time in possession and scoring. The examples given here are taken from soccer, rugby union and basketball although the techniques could just as easily apply to American football, netball, hockey, etc.

14.3.1 Soccer

The 'beautiful game' attracts massive media interest in much of the world and currently seems to be increasing its worldwide audience. The rules of the game are simple, although the offside laws may stretch this contention somewhat, but performance analysis of 22 players interacting intermittently is somewhat more complex. Newspapers in the UK devote more column inches to soccer than any other sport but the extent to which they portray performance analysis statistics is relatively limited (Figure 14.1).

The chart presented in Figure 14.1 was replicated in virtually every British newspaper at the time of writing using the same performance indicators, although

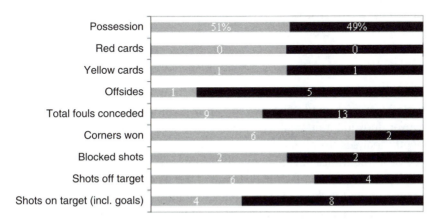

Figure 14.1 Match stats as presented in *The Sunday Times* newspaper for an FA Cup match won 3–0 by the League One side

some chose not to include all of them. This suggests that one or two independent companies collect these statistics and sell them to the newspapers, e.g. Opta Sportsdata (www.sportingstatz.com) provide statistics for a number of media companies. However, if this was the case, you would expect the same values in each newspaper. To test this hypothesis O'Donoghue (2007) compared seven Sunday newspaper reports on three FA Premier League soccer matches, using the same indicators as Figure 14.1, and found limited agreement between them. This would suggest that the reliability of this information is questionable which is surprising given that in many instances a lot of time, effort and money has been invested in their collection. The extent, to which this potential lack of precision is important, however, is determined by what the statistics are to be used for. In the main, of course, they are simply to provide additional information for the reader, and in this instance, it may be argued that precision is not essential. However, if the statistics and the way in which they are presented are also utilized by sports teams then incorrect statistics could well be problematical. My experience of sports coaches and players involved in high level sport, suggests that they tend to prefer to use the statistics provided by their own performance analysts. This is because the collection of performance information is then under the control of the coaches who can determine what and how this information is collected.

Television coverage of soccer presents similar information although in a far more visual manner, e.g. shots are often presented as arrows starting from the point of the kick and finishing where the ball crossed the goal line. Recently, Sky television introduced an interactive service which can present the match statistics as they change throughout the match. For example, ball possession is presented as a percentage (in the style of Figure 14.2), which is continuously updated by Sky's analyst and refreshed on the television screen at the end of each possession. For the interested future performance analyst therefore, it is possible to work out how Sky defines possession by timing the possessions and comparing these results with Sky's.

The statistics presented thus far are fairly common and utilized regularly. However, individual newspapers and television companies also provide more in depth analyses from time to time. For example, *The Guardian* (19 January 2007) and *The Times* (22 January 2007) ran articles on Thierry Henry, the Arsenal striker who had recently been out of the team due to injury. Both newspapers attempted to show, via performance analysis, how Henry had influenced Arsenal's performances. *The Times* compared the touches of the ball for the two Arsenal strikers (Emmanuel Adebayor and Thierry Henry, Figure 14.3) in the 2–1 win against Manchester United (21 January 2007).

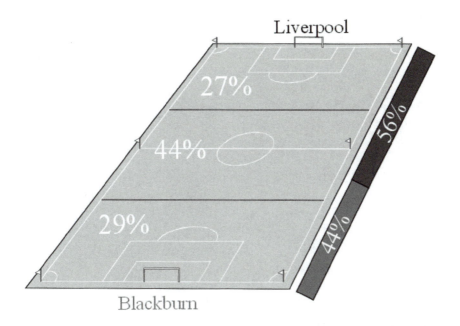

Figure 14.2 Possession percentages for a FA Premier League soccer match

The touch graphics in Figure 14.3 represent the whole match and so therefore the two halves have been combined. No explanation is given for the direction of attack although in this instance it is fairly self-explanatory given the attacking roles of both players. *The Guardian* chose to depict the passing endpoints for two of Arsenal's previous matches to show how Arsenal play with more varied passing when Henry is present in the side (Figure 14.4).

As Figure 14.4 shows, the match depicting Arsenal without Henry is characterized by less passing end points in comparison to the match with Henry. Also, when Henry was playing there was a greater tendency to use the left side of the pitch, which is where he tends to operate. However, this type of analysis risks erroneous conclusions. Why? The selection of just one match to represent typical play is dangerous. How do we know that the matches selected were not very unusual ones, quite unlike the normal matches played by Arsenal? Of course it is also possible that they are very representative. The point is that it is impossible to know on the basis of one match. Thus a performance analyst would collect passing end points for a number of matches both with and without Henry to make conclusions more reliable.

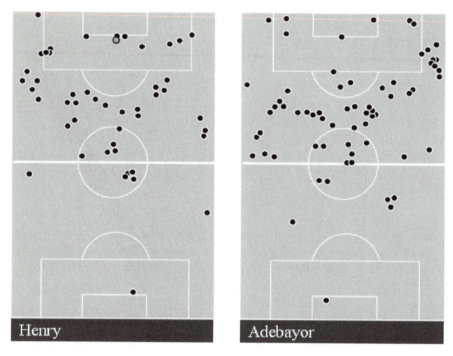

Figure 14.3 Touch graphics for Thierry Henry and Emmanuel Adebayor (grey dot represents Henry's headed goal)

Without Henry Wigan 0 Arsenal 1 13/12/06				With Henry Arsenal 4 Charlton 0 02/01/07			
40	45	33	30	27	44	61	63
37	20	21	13	44	64	59	46
24	24	40	25	24	52	47	32

>>Direction of play   >>Direction of play

Figure 14.4 Passing end points for Arsenal with and without Thierry Henry

14.3.2 Rugby union

Rugby union involves teams of 15 players, each of whom can be classified as either a forward or a back. The play of the forwards tends to involve the eight players working as a single unit, often in small areas of the pitch. For the majority of viewers, the complexities of the forward's play is difficult to understand. In comparison the backs tend to spread out over the pitch and their play is relatively simple to understand. Consequently, television pundits often try to explain what has happened and provide replays of the action to help analyse the events. Statistical summaries are often provided (Table 14.1) as a means of showing where one team had superiority over the other.

When comparing performances such as those depicted in Table 14.1, it is easy to look at the values in isolation, without regard to the other values or other potentially important information. For example, the tackles made and tackles missed should be considered together. In the example above, Wales missed, what appears to be a very high 25.0 per cent (8 out of 32, 8 + 24) of tackles compared with 10.0 per cent by Ireland (4 out of 40). The fact that Ireland attempted more tackles suggests that Wales had more possession of the ball, confirmed by the possession percentage, but also that Wales used their possession to run at the Irish defence more so than Ireland did against Wales. This factor also needs to be considered when looking at the errors made by Wales, who, although they made more than Ireland (10 against 9), would not consider this an inferior performance as the handling errors should be considered with respect to the

Table 14.1 Summary statistics for the first half of the Six Nations match between Wales and Ireland played on 4 February 2007

	Wales	Ireland
Total possession	51%	49%
Total territory	56%	44%
Tackles made	24	36
Tackles missed	8	4
Ball won in opposition 22	9	3
Passes completed	52	40
Possession kicked	22	18
Errors made	10	9

total number of times the ball was handled (Hughes and Bartlett 2002), in this case the evidence suggests that Wales handled the ball more than Ireland.

It is usually the case that an individual's or a team's statistics need to be considered in light of other information. For example, Hughes and Bartlett (2002) suggest that performances may be considered relative to typical performance standards by similar teams or previously accomplished standards by the same team. Thus the values in Table 14.1 do not provide evidence of a particularly good or poor performance by either team as, for example, in isolation; we do not know whether winning the ball nine times in the opposition's 22 is a particularly good or bad performance. We do know that Wales won the ball three times as often in the opponent's 22 as Ireland did, which indicates superiority, but is this a typical value for a team of this standard? Also, what the statistics do not reveal is that Ireland scored a try from one of these three turnovers in the opposition 22, something that Wales were unable to do from their nine. Hence, while the total territory values gives an indication of how the match had been played, the score at half-time was Wales 9/Ireland 12 and indicates a marked difference in success rate.

The statistics presented in Table 14.1 reflected overall team performance. However, the media often provide statistics in relation to individuals, usually to highlight outstanding performances or those of the supposed key players, be it during or after the match. For example, Sky television showed Opta Index statistics for Lawrence Dallaglio's performance in a match between Wasps and Perpignan (13 January 2007) to indicate that he had made 10 tackles and carried the ball seven times. Without knowledge of what a player in his position usually does in matches of this sort, it is impossible to know whether his performance is out of the ordinary or not. Performance analysts working for rugby teams will collect this sort of information for all of their players on a match by match basis (e.g. James *et al.* 2005). This will enable them to assess whether players had good or bad games and coaches can utilize summary information gained from a number of matches to determine where players strengths and weaknesses lie which in turn can suggest training drills to improve performance or form the basis of selection decisions.

14.3.3 Basketball

Basketball involves teams of five players trying to score baskets which are usually worth 2 points but if the shot is from outside the 3-point line, then an extra point is awarded. Fouls can result in free throws which are worth 1 point each, although usually two free throws are awarded. Once a basket is scored, possession passes to the team scored against which results in rapid turnovers of possession. Since elite teams (this refers to NBA data) have relatively high successful shooting percentages (approximately 45 per cent field goal; 35 per cent 3 point and 80 per cent free throw), basketball is characterized by high scores (about 100 points/team). The nature of the game also means that each player's contribution to the team's performance can be broken down into scoring indices (assists, field goals, 3 point shots, free throws) and attempts to win possession (rebounds, steals, blocks and turnovers). A typical team's performance over a season is given in Table 14.2 (data from http://www.nba.com/bulls/stats).

The NBA website provides up to date statistics throughout the season and includes archive information from previous seasons. This information is used by the media to identify individual player's histories and to compare current form with previous accomplishments. This use of previous accomplishments is a good method of putting statistics into perspective. Hughes and Bartlett (2002) recommend presenting statistical information with respect to previous performance standards, both of the same team or player and other teams. For example, Ben Gordon's shooting performance (0.422 FG per cent, 0.435 3pt per cent, 0.787 FT per cent, see Table 14.2) could be put into perspective by comparing these statistics with his career statistics (0.428 FG per cent, 0.414 3pt per cent, 0.841 FT per cent; www.nba.com/playerfile/ben_gordon/inde14.html?nav=page). The two sets of statistics are relatively similar although these are based on 80 games for the 2005/6 season and 207 for his career. From this comparison, we can only say that he appears pretty consistent but we do not know how good this performance is. If we also compare his shooting performance with the best performer during the 2005/6 season, Kobe Bryant (0.45 FG per cent, 0.347 3pt per cent, 0.85 FT per cent; www.nba.com/playerfile/ben_gordon/index.html?nav=page), we can see that his percentages are slightly better for 3 pointers but lower for free throws. Interestingly, Gordon was only ranked 47 in shooting (although this is out of 434 players). This is because the shooting ranking is based on points per game (Kobe Bryant scored 35.4 points/game) and not the success rate of shots. Clearly Gordon did not take as many shots/game as Bryant. In order to put Gordon's shooting prowess into perspective, it might be advisable to compare his performance with, e.g. the top 50 in the shooting rankings. Figure 14.5 shows that Gordon's field goal and free throw success rates are pretty typical of the performances of the top 50 rated scoring players that season. His 3 point shooting is one standard deviation better than the top 50 average, which equates to one more basket every 10 attempts. It may be the case therefore, that Gordon, who has less than three full seasons of NBA

Table 14.2 Player averages for the Chicago Bulls 2005/6 regular season

CHICAGO BULLS

Player averages 2005/6 regular season

Player	G	GS	MPG	FG%	3pt%	FT%	OFF	DEF	TOT	APG	SPG	BPG	TO	PF	PPG
Ben Gordon	80	47	31.0	0.422	0.435	0.787	0.50	2.20	2.70	3.0	0.94	0.06	2.25	3.00	16.9
Kirk Hinrich	81	81	36.5	0.418	0.370	0.815	0.40	3.20	3.60	6.3	1.16	0.26	2.32	3.10	15.9
Luol Deng	78	56	33.4	0.463	0.269	0.750	1.60	5.00	6.60	1.9	0.92	0.64	1.35	1.60	14.3

G, games played; GS, games started; MPG, min/game; FG%, field goal percentage; 3pt%, 3 point percentage; FT%, field throw percentage; OFF, offensive rebounds; DEF, defensive rebounds; TOT, total rebounds per game; APG, assists per game; SPG, steals per game; BPG, blocks per game; TO, turnovers per game; PF, personal fouls; PPG, points per game.

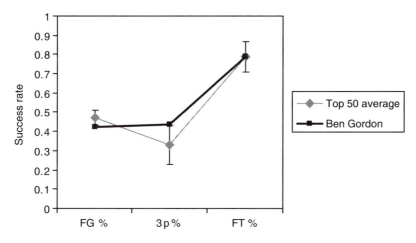

Figure 14.5 Ben Gordon's shooting success rate compared with the top 50 rated shooters during the 2005/6 season. Error bars signify 1 SD

experience, may in future be given the opportunity to shoot more often, by his team mates and coaches, in recognition of his excellent shooting success rate.

14.4 NET AND WALL GAMES

Net and wall games are characterized by opponents sequentially trading shots until a shot is not returned or is played out of the boundaries of the playing area. In this manner points are won or lost until a winner is declared. Net and wall games tend to be played by individuals, pairs and teams with different games often played in small isolated parts of the world, e.g. squash and racketball are very similar but different games popular in different parts of the world. The common characteristics of these sports include serving, court coverage, shot selection and shot execution. General interest tends to centre on certain aspects of play such as the influence of serving, winners, errors and points won, although the media coverage of these statistics is sporadic. This section will focus on tennis as it is has the most media coverage in this sports category.

The 2007 Australian Open tennis championships, like the other tennis Grand Slam events, produce all of the statistics typically used in the media for tennis (www.australianopen.com). The statistics for the first round of the men's event are presented in Table 14.3. This format has limited potential for trying to determine how individual matches progressed but does offer some insights into men's tennis in general, albeit on this type of playing surface, as court surface has

Table 14.3 Summary statistics of the men's event of the 2007 Australian Open tennis championships

	1st round
Matches played	64
5 set matches	15
4 set matches	18
3 set matches	28
Sets played	235
Tie breaks played	42
Total games	2,269
Winners	4,980
Return games won	532
Server points won	8,858
Unforced errors	4728
Total points	14,197
First serves in	8485
% 1st serves in	57
Total aces	1,232
Total double faults	553
1st serve points won	6,066
% 1st serve points won	71
% 2nd serve points won	44

been shown to effect the way in which rallies are played (O'Donoghue and Ingram 2001). For example, there was an unforced error every three rallies (unforced errors/number of points). This seems quite high but would need to be checked against values achieved in previous tournaments to see whether this is normal or not. It may be indicative of the way men's tennis is played currently, i.e. players go for their shots, since there was also a winner played every 2.85 rallies. However, these values can only be interpreted sensibly by comparing the values with previous match values.

Event statistics are also available on an individual basis for a number of statistics. For example, the effectiveness of the women's first serve can be assessed via Table 14.4.

Comparison data are only effective if all factors are considered however. In Table 14.4, the first serve points won are based on only two matches. If a particular player had been unlucky enough to play two very difficult matches, in comparison to another who had two easy wins, then the percentages would likely reflect this disparity rather than indicate a superior serving ability. In this instance a check of the number of points played would help distinguish if

254

Table 14.4 Individual first serve statistics from the women's event of the 2007 Australian Open tennis championships

Rank	Player	Country	Matches	First serve points won
1	S Kuznetsova	RUS	2	43 of 52 = 83%
2	S Williams	USA	2	55 of 68 = 81%
3	A Molik	AUS	2	65 of 83 = 78%
4	A Ivanovic	SRB	2	49 of 63 = 78%
5	V Zvonareva	RUS	2	51 of 66 = 77%
6	A Chakvetadze	RUS	2	59 of 77 = 77%
7	P Schnyder	SUI	2	62 of 81 = 77%
8	L Safarova	CZE	2	52 of 68 = 76%
9	M Sharapova	RUS	2	63 of 83 = 76%
10	D Safina	RUS	2	53 of 70 = 76%

this had happened. On doing so, it is apparent that the number one player, Kuznetsova, only served 52 service points, less than any of the other players in the top 8, suggesting she may well have had an easier draw than the others.

Technology was highly visible at the 2007 Australian Open, such that performance analysis was available live on the internet site as well as being available for players to utilize to check line calls (a maximum of two per set). IBM's 'Point-tracker' system (Figure 14.6) was available on the Australian Open website to view ongoing matches and replay previous ones. The viewpoint could be altered as well as other factors such as the number of visible shots, the display of serve and return of serve speeds as well as the speed of a winner. A further interesting feature was the ability to select a single category of shot, e.g. backhand unforced errors. This type of analysis can be useful for individual player feedback to highlight strengths and weaknesses.

The collection of live performance data has great potential but is also liable to error. Depending on the technology used, the chance of making mistakes is related to the time in which the data need to be captured. In tennis, the ball is hit between the players in a relatively small period of time, meaning that there is limited time frame in which to record the necessary details. If you consider Table 14.3 it can be appreciated that some of the statistics can be derived from the match score, e.g. number of sets. More detail is required to determine the number of points and further information is required to determine the number of net points, winners, etc. If these details are recorded by hand then as the number of things that are needed to be recorded per point increases so to does

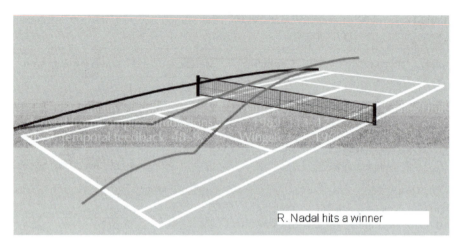

R. Nadal hits a winner

Figure 14.6 Visual representation of the 'IBM Pointtracker' system used at the 2007 Australian Open tennis championships

the likely error rate. If an automated system is possible, of course, then the error rate can theoretically be reduced to zero.

It is not uncommon for performance analysis researchers to utilize statistics gained from websites for their publications. Clearly some account needs to be taken as to the accuracy of these match statistics. O'Donoghue (2007) compared the number of points he deemed to be net points in US Open tennis matches with the values reported on the US Open internet site (www.usopen.org). He found a systematic bias with 1.95 more net points being reported on average for each player in each set on the internet site than he recorded. O'Donoghue suggested that this difference was likely to have been due to how one defines a net point. However, while he could detail his definition it was impossible to determine the definition used by the US Open since this detail is not reported.

14.5 STRIKING AND FIELDING GAMES

Striking and fielding games tend to lend themselves well to the collection of performance statistics. This is because the different skills required can be broken down into many parts, each of which can be represented statistically. However, the two exemplar sports illustrated here show how the media's portrayal of the different sports can be dramatically different. Golf coverage on television tends to minimize the role of statistics whilst cricket has invested in the latest technology to produce visually stunning and informative performance analysis.

14.5.1 Golf

Golf has a long tradition (complete records go back to 1980 on the PGA website, www.pgatour.com) of collecting performance statistics, presumably, as just stated, there are many easily distinguishable skills involved in the game, e.g. driving distance, greens in regulation (GIR) and number of putts. The PGA website lists and continuously updates 30 different performance statistics although 17 of these relate directly to scoring outcomes, e.g. number of birdies.

Surprisingly, television companies do not avail themselves of these statistics very much. It is usual for them to select just a few statistics for one player, e.g. fairways hit, GIR and number of putts, to illustrate their performance on a particular round. This is useful if the viewer is knowledgeable about these statistics and more importantly the range in values that correspond to good and poor performances. In contrast to this limited presentation, the PGA website provides comprehensive statistics as well as visual and statistical information for each player on each hole of all PGA events. For example, using 'TourCast', powered by IBM's ShotLink system, each shot played in the FBR Open (1–4 February 2007) at TPC Scottsdale can be viewed with detailed information regarding shot distances also given. Figure 14.7 shows the outcome of the eventual winner, Aaron Baddeley's, first two shots on the par 4, 11th hole (rated the hardest hole on the day averaging 4.18 shots) during his first round, with details regarding the distance of each shot and the resulting distance to the flag. The accuracy of this information appears to be considerable, given that distances are measured to inches. However, the measurement devices used (laser rangefinders and GPS systems) are typically accurate to about 1 yard at best although this is still pretty impressive.

A recent innovation on the PGA website is an attempt to simplify the various performance statistics into four values, power, accuracy, short game and putting, called the PGA Tour Skill Rating. Power relates to the power off the tee (average driving distance) but also factors in the percentage of drives that go over 300 and 320 yards. Accuracy combines driving accuracy with GIR and proximity to the hole for approach shots over 100 yards only. Short game uses all statistics for shots to the green from <100 yards, i.e. rough, sand and utilizes scrambling and GIR percentages from this distance. Putting uses all putting performances split

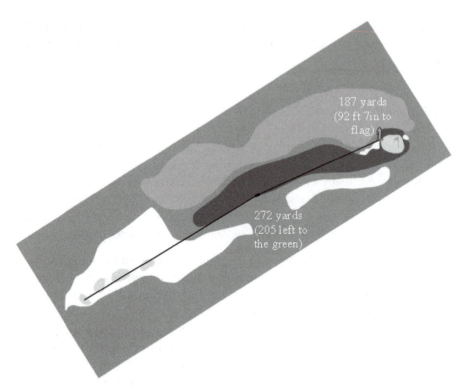

Figure 14.7 Visual representation of the 'IBM TourCast' system used on the PGA website

into distances from the hole. This is an interesting attempt to answer one of the criticisms of performance statistics in golf, namely that they are not distinct variables. For example, GIR is widely regarded as a good indication of approach shot accuracy. However, if one player drives on average 300 yards compared with another player only 250 yards, then if everything else was equal, the longer driver would typically have much easier approach shots and consequently the GIR would not be a fair comparison. In practice the longer drivers tend to be less accurate and therefore play more approach shots from the rough. However, the GIR statistic is bound to be a composite measure of both approach shot accuracy and driving performance. Hence the new accuracy measure explicitly combines elements of both driving and approach shots. It is too early to say how well these new measures will be received by players, scientists and sports fans but this does appear to have some merit.

14.5.2 Cricket

Fielding games are characterized by playing areas into which one team hits a ball and the other tries to retrieve it. While the rules for the different sports in this category differ the objective is for the fielding side to minimize the opponent's score by catching, throwing and bowling successfully. General interest in games such as cricket and baseball tends to centre on aspects of play such as scoring rates, types of bowling delivery and shot selection. Fielding games are extremely popular, although not all over the world, and the media tends to produce very impressive performance analysis statistics.

Cricket has a long record of collecting statistics, recorded each year in the book *Wisden*. Records are accessible online (http://content-usa.cricinfo.com/wisdenalmanack) and date back to 1864. These records are comprehensive and easily available to the media and public alike. The following example is primarily taken from Sky Sports live coverage of the Commonwealth Bank One Day International (ODI) Series between Australia and England at the MCG, Melbourne on 12 January 2007. Figure 14.8 shows how the runs were accumulated by both teams as they progressed through the allotted 50 overs. The chart also indicates where wickets fell and shows how Australia was always ahead of England's scoring rate. However, what is not so clear from this chart is how dramatically Australia outscored England in the early overs (Figure 14.9).

Hughes and Bartlett (2002) suggest that performance indicators such as scoring rate should not be viewed in isolation of the opponent's performance. This does

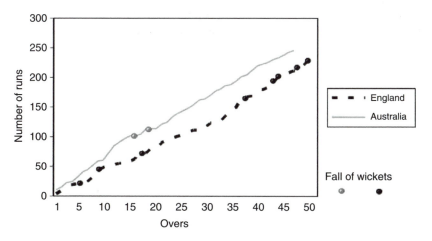

Figure 14.8 Cumulative runs scored in the One Day International (ODI) between Australia and England on 12 January 2007

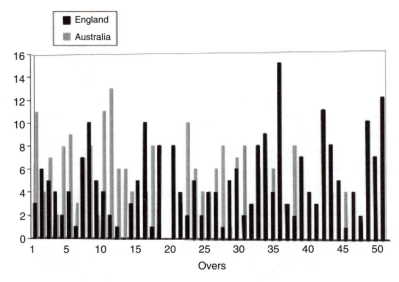

Figure 14.9 Runs scored each over in the One Day International between Australia and England

not mean a comparison, as in Figures 14.8 and 14.9, is sufficient. Rather they mean that a team's scoring is not only a reflection of their batting performance but also is dependent on the opposition's bowling performance. The television coverage gave the bowling statistics for both the current match (Table 14.5) as well as ODI career averages (Table 14.6).

Although the commentators did not explicitly link the England batting to the Australian bowling, the two sets of statistics were regularly displayed. From a

Table 14.5 Australian bowling statistics for the One Day International between Australia and England

Bowler	Overs	Maidens	Runs	Wickets	Strike rate	Econ
G D McGrath	10	0	40	2	20.00	4.00
N W Bracken	9	0	46	3	33.33	5.11
S R Clark	10	0	58	1	10.00	5.80
M G Johnson	10	2	34	2	20.00	3.40
M J Clarke	8	0	35	0	0.00	4.38
C L White	3	0	27	0	0.00	9.00

Strike rate is the number of wickets taken per 100 overs bowled. Econ is the number of runs conceded per over bowled.

Table 14.6 Australian bowling One Day International career statistics

Bowler	Strike rate	Econ
G D McGrath	35.00	3.82
N W Bracken	28.20	4.36
S R Clark	36.00	5.50
M G Johnson	30.00	5.15
M J Clarke	41.30	5.24
C L White	48.00	7.50

performance analyst's point of view the Econ statistics (Tables 14.5 and 14.6) are most informative as they show that only two of the Australian bowlers (M G Johnson and M J Clarke) had better Econ rates during this match than their ODI averages. This would suggest that the Australian bowlers as a team, performed at around their average suggesting that the English batsmen did not have a particularly bad day rather they were only allowed to score at the typical rate allowed by the Australian bowlers. Of course, other factors come into play in a single match, such as conditions that favour the batsmen rather than the bowlers. Performance analysts working with a team are thus cautious about reading too much into the statistics from one match and prefer to look at trends over a series of matches.

The Hawk-Eye system (http://www.hawkeyeinnovations.co.uk), owned by The Television Corporation and introduced by Channel 4 in the UK in 2001, enables broadcasters to calculate the speed of each bowl as well as a range of visual information. This system has also reportedly been used by the England cricket team for post-match analysis. Figure 14.10 shows how the batsman (Cook) responded to balls delivered by McGrath. This type of analysis can be useful for both bowlers and batmen to identify strengths and weakness in technique.

Other facets of performance can be visually represented, such as where a bowler's deliveries land for each batsman, or for all right-handed batsmen. This is the strength of the Hawk-Eye system, particularly for media presentations, as this flexibility is immediately available and allows presenters to select the aspect of play they wish to display. This visual information also provides some objective information to the long enduring debate regarding LBW decisions (Figure 14.11), which must be a good thing!

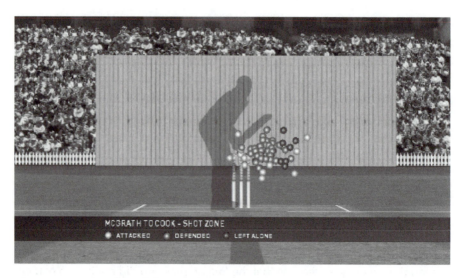

Figure 14.10 Bowling deliveries by McGrath to Cook in the 4th day of the 3rd Test between England and Australia in Perth, 14–18 December 2006 (Reproduced with permission from Hawk-Eye Innovations)

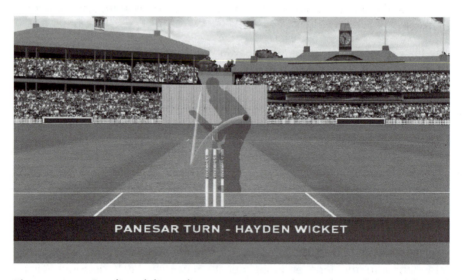

Figure 14.11 Bowling delivery by Panesar to Hayden in the 3rd day of the 3rd Test between England and Australia in Perth, 14–18 December 2006 (Reproduced with permission from Hawk-Eye Innovations)

SUMMARY

It would seem that the media currently utilizes a wide range of techniques to display the outputs of performance analysis. However, the extent to which performance analysis is used is dependent on the sport and the medium in which the results are presented. The most comprehensive statistics are, not surprisingly, available on the internet whilst the most sophisticated technology is primarily used on television. Television companies and newspapers tend to use statistics to illustrate a point they wish to make and consequently do not overly concern themselves with scientific rigour. For this reason, sports teams prefer to utilize their own performance analysts rather than rely on statistics published in the media. In conclusion, it is suggested that the media provides variable quality performance analysis, which should not always be relied upon, but adds significantly to the enjoyment of the sports fans.

CHAPTER FIFTEEN

NOTATIONAL ANALYSIS OF COACHING BEHAVIOUR

Kenny More

In this chapter we:

- describe how, on a theoretical and practical level, coaching behaviour in the training environment can be observed and analysed to improve coaching effectiveness.
- will inform on the sequential development of systematic observation and analysis for the measurement and modification of verbal coaching behaviour.

15.1 INTRODUCTION: THE COACHING PROCESS

A primary function of every coach is to provide athletes with the opportunity to acquire, refine, and learn skills that will produce a successful performance in competition. This requires the coach to:

1 Identify the technical and strategic skills required for successful performance.
2 Observe and analyse their athlete's competence in the execution of these skills.
3 Design training opportunities to assist the acquisition and learning of these skills.
4 Provide instruction and feedback on these skills in the training environment.

In relation to these requirements, previous chapters have provided guidance and methods on how to identify, then systematically observe and analyse key aspects of individual and team performance, while National Governing Bodies and coaching materials typically provide the coach with support in the design of appropriate training content, and guidance on their instructional behaviour.

The coaching skills of observation, planning and delivery naturally flow from athlete performance, and the position of Notational Analysis as a means of supporting innate observation is well documented. However, less well established is the role of Notational Analysis in monitoring the instruction and feedback the coach delivers during training.

If we consider the significant time devoted to the formal analysis of performance, followed by the careful and informed selection of training content, it would seem folly to have no rationale for, or means of, monitoring effectiveness in providing instruction and feedback (Figure 15.1).

15.2 NOTATIONAL ANALYSIS OF COACHING BEHAVIOUR

15.2.1 Effective coaching

Effective coaching is crucial to the pursuit of optimal sporting performance. The more effective the coaching, the more fully the coach's role will benefit athlete performance. To this end, research into coaching effectiveness has increased in recent years, and now planning, management, instruction and monitoring skills are being analysed. To direct this work, coaching effectiveness research has drawn its theoretical framework from the teacher effectiveness domain, where teaching skills were viewed as a science and, therefore, amenable to systematic observation and analysis. While it is not yet possible to assess completely the full range of skills that are blended into effective coaching, there is a will to assess specific skills where and when possible.

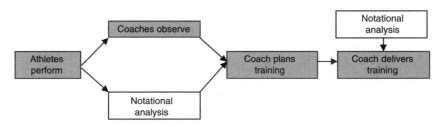

Figure 15.1 The diagram represents the inclusion of notational analysis into the coaching process

Notational analysis of the instructional process promotes the objective assessment of coaching behaviour and can, therefore, provide insight into variables deemed important in determining effectiveness. This systematic process can provide valid and reliable information that can accurately describe coaching behaviour, and advances in computer and video technology have enhanced the process of data acquisition, analysis and feedback. It is now possible, for example, to analyse verbal coaching behaviour using an interactive video software tool that provides a meaningful and timely output of statistical and video data on the coach's performance. The utility of such methods as part of an intervention strategy has real application for those in supervisory capacities in physical education and sport settings, and has also been adopted by professionals in medical practice and banking as a means of monitoring consultancy interactions.

15.2.2 Teaching and coaching behaviour – a historical perspective

In the 1950s, the American Education Research Association stated that after 40 years of research into teacher effectiveness, during which a vast number of studies were carried out, few outcomes had advanced the assessment and modification of teacher behaviour. It was ultimately criticized as being a blind search for the qualities of good teaching. However, the late 1950s saw a shift in how teaching variables were understood and by the early 1970s teacher process variables (the variables concerned with the actual activities of classroom teaching) became the focus. Researchers began to study skills and strategies for organization, instruction, and feedback provision, as these were shown to directly relate to teacher performance (as measured by student achievement).

It became clear that teachers should have their teaching observed, receive regular feedback on these observations, and be provided with the necessary support to effect improvement. To this end, the quality and accuracy of feedback the teachers received was central to efforts to modify their teaching behaviour. A substantial body of evidence suggested that this feedback should be based on information gathered through systematic observation (the adoption of notational analysis techniques) because intuitive observation and analysis was unlikely to be a powerful enough tool to create lasting improvement. Creating a systematic and objective process would help ensure a more complete description and understanding of performance was gained and more quantifiable evidence to present to the teacher. This would allow greater precision of information, allowing goals to be set and, subsequently, monitored.

15.2.3 Systematic observation

Observation is a key element in efforts to improve teaching skills, and the turning point in research was the development of a methodology for objectively observing teachers as they taught. Only through 'systematic observation' methods could the observation and data acquisition process provide reliable, accurate and consistent information for the assessment of teacher effectiveness. Systematic observation permits a trained observer to use a set method (the observational instrument) to observe, record, and analyse events and behaviours, with the assumption that other observers, using the same observational instrument, and viewing the same sequence of events, would agree with the recorded data. These instruments gave researchers, or those in supervisory capacities, a great advantage over traditional 'eyeballing' or rating scale methods.

Observation methods are designed to produce information on specific teacher and student variables, and the instrument chosen should be tailored to the goals of the particular observation. For example, event recording, which gathers information relating to the frequency of event occurrence, may, in some instances, be more informative than assessment by duration recording. Regardless, once the technique best suited to the observational goal is identified, a means for data acquisition and analysis is then chosen. This would consider whether real-time or post-event acquisition was desirable or achievable, and whether it required hand notation or the recruitment of a computer-assisted tool. Over the last 30 years, these instruments have been adapted for sports coaching, and have benefited from significant advances in computer and video technology.

The data obtained from systematic observation can serve as information by which teaching skills can be improved. For example, systematic observation produced valuable information on how much lesson time students were engaged with content suitable to their stage of learning, and through systematic observation, successful classroom management techniques were identified, and then actively promoted in physical education teachers. In both cases, the acquired information provided a database of behaviour, and was used as an integral part of the feedback process.

15.2.4 Systematic observation instruments

One of the first instruments used to observe instructional behaviour was the Flanders Interaction Analysis System (FIAS). It was designed to analyse verbal teaching behaviour under the headings of teacher talk, student talk and silence/

confusion. The strengths of the FIAS were compelling and the first attempts to analyse teaching in physical education were modifications of that system. Since then there have been numerous observation systems specific to the physical education and sport environment (Figure 15.2).

During the late 1980s and early 1990s The Centre for Sports Analysis, at the University of British Columbia, undertook the task of extending and improving upon the existing techniques and instruments. Specific attention was directed towards the recording of coaching and athlete behaviours during team sport practices. The Computerized Coaching Analysis System (CCAS) collected data on the individual comments made by the coach (CAI), the technical success of athletes during practice sessions (AAI), and the time management skills of the coach (ATEI). From its inception the CCAS was designed to be an on-site, real-time computer-driven system, capable of in-depth analysis of coaching behaviour.

The CAI part of this system was designed to analyse the verbal behaviour of the coach when organizing and instructing within a defined segment of practice. Although previous instruments had identified the nature of verbal coaching behaviours, they did not fully describe the instructional style in use. Any strategy to modify coaching behaviour, based on selected and independent findings, failed to recognize the complexity of effective instruction, and would be limited

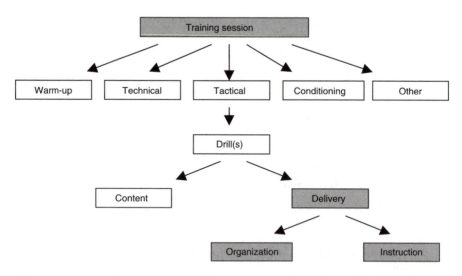

Figure 15.2 A training session can be represented as a hierarchical model with a continuous time-line of activity segments. Each segment is composed of a number of drills that are devoted to coaching the skills and concepts of that particular segment

notational analysis of coaching behaviour

to the scope of the original instrument. After refinements were made to its original structure, the CAI produced a quantitative analysis profile reflective of every comment made during the observed practice. It was used in conjunction with a video-taped recording of the session, allowing the user to recall the audio-visual representation of the previously recorded behaviour.

The CAI was presented to a panel of observational analysis experts, members of the Coaching Association of Canada, and other members of the coaching fraternity. There was a clear consensus as to its completeness and validity as a measuring tool, and as a mechanism of professional development. Appropriate intra- and inter-observer reliability measures were conducted to ensure that recorded changes in behaviour were attributable to the coach and not the observer.

The CAI was designed to allow an observer to collect and subsequently analyse data pertaining to the organization and instruction components of these drills. The organizational component consists of the verbal behaviour displayed while explaining the organizational goals of the drill. As such, all comments are grouped and separated from the instructional component. The instructional component consists of all other coaching information, with clear operational criteria for each separate and definable comment (Figure 15.3). For a fuller description of the CAI and its operational definitions, readers are directed to More and Franks (1996).

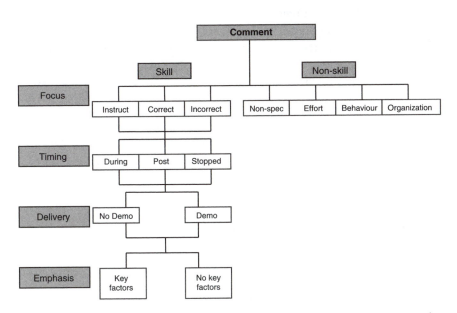

Figure 15.3 The structure of the instructional component, representing four levels of data entry for each verbal comment

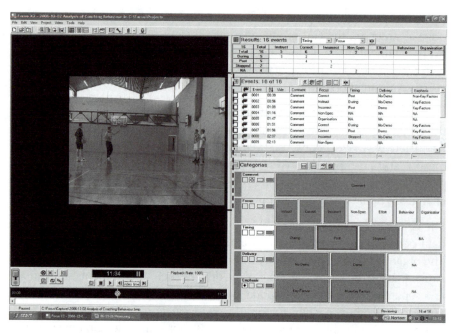

Figure 15.4 Display of screen from Focus X2

While this structure was originally mapped onto the keyboard of a computer, its most recent application has been through the Performance Analysis software Focus X2 (www.elitesportsanalysis.com). This software has maintained the integrity of the data being logged on each comment, but permits instant compilation and display of summary data, and instant interactive access to the video associated with the data.

The architecture of Focus X2 shows the video being captured to the left hand side of the screen, while category buttons on the bottom right hand side allow the entry of comment details (Figure 15.4). All entries are displayed in an event list, before being exported to excel for display.

15.3 EFFECTIVE COACHING BEHAVIOURS

15.3.1 Understanding the data

In the example of the CAI, the major source of information is the quantitative comment summary data. As a result, the researchers at UBC decided to create quantitative targets for the different dimensions of verbal behaviour. However, while the precise value of any specific target was not considered critical, it was anticipated that these targets would benefit the coaches when interpreting their data, generate motivation to change a particular behaviour, and provide a reference whereby they could evaluate the magnitude of the resulting change. These targets were estimates of effective coaching behaviour based upon an understanding of relevant research literature, and dialogue with coach educators. Chapters 1 and 2 highlighted some of the relevant literature that we now illustrate in a more practical learning setting. After each of the following sections, it may be useful to re-review the material in these chapters.

The results table (Table 15.1) provides a typical display of summary data on the instructional component of the CAI. Target behaviours (discussed in the next section) are provided in brackets for comparative purposes only and may be changed as needed.

15.3.2 Should comments be skill- or non-skill related?

Skill-related comments are interactions directed at the athletic performance of the learners, while non skill-related comments are interactions directed at the organization and social behaviour of the learners. More effective coaches spend

Table 15.1 Example data from an analysis of coaching behaviour

Analysis of Coaching Behaviour: Coach 1			
Skill comments	**83%**	**(>80%)**	**Non-skill comments 17% (<20%)**
Focus:			Focus:
Instruction	56%	(40%)	Organizational
Feedback on correct performance	32%	(40%)	Social (behaviour/effort)
Feedback on incorrect performance	12%	(20%)	Non-specific
Timing:			
During performance	45%	(30%)	
Post performance	43%	(60%)	
Stopped (freeze)	12%	(10%)	
Delivery:			
Demonstration	n = 4		
Emphasis:			
Key factors	81%	(80%)	
Non-key factors	19%	(20%)	

more time instructing the proposed content of the session and providing skill-related feedback than do those who are less effective. Intuitively, this suggests that more effective coaches spend less time organizing the athletes and providing behavioural feedback. It is believed that a necessity for increased amounts of behavioural feedback may reflect a lack of effective planning or organization. Improving those coaching qualities would allow them to spend a greater proportion of time giving skill-related instruction and feedback.

15.3.3 The focus of skill-related comments

The need for coaching comments to include information is compelling. When given in the form of instructions, the comments will relate to how the skill should be performed, and should pertain specifically to the skills and concepts that the drill is designed to improve. For example, in a soccer drill designed to improve the skill of crossing, verbal instruction should concentrate on the player's ability to gain the required pace, direction and flight of the ball.

Once the skill has been executed the coach can make comment on the quality of the performance in relation to its goal. Motor learning research promotes feedback as the single most important variable (except for practice itself) in learning a motor task. As coaches, by nature of their roles, are responsible for much of the augmented feedback received by athletes as they perform, it is crucial that the feedback they give reflect effective strategies. Augmented feedback produces learning, not by reward or punishment, but by the provision of information on the action and, where necessary, on how to change and improve subsequent action.

Coaches, therefore, should ensure that their feedback goes beyond simple reward or punishment (e.g. 'Nice job' or 'Not that way') and include some information (e.g. 'Nice job – great pace on the ball'). The information should reinforce the specific aspects that are 'correct', or should identify discrepancies between actual and desired performance, so that 'incorrect' aspects can be modified. Thus, regardless of the success of the action, the inclusion of information ensures comments are neither general nor 'non-specific'. In terms of seeking a balance to feedback on 'correct' and 'incorrect' performance, research suggests a differential use of strategy based on the age and ability of athlete involved. For example, with younger athletes, an effective strategy would be to concentrate on feedback that would reinforce correct performance. This is not to suggest that coaches ignore incorrect performance, but rather that they favour information that reinforces correct actions.

272

15.3.4 The timing of skill-related comments

In developing a strategy for their verbal behaviour, the coach should be aware of the attention capacity of athletes as they learn. If the skill is low in complexity, or familiar to the athlete, the athlete's information-processing system can effectively handle other stimuli at that time. This is not true if the task requires full allocation of their attention. Consideration must be given to the amount and timing of instruction and feedback. Successful coaches have been shown to deliver a significant amount of information as soon as their athletes are free from the immediate demands of performance. For example, in our crossing example, this could be after the player has delivered the cross, and is returning to the 'start position'. This temporal location allows a strong association between the athlete's perception of the action and the augmented feedback delivered by the coach.

A related issue to the timing of instruction and feedback is the frequency with which it is given. Practice with the athletes receiving feedback after every performance has been shown to be beneficial for the (temporary) performance of skill, but detrimental to the (relatively permanent) learning of skill. This principle known as the Guidance Hypothesis, suggests that immediate performance is facilitated because the athlete is guided toward the target performance, but that learning is degraded as the athlete is not forced to attend to sensory feedback or detect errors. In practice (and depending on the specific activity), feedback should be frequent in initial practice to guide the athlete toward the goal of the action, then systematically smaller as practice continues to force these self-detection processes.

15.3.5 The delivery of skill-related comments

A very effective way of delivering information is to support it with a visual demonstration. Also known as modelling, demonstrations can aid learning by accurately and skilfully portraying the critical features of performance. This creates an internal model which guides the athlete's response and provides a standard against which feedback is compared. The demonstration should be accompanied by succinct verbal instructions that ensure the athlete's attention is directed to the key aspects of performance.

Demonstrations can occur before the skill is attempted, to give the learners the idea of the movement, or during practice to confirm and extend the athlete's understanding of the performance; they can be performed by the coach or one of the athletes, provided the person is skilled in the act of demonstration; and can be delivered in slow-motion to give a clear representation of physical relationships of body parts, or at normal speed to give a clear representation of the timing necessary for optimum performance.

15.3.6 The emphasis of skill-related comments

The need for coaching comments to include information seems conclusive. However, it would seem vital that the information given should pertain to the skills and concepts that the drill is designed to improve. In our football 'crossing' example, information was to be based on the required pace, direction and flight of the crossed ball, and not to be concerned with issues such as ball reception or dribbling prior to the delivery of the cross. While these may, instinctively, be commented upon, it is clearly desirable that the majority of information be focussed on the 'key factors', these are factors that the coach has deemed beforehand to be critical to successful performance of the skill (in this example 'crossing').

15.3.7 The case for non-skill-related comments

Those comments considered to be non-skill-related, i.e. organizational, effort, behaviour and non-specific, also contribute to the quality of the learning environment. For example, occasional use of an enthusiastic or forcefully delivered comment to motivate or bring back on-task behaviour will have a positive effect on the concentration and application of the athletes. However, should these types of comments become commonplace, the lesson will not engage the athletes, and issues such as the original organization or content selection may be in need of revision.

15.4 MODIFICATION OF COACHING BEHAVIOUR

The opportunity to practise relevant skills, with the provision of systematic feedback, has long been shown to improve sporting skills. However, it is now widely recognized that this process will also benefit teaching and coaching skills. For example, educational research has shown that change can be expedited if attention is on one process variable, and only a few teaching behaviours are selected for change at any one time. In the example given of the CAI above, the process variable is verbal coaching behaviour, and behaviours for change may be limited to say the 'timing' and 'emphasis' of comments.

notational analysis of coaching behaviour

There are a number of components that help guide the modification of behaviour process. First, a baseline of coaching behaviour from three or more observations should be established; second, behaviour(s) for change or reinforcement should be identified from the data generated; third, strategies to facilitate the change or reinforcement of targeted behaviour(s) should be specified; fourth, criteria for evaluating the targeted behaviour(s) should be established and finally, start and finish dates for the targeted behaviour(s) can be indicated.

As previously mentioned, researchers at the Centre for Sports Analysis modified the CAI to provide a more complete description of the verbal comments of coaches. This instrument was then used to analyse the coach's verbal behaviour, and to modify aspects of their ineffective behaviour. Four coaches were observed and analysed across 12 soccer practice sessions. (This constituted four sessions during 'baseline', four sessions during 'intervention' and four sessions during 'follow-up'.) Coaches A, B and C received intervention feedback through the CAI data, where selected behaviours were highlighted for discussion, and video-taped evidence was used to illustrate discussion points. Coach D was provided with video tapes of his own performance, and told to formulate and implement any of his own recommendations. Written journals and audio-tape recordings were also utilized to promote insight into the complexity of verbal behaviour and the 'human factors' that affect behaviour modification.

Change was quantified according to the 'organizational' and 'instructional' components of the CAI. Interpretation of cumulative values for organizational effectiveness revealed marked improvement in Coaches A and B's behaviour following intervention, and marginal improvement in the clarity and conciseness of Coach C. Marginal change was also reported in the organizational behaviour of Coach D, although this was not maintained. Instructional effectiveness was assessed by Time-Series Analysis, according to recognized criteria. There was evidence from each behaviour dimension that change can occur and be maintained as a result of exposure to the CAI intervention strategy. However, this was clearly contingent on the coaches understanding of what was asked of them, and remaining focussed and committed to changing these particular behaviours. The analysis of Coach D's behavioural change suggested that there were limitations to the sensitivity of discretionary viewing, as only two dimensions of behaviour resulted in positive change.

This research provided support that the modification of behaviour can occur through the systematic collection of valid and reliable information. Such intervention can oversee the fine-tuning of existing skills and/or the identification and acquisition of new skills; the information generated being used as direct feedback to reinforce appropriate performance, or to identify weakness and recommend change. However, it is difficult to ascertain why consistent, desirable change did not occur in all dimensions of analysed behaviour, or as readily for one coach as for another. Three reasons were proposed for this differential success in modifying behaviour, and these resonate with findings from contemporary studies.

First, the information that is delivered should be linked to the overall goal of more effective coaching performance. The coaches need to understand the consequences of more effective verbal behaviour, i.e. the link to the learning properties of feedback, and the resultant effect on athlete performance and improvement. Second, the coach should feel supported by the 'supervisors' attention. While the intervention sessions of this study tried to address areas for change in a supportive and collaborative manner, it is likely that not all information was accepted in the same way by different individuals. Such perceptions were evident in the reactions of the coaches and their journal entries. It has since proved beneficial for the 'supervisor' to use instances of positive behaviour even when addressing areas of weakness. Third, the context in which the intervention strategy occurs has an impact on likely success. If not enough importance is attached to the results of the intervention, there may be little incentive for the coach to accept prescriptive comment and strive for improvement. Where, for example, certification is not the end result, significant intrinsic motivation is required to commit to the need for change, and remain focussed on any targets set.

SUMMARY

While the CAI and other intervention strategies have provided evidence that modification can occur across a range of coaching behaviours, including those that require the balancing and orchestration of behaviour, further research could investigate the optimal dissemination of any intervention strategy. In recent years, the delivery of the CAI to both soccer and rugby coaches has 'packaged' information in two stages. Benefits were gained by educating coaches on the nature and complexity of their verbal behaviour in advance of them becoming the focus of analysis and modification. Their increased sensitivity to their baseline behaviour provided a much better platform for subsequent prescription.

BIBLIOGRAPHY

Al-Abood, S. A., Davids, K. and Bennett, S. J. (2001) 'Specificity of Task Constraints and Effects of Visual Demonstrations and Verbal Instructions in Directing Learner's Search During Skill Acquisition', *Journal of Motor Behavior* 33, 295–305.

Altman, D. G. (1991) *Practical Statistics for Medical Research*, London: Chapman & Hall, p. 404.

Annett, J. (1993) 'The Learning of Motor Skills: Sports Science and Ergonomics Perspectives', *Ergonomics*, 37, 5–16.

Atkinson, G. and Nevill, A. M. (1998) 'Statistical Methods for Assessing Measurement Error (Reliability) in Variables Relevant to Sports Medicine', *Sports Medicine*, 26, 217–38.

Balsom, P. D., Seger, J. Y., Sjodin, B. and Ekblom, B. (1992) 'Maximal intensity intermittent exercise: effect of recovery duration', *International Journal of Sports Medicine*, 13, 528–33.

Bangsbo, J. (1993) *The Physiology of Soccer – With Special Reference to Intense Intermittent Exercise*, Copenhagen: HO & Strom.

Bangsbo, J. (1997) 'The Physiology of Intermittent Activity in Football', in Reilly, T., Bangsbo J. and Hughes M. (eds) *Science and Football III*, London: E&FN Spon, pp. 43–53.

Bangsbo, J., Nørregaard, L. and Thorsøe, F. (1991) 'Activity Profile of Professional Soccer', *Canadian Journal of Sports Sciences*, 16, 110–116.

Bartlett, R. M. (1999) *Sports Biomechanics: Reducing Injury and Improving Performance*, London: E&FN Spon.

Bartlett, R. M. (2001) 'Performance Analysis: Can Bringing Together Biomechanics and Notational Analysis Benefit Coaches?' *The International Journal of Performance Analysis in Sport*, 1, 122–6.

Bartlett, R. M. (2004) 'Artificial Intelligence in Performance Analysis', in

O'Donoghue, P. and Hughes, M. (eds) *Notational Analysis of Sport VI*, Cardiff: UWIC

Bate, R. (1988) 'Football Chance: Tactics and Strategy', in Reilly, T., Lees, A., Davids, K. and Murphy, W. (eds) *Science and Football*, London: E&FN Spon.

Beck, C. and O'Donoghue, P. G. (2004) 'Time-Motion Analysis of Intervarsity Rugby League Competition', in O'Donoghue, P. G. and Hughes, M. D. (eds) *Performance Analysis of Sport 6*, Cardiff: CPA Press, UWIC, pp. 150–5.

Behan, H. (2006) Personal communication. August.

Bekkering, H., Wohlschläger, A. and Gattis, M. (1996) 'Motor Imitation: What is Imitated?', *Corpus, Psyche et Societas*, 3, 68–74.

Bland, J. M. and Altman, D. G. (1986) 'Statistical Methods for Assessing Agreement between Two Methods of Clinical Measurement', *The Lancet*, 1, 307–10.

Bloomfield, J., Polman, R. and O'Donoghue, P. G. (2004) 'The "Bloomfield Movement Classification": Movement Analysis of Individual Players in Dynamic Movement Sports', *International Journal of Performance Analysis of Sport (e)*, 4, 20–31.

Bloomfield, J., Polman, R. and O'Donoghue, P. G. (2007) 'Reliability of the Bloomfield Movement Classification', *International Journal of Performance Analysis of Sport (e)*, 7, 20–27.

Boddington, M., Lambert, M., St Clair Gibson, A. and Noakes, T. (2001) 'Time-Motion Study of Female Field Hockey', in Hughes M. and Franks I. M. (eds) *pass.com*, Cardiff: CPA, UWIC, pp. 333–5.

Bogdanis, G., Nevill, M., Boobis, L., Lakomy, H. and Nevill, A. (1995) 'Recovery of Power Output and Muscle Metabolites Following 30s of Maximal Sprint Cycling in Man', *Journal of Physiology*, 482, 467–80.

Boobis, L. H. (1987) 'Metabolic Aspects of Fatigue During Sprinting', in McLeod, D., Maughan, R., Nimmo, M., Reilly, T. and Williams, C. (eds) *Exercise – Benefits, Limits and Adaptations*, London: E&FN Spon, pp. 116–40.

Booth, D. and Doyle, G. (1997) 'UK Television Warms Up for the Biggest Game Yet: Pay-Per-View', *Media, Culture and Society*, 19, 277–84.

Boyle, R. and Haynes, R. (2000) *Power Play: Sport, the media and popular culture*. London: Longman.

Brooks, G. A. (1987) 'Lactate Production During Exercise: Oxydizable Substrate Versus Fatigue Agent', in McLeod, D., Maughan, R., Nimmo, M., Reilly, T. and Williams, C. (eds) *Exercise – Benefits, Limits and Adaptations*, London: E&FN Spon, pp. 144–57.

Brown, D. and Hughes, M. D. (1995) 'The Effectiveness of Quantitative and Qualitative Feedback on Performance in Squash', in Reilly, T., Hughes, M. D. and Lees, A (eds) *Science and Racket Sports*, London: E&FN Spon, pp. 232–7.

Brown, E. (2005) 'Running Strategy of Female Middle Distance Runners Attempting the 800m and 1500m "Double" At a Major Championship: a Performance Analysis and Qualitative Investigation', *International Journal of Performance Analysis of Sport (e)*, 5, 73–88.

Brown, E. and O'Donoghue, P. G. (2006) 'Analysis of Performance in Running Events', in Dancs, H., Hughes, M. and O'Donoghue, P. G. (eds) *Performance Analysis of Sport 7*, Cardiff: CPA UWIC Press, pp. 337–48.

Brown, E. and O'Donoghue, P. G. (2007) 'Relating Reliability to Analytical Goals in Performance Analysis', *International Journal of Performance Analysis of Sport (e)*, 7, 28–34.

Bruggeman, G-P., Koszewski, D. and Muller, H. (1999) *Biomechanical Research Project: Athens 1997 – Final Report*, International Athletic Federation, Oxford, UK: Meyer and Meyer Sport.

Buekers, M. J. A., Magill, R. A. and Hall, K. G. (1992) 'The Effect of Erroneous Knowledge of Results on Skill Acquisition When Augmented Information is Redundant', *Quarterly Journal of Experimental Psychology* 44, 105–17.

Burry, H. C. and Calcinai, C. J. (1988) 'The Need to Make Rugby Safer', *British Medical Journal*, 6616, 149–50.

Cadopi, M., Chatillon, J. F. and Baldy, R. (1995) 'Representation and Perform-ance: Reproduction of Form and Quality of Movement in Dance by Eight and Eleven-Year-Old Novices', *British Journal of Psychology*, 86, 217–25.

Carling, C., Williams, A. M. and Reilly, T. (2005) *Handbook of Soccer Match Analysis: a Systematic Approach to Improving Performance*, Abingdon, Oxon: Routledge.

Carroll, W. R. and Bandura, A. (1982) 'The Role of Visual Monitoring in Obser-vational Learning of Action Patterns: Making the Unobservable Observable', *Journal of Motor Behavior*, 14, 153–67.

Carroll, W. R. and Bandura, A. (1985) 'Role of Timing of Visual Monitoring and Motor Rehearsal in Observational Learning of Action Patterns', *Journal of Motor Behavior*, 17, 269–81.

Carroll, W. R. and Bandura, A. (1990) 'Representational Guidance of Action Production in Observational Learning: a Causal Analysis', *Journal of Motor Behavior*, 22, 85–97.

Carter, A. (1996) 'Time and Motion Analysis and Heart Rate Monitoring of a Back-Row Forward in First Class Rugby Union Football'. in Hughes M. (ed.) *Notational Analysis of Sport I & II*, Cardiff: UWIC, pp. 145–60.

Chandler, J. M. (1988) *Television and National Sport: The United States and Britain*. Chicago: University of Illinois Press.

Chapman, A. E. and Sanderson, D. J. (1990) 'Muscular Coordination in Sporting Skills', in Winters, J. M. and Woo, S. L-Y (eds) *Multiple Muscle Systems:*

Biomechanics and Movement Organization, New York: Springer-Verlag: pp. 608–20.

Chiviacowsky, S. and Wulf, G. (2005) 'Self-Controlled Feedback is Effective if it is Based on the Learner's Performance', *Research Quarterly for Exercise and Sport*, 76, 42–8.

Church, S. and Hughes, M. D. (1986) Patterns of Play in Association Football – A computerised Analysis. *Communication to First World Congress of Science and Football*, Liverpool, 13–17 April.

Clifford, B. and Hollin, C. (1980) 'Effects of Type of Incident and the Number of Perpetrators on Eyewitness Memory', *Journal of Applied Psychology*, 65, 364–70.

Coakley, J. (2001) *Sport in Society: Issues and Controversies*. New York: McGraw-Hill.

Collier, G. L. and Wright, C. E. (1995) 'Temporal Rescaling of Simple and Complex Ratios in Rhythmic Tapping', *Journal of Experimental Psychology: Human Perception and Performance*, 21, 602–27.

Collinson, L. and Hughes, M. (2002) 'Surface Effect on Strategy of Elite Female Tennis Players', *Journal of Sports Sciences*, 21, 266–7.

Cooper L. A. and Shepard R. N. (1973) 'Chronometric Studies of the Rotation of Mental Images', in Chase W. G. (ed.) *Visual information processing*, New York: Academic Press. pp. 75–176

Cooper, D. L. (1994) 'Sports Rule Changes Over the Years', *Strength and Conditioning*, 16, 70–3.

Cousens, L. (1997) from Diamonds to Dollars: the Dynamics of Change in AAA Baseball Franchises', *Journal of Sports Management*, 11, 316–34.

Craik, F. I. M. and Lockhart, R. S. (1972) 'Levels of Processing: a Framework for Memory Research', *Journal of Verbal Learning and Verbal Behavior*, 11, 671–84.

Crossman, E. R. F. W. (1959) 'A Theory of Acquisition of Speed Skill', *Ergonomics*, 2, 153–66.

Croucher, J. S. (1996) 'The Use of Notational Analysis in Determining Optimal Strategies in Sports', in Hughes, M. (ed.) *Notational Analysis of Sport – I & II*, Cardiff: UWIC, pp. 3–20.

Dancs, H., Hughes, M. and O'Donoghue, P. (eds) (2006) *Notation of Sport VII*. Cardiff: CPA, UWIC.

Davies, G. (1999) 'Screen Tests Could Turn off Rugby's Faithful Supporters', *The Times*, 3 December, p. 60.

Di Salvo, V., Collins, A., McNeill, B. and Cardinale, M. (2006) 'Validation of Prozonefi: a New Video-Based Performance Analysis System', *International Journal of Performance Analysis of Sport (e)*, 6, 108–19.

Docherty, D. (1982) 'A Comparison of Heart Rate Response in Racket Sports', *British Journal of Sports Medicine*, 16, 96–100.

Doggart, L., Keane, S., Reilly, T. and Stanhope, J. (1993) 'A Task Analysis of Gaelic Football', in Reilly, T., Clarys, J. and Stibbe, A. (eds) *Science and Football II*. London: E&FN Spon, pp. 186–9.

Downey, J. C. (1973) *The Singles Game*. London: EP Publications.

Drianovski, Y. and Otcheva, G. (2002) 'Survey of the Game Styles of Some of the Best Asian Players At the 12th World University Table Tennis Championships (Sofia, 1998)', in *Table Tennis Sciences 4*, Lausanne: ITTF, pp. 3–9.

Elliott, B., Burnett, A., Stockill, N. and Bartlett, R. M. (1996) 'The Fast Bowler in Cricket: a Sports Medicine Perspective', *Sports Exercise and Injury* 1, 201–6.

Eom, H. J. (1988) 'A Mathematical Analysis of Team Performance in Volleyaball'. *Canadian Journal of Sports Sciences*, 13, 55–6.

Feiner, S. K. (2002) Augmented reality: a new way of seeing. *Scientific American*, April, 50–5.

Fennell, T., Jenish, D., Cazzin, J., Todd, D., Daly, J., Harrison, M. and Gregor, A. (1990) 'The Riches of Sport', *Macleans* April, 42–5.

Flanagan, J. C. (1954) 'The Critical Incident Technique', *Psychological Bulletin*, 51, 327–58.

Franks, I. M. (1988) 'Analysis of Association Football', *Soccer Journal*, September/October, 35–43.

Franks, I. M. (1992) 'Computer Technology and the Education of Soccer Coaches', in Reilly, T. (ed.) *Science and Football II*, London: E&FN Spon.

Franks, I. M. (1993) 'The Effects of Experience on the Detection and Location of Performance Differences in a Gymnastic Technique', *Research Quarterly for Exercise and Sport*, 64, 227–31.

Franks, I. M. (1993) 'The Effects of Experience on the Detection and Location of Performance Differences in a Gymnastic Technique', *Research Quarterly for Exercise and Sport*, 64, 227–31.

Franks, I. M. (1993) 'The Effects of Experience on the Detection and Location of Performance Differences in a Gymnastic Technique', *Research Quarterly for Exercise and Sport*, 64, 227–31.

Franks, I. M. (1996) 'Use of Feedback by Coaches and Players', in Reilly, T., Bangsbo, J. and Hughes, M. (eds) *Science and Football III*. London: E&FN Spon.

Franks, I. M. (1996b) 'The Science of Match Analysis', in Reilly, T. (ed.) *Science and Soccer*, London: E&FN Spon.

Franks, I. M. (2000) 'The Structure of Sport and the Collection of Relevant Data', in Baca, A. (ed.) *Computer Science in Sport*, Vienna, Austria: OBV and HPT publishers, pp. 226–40.

Franks, I. M. and Goodman, D. (1984) 'A Hierarchical Approach to Performance Analysis', *SPORTS*, June.

Franks, I. M. and Goodman, D. (1986a) 'A Systematic Approach to Analyzing Sports Performance', *Journal of Sports Sciences* 4, 49–59.

Franks, I. M. and Goodman, D. (1986b) 'Computer-Assisted Technical Analysis of Sport', *Coaching Review*, May/June, 58–64.

Franks, I. M. and McGarry, T. (1996) 'Development, Application and Limitation of a Stochastic Markov Model in Explaining Championship Squash Performance', *Research Quarterly for Exercise and Sport*, 67, 406–15.

Franks, I. M. and Miller, G. (1986) 'Eyewitness Testimony in Sport', *Journal of Sport Behavior* 9, 39–45.

Franks, I. M. and Miller, G. (1991) 'Training Coaches to Observe and Remember', *Journal of Sports Sciences*, 9, 285–97.

Franks, I. M. and Nagelkerke, P. (1988) 'The Use of Computer Interactive Video Technology in Sport Analysis', *Ergonomics*, 13, 1593–1603.

Franks, I. M. and Nagelkerke, P. (1988) 'The Use of Computer Interactive Video Technology in Sport Analysis', *Ergonomics*, 31, 1593–1603.

Franks, I. M., Goodman, D. and Miller, G. (1983a) 'Analysis of Performance: Qualitative or Quantitative', *SPORTS*, March.

Franks, I. M., Goodman, D. and Miller, G. (1983b) 'Human Factors in Sport Systems: an Empirical Investigation of Events in Team Games', *Proceedings of the Human Factors Society – 27th Annual meeting*, pp. 383–6.

Franks, I. M., Goodman, D. and Paterson, D. (1986) 'The Real Time Analysis of Sport: an Overview', *Canadian Journal of Sports Sciences*, 11, 55–7.

Franks, I. M., Nagelkerke, P. and Goodman, D. (1989) 'Computer Controlled Video: an Inexpensive IBM Based System', *Computers in Education*, 13 (1), 33–44.

Franks, I. M., Wilberg, B. R., and Fishburne, G. (1982) 'The Process of Decision Making: an. Application to Team Games', *Coaching Science Update*, 12–16.

Fuller, N (1990) 'Computerised Performance Analysis in Netball', in Alderson, J., Fuller, N. and Treadwell, P. (eds) *Match Analysis in Sport: A 'State of Art' Review*, Leeds: National Coaching Foundation.

Fullerton, H. S. (1912) 'The Inside Game: the Science of Baseball', *The American Magazine*, LXX, 2–13.

Gaitanos, G. C., Williams, C., Boobis, L. H. and Brooks, S. (1993) 'Human Muscle Metabolism During Intermittent Maximal Exercise', *Journal of Applied Physiology*, 75, 712–9.

Gamble, D., Young, E. and O'Donoghue, P. G. (2007) 'Activity Profile and Heart Rate Response of Referees in Gaelic Football', *World Congress of Science and Football VI*, 16–20th January 2007, Antalya, Turkey.

Gardiner, S., Felix, A., James, M., Welch, R. and O'Leary, J. (1998) *Sports Law*. London: Cavendish Publishing.

Garganta, J. and Gonçalves, G. (1997) 'Comparison of Successful Attacking Play in Male and Female Portuguese National Soccer Teams', in Hughes, M. D. (ed.) *Notational Analysis of Sport – I & II*, Cardiff: UWIC, pp. 79–85.

Gerrard, D. F. (1998) 'The Use of Padding in Rugby Union', *Sports Medicine*, 25, 329–32.

Giatsis, G. (2003) 'The Effect of Changing the Rules on Score Fluctuation and Match Duration in the FIVB Women's Beach Volleyball', *International Journal of Performance Analysis in Sport*, 3, 57–64.

Gissane, C., Jennings, D., White, J. and Cumine, A. (1998) 'Injury in Summer Rugby League Football: the Experience of One Club', *British Journal of Sports Medicine*, 32, 149–52.

Goodwin, J. E. and Meeuwsen, H. J. (1995) 'Using Bandwidth Knowledge of Results to Alter Relative Frequencies During Motor Skill Acquisition', *Research Quarterly for Exercise and Sport*, 66, 99–104.

Green, T. (1985) 'Rule Changes for Safety in Canadian Amateur Football', *Audible*, Spring, 26–30.

Haake, S. J., Chadwick, S. G., Dignall, R. J., Goodwill, S. and Rose, P. (2000) 'Engineering Tennis – Slowing the Game Down', *Sports Engineering*, 3, 131–43.

Hackney, R. G. (1994) 'Nature, Prevention, and Management of Injury in Sport. (ABC of Sports Medicine)'. *British Medical Journal*, 308, 1356–60.

Hall, C., Moore, J., Annett, J. and Rodgers, W. (1997) 'Recalling Demonstrated and Guided Movements Using Imaginary and Verbal Rehearsal Strategies', *Research Quarterly for Exercise and Sport*, 68, 136–44.

Hammond, J., Hosking, D. and Hole, C. (1999) 'An Exploratory Study of the Effectiveness of Rule Changes in Netball. Communications to the Fourth International Conference on Sport', *Journal of Sport Sciences*, 17, 916–17.

Hayes, S. J., Hodges, N. J., Scott, A. M., Horn, R. R. and Williams, A. M. (2007). 'The Efficacy of Demonstrations in Teaching Children an Unfamiliar Movement Skill: the Effects of Object Orientated Actions and Point-Light Demonstrations', *Journal of Sports Sciences*, 25, 599–675.

Held, R. (1965) 'Plasticity in the Sensory-Motor System', *Scientific American* 213, 84–94.

Held, R. and Hein, A. (1958) 'Adaptation of Disarranged Hand-Eye Coordination Contingent Upon Re-Afferent Stimulation', *Perceptual and Motor Skills*, 8, 87–90.

Held, R. and Hein, A. (1963) 'Movement-Produced Stimulation in the

Development of Visually Guided Behavior', *Journal of Comparative and Physiological Psychology*, 56, 872–76.

Herbert, P. and Tong, R. (1996) 'A Comparison of the Positional Demands of Wingers and Back Row Forwards Using Movement Analysis and Heart Rate Telemetry', in Hughes, M. D. (ed.) *Notational Analysis of Sport I & II*, Cardiff: UWIC, pp. 177–82.

Hodges, N. J. and Franks, I. M. (2000) 'Focus of Attention and Coordination Bias: Implications for Learning a Novel Bimanual Task', *Human Movement Science*, 19, 843–67.

Hodges, N. J. and Franks, I. M. (2001) Learning a Coordination Skill: Interactive Effects of Instruction and Feedback', *Research Quarterly for Exercise and Sport*, 72, 132–42.

Hodges, N. J. and Franks, I. M. (2002) 'Learning As a Function of Coordination Bias: Building Upon Pre-Practice Behaviours', *Human Movement Science*, 21, 231–58.

Hodges, N. J. and Franks, I. M. (2002) 'Modelling Coaching Practice: the Role of Instruction and Coaching', *Journal of Sports Sciences*, 21, 793–811.

Hodges, N. J. and Franks, I. M. (2004) 'Instructions, demonstrations and the learning process: creating and constraining movement options', in Williams, A. M. and Hodges, N. J. (eds), *Skill Acquisition in Sport: Research, Theory and Practice*, London: Routledge, pp. 145–74.

Hodges, N. J. and Lee, T. D. (1999) 'The Role of Augmented Information Prior to Learning a Bimanual Visual-Motor Coordination Task: Do Instructions of the Movement Pattern Facilitate Learning Relative to Discovery Learning', *British Journal of Psychology*, 90, 389–403.

Hodges, N. J., Chua, R. and Franks, I. M. (2003) 'The Role of Video in Facilitating Perception and Action of a Novel Coordination Movement', *Journal of Motor Behavior*, 35, 247–60.

Hodges, N. J., Hayes, S. J., Eaves, D., Horn, R. and Williams, A. M. (2006) 'End-Point Trajectory Matching as a Method for Teaching Kicking Skills', *International Journal of Sport Psychology*, 37, 230–47.

Hodges, N. J., Hayes, S., Breslin, G. and Williams, A. M. (2005) 'An Evaluation of the Minimal Constraining Information during Movement Observation and Reproduction', *Acta Psychologica*, 119, 264–82.

Hodges, N. J., Williams, A. M., Hayes, S. J. and Breslin, G. (2007) 'End-Point and End-Effector Information in Modeling', *Journal of Sports Sciences*, (in press)

Hodgson Phillips, L., Standen, P. J. and Batt M. E. (1998) 'Effects of Seasonal Change in Rugby League on the Incidence of Injury', *British Journal of Sports Medicine*, 32, 144–8.

Hogan, J. C. and Yanowitz, B. A. (1978) 'The Role of Verbal Estimates of

Movement Error in Ballistic Skill Acquisition', *Journal of Motor Behavior* 10, 133–8.

Hope, W. (2002) 'Whose All Blacks?', *Media, Culture and Society 24*, 235–53.

Hopkins, W. G. (2000) 'Measurement of Reliability in Sports Medicine and Science', *Sports Medicine*, 30, 1–15.

Horn, R., Williams, A. M. and Scott, M. A. (2002) 'Learning from Demonstration: the Role of Visual Search from Video and Point-Light Displays', *Journal of Sport Sciences*, 20, 253–69.

Howells, C. (2000) A comparison of the tactics used by three groups of teams in the first 15 overs of the 1999 cricket World Cup. *Unpublished dissertation, B.Sc. Sport and Exercise Science*, Cardiff.

Hubbard, M. and Alaways, L. W. (1989) 'Rapid and Accurate Estimation of Release Conditions in the Javelin Throw', *Journal of Biomechanics*, 22, 583–95.

Hughes, M. D. (1985) 'A Comparison of the Patterns of Play of Squash', in Brown, I. D., Goldsmith, R., Coombes, K. and Sinclair, M. A. (eds) *International Ergonomics '85*, London: Taylor & Francis, pp. 139–41.

Hughes, M. D. (1986) 'A Review of Patterns of Play in Squash', in Watkins, J., Reilly, T. and Burwitz, L. (eds) *Sports Science*, London: E&FN Spon, pp. 363–8.

Hughes, M. D. (1988) 'Computerised Notation Analysis in Field Games', *Ergonomics*, 31, 1585–92.

Hughes, M. D. (1993) 'Notational Analysis of Football', in Reilly, T., Clarys, J. and Stibbe, A. (eds) *Science and Football II*, London: E&FN Spon, pp. 151–9.

Hughes, M. D. (1995a) 'Using notational analysis to create a more exciting scoring system for squash', in Atkinson, G. and Reilly, T. (eds) *Sport, Leisure and Ergonomics*, London: E&FN Spon, 243–7.

Hughes, M. D. (1995b) 'Computerised Notation of Racket Sports', in Reilly, T., Hughes, M. and Lees, A. (eds) *Science and Racket Sports*, E&FN Spon: London, pp. 249–56.

Hughes, M. D. (1998) 'The Application of Notational Analysis to Racket Sports', in Lees, A., Maynard, I., Hughes, M. and Reilly T. (eds) *Science and Racket Sports II*, London: E&FN Spon, pp. 211–20.

Hughes, M. D. (ed.) (2000a) *Notational Analysis of Sport III*, Cardiff: UWIC.

Hughes, M. D. (2000b) 'Do Perturbations Exist in Soccer?', in Hughes, M. (ed.) *Notational Analysis of Sport III*, Cardiff: UWIC, pp. 16–24.

Hughes, M. D. (2001a) 'Perturbations and Critical Incidents in Soccer', in Hughes, M. and Tavares, F. (eds) *Notational Analysis of Sport IV*, Porto: Faculty of Sports Sciences and Education, University of Porto, Portugal, pp. 23–33.

Hughes, M. D. (2004) Performance Analysis – a mathematical perspective.

EIJPAS, International Journal of Performance Analysis Sport (Electronic), 4, 97–139.

Hughes, M. D. and Bartlett, R. (2002) 'The Use of Performance Indicators in Performance Analysis', *Journal of Sports Sciences*, 20, 739–54.

Hughes, M. D. and Clarke, S. (1995) 'Surface Effect on Patterns of Play of Elite Tennis Players', in Reilly, T., Hughes, M. and Lees, A. (eds) *Science and Racket Sports*, London: E&FN Spon, pp. 272–8.

Hughes, M. D. and Cunliffe, S. (1986) Notational Analysis of Field Hockey. *Proceedings of the BASS Conference*, Birmingham University, September.

Hughes, M. D. and Franks, I. M. (1991) 'A Time-Motion Analysis of Squash Players Using a Mixed-Image Video Tracking System', *Ergonomics*, 37, 23–9.

Hughes, M. D. and Franks, I. M. (1997) *Notational Analysis of Sport*, London: E&FN Spon.

Hughes, M. D. and Franks, I. M. (2004) *Notational Analysis of Sport II – Improving Coaching and Performance in Sport*, E&FN Spon. London.

Hughes, M. D. and Franks, I. M. (2005) 'Analysis of Passing Sequences, Shots and Goals in Soccer', *Journal of Sports Science*, 23, 509–14.

Hughes, M. D. and Knight, P. (1995) 'Playing Patterns of Elite Squash Players, Using English and Point-per-Rally Scoring', in Reilly, T., Hughes, M. and Lees, A. (eds) *Science and Racket Sports*, E&FN Spon: London, pp. 257–9.

Hughes, M. D. and McGarry, T. (1989) 'Computerised Notational Analysis of Squash', in Hughes, M. (ed.) *Science in Squash*, Liverpool: Liverpool Polytechnic.

Hughes, M. D. and Reed, D. (2005) Creating a performance profile using perturbations in soccer. *Proceedings of 4th International Scientific Conference on Kinesiology*, Opatija, University of Zagreb, Croatia, September.

Hughes, M. D. and Robertson, C. (1997) 'Using Computerised Notational Analysis to Create a Template for Elite Squash and its Subsequent use in Designing Hand Notation Systems for Player Development', in Lees, A., Hughes, M., Reilly, T. and Maynard, I. (eds) *Science and Racket Sports II*, London: E&FN Spon, pp. 227–34.

Hughes, M. D. and Sykes, I. (1994) 'Computerised Notational Analysis of the Effects of the Law Changes in Soccer upon Patterns of Play', *Journal of Sport Sciences*, 12, 180.

Hughes, M. D. and Tavares, F. (eds) (2001) *Notational Analysis of Sport IV*, Porto: Faculty of Sports Sciences and Education.

Hughes, M. D. and Taylor, M. (1998) 'A Comparison of Patterns of Play between the Top Under 18 Junior Tennis Players in Britain and the Rest of the World', in Lees, A., Maynard, I., Hughes, M. and Reilly, T. (eds) *Science and Racket Sports II*, London: E&FN Spon, pp. 260–64.

Hughes, M. D. and Wells, J. (2002) 'Analysis of Penalties Taken in Shoot-Outs', eIJPAS International Journal of Performance Analysis Sport (Electronic), 2, 55–72.

Hughes, M. D., Cooper, S. M. and Nevill, A. (2004) 'Analysis of Notation Data: Reliability', in Hughes, M. and Franks, I. M. (eds) Notational Analysis of Sport, 2nd Edition, London: Routledge, pp. 189–204.

Hughes, M. D., Dawkins, N. and David, R. (1997a) Perturbation effect in soccer. Notational Analysis of Sport III, Cardiff: CPA, UWIC, pp. 1–14.

Hughes, M. D., Dawkins, N. and Langridge, C. (2000) 'Perturbations not Leading to Shots in Soccer', in Hughes, M. (ed.) Notational Analysis of Sport III, Cardiff: CPA, UWIC, pp. 108–16.

Hughes, M. D., Dawkins, N., David, R. and Mills, J. (1997b) 'The Perturbation Effect and Goal Opportunities in Soccer', Journal of Sports Sciences 16, 20.

Hughes, M. D., Dawkins, N., David, R. and Mills, J. (1998) 'The Perturbation Effect and Goal Opportunities in Soccer', Journal of Sports Sciences 16, 20.

Hughes, M. D., Fenwick, B. and Murray, S. (2006) 'Expanding Normative Profiles of Elite Squash Players Using Momentum of Winners and Errors', eIJPAS International Journal of Performance Analysis Sport (Electronic) 6, 145–54.

Hughes, M. D., Franks, L. M. and Nagelkerke, P. (1989) 'A Video System for the Quantitative Motion Analysis of Athletes in Competitive Sport', Journal of Human Movement Studies 17, 212–27.

Hughes, M. D., Ponting, R., Murray, S. and James, N. (2002) Some example of computerised systems for feedback in performance analysis. UKSI website: www.uksi.com, October.

Hughes, M. D., Robertson, K. and Nicholson, A. (1988) 'An Analysis of 1984 World Cup of Association Football', in Reilly, T., Lees, A., Davids, K. and Murphy, W. (eds) Science and Football, London: E&FN Spon, pp. 363–7.

Hughes, M. G., Rose, G. and Amaral, I. (2005) 'The Influence of Recovery Duration on Blood Lactate Accumulation in Repeated Sprint Activity', Journal of Sports Sciences, 23, 130–1.

Hughes, M. T. and Hughes, M. D. (2005) 'The Evolution of Computerised Notational Analysis Through the Example of Squash', International Journal of Computers in Sport Science, 4, 5–20.

Hughes, M. T., Howells, M., Hughes, M. and Murray, S. (2007) 'Using Perturbations in Elite Men's Squash to Generate Performance Profiles', in Lees, A., Kahn, J-F. and Maynard, I. (eds) Science and Racket Sports IV, London: E&FN Spon.

International Rugby Board (1997) Charter on the Game. Dublin: International Rugby.

James, N. (2006) 'Notational Analysis in Soccer: Past, Present and Future', in

Dancs, H., Hughes, M. and O'Donoghue, P. (eds) *Notation of Sport VII*. Cardiff: CPA, UWIC, pp. 35–53.

James, N., Mellalieu, S. D. and Jones, N. M. P. (2005) 'The Development of Position-Specific Performance Indicators in Professional Rugby Union', *Journal of Sports Sciences*, 23, 63–72.

Johansson, G. (1975) 'Visual Motion Perception', *Scientific American*, 232, 76–89.

Johnson, W. O. (1971) *Super Spectator and the Electric Lilliputians*, Boston: Little, Brown and Co.

Keating, P. and O'Donoghue, P. G. (1999) 'A Time-Motion and Heart Rate Analysis of Netball Competition', *Book of Abstracts, Exercise and Sports Science Association of Ireland*, Limerick, 19th November 1999.

Kelly, M. and Pedersen, P. (2001) 'Hardball-Hardbat: a Call for Change from Aluminium to Wooden Baseball Bats in the NCAA', *The Sport Journal*, 4, 3.

Kelso, S. (1999) *Dynamic Patterns. The Self Organization of Brains and Behaviour*, Cambridge: Bradford Book.

Kernodle, M. W. and Carlton, L. G. (1992) 'Information Feedback and the Learning of Multiple-Degree-of-Freedom Activities', *Journal of Motor Behaviour*, 24, 187–96.

Kernodle, M. W., Johnson, R. and Arnold, D. R. (2001) 'Verbal Instruction for Correcting Errors Versus Such Instructions Plus Videotape Replay on Learning the Overhand Throw', *Perceptual Motor Skills*, 92, 1039–51.

Kew, F. (1986) 'Playing the Game: an Ethnomethodological Perspective', *International Review for the Sociology of Sport*, 21, 305–21.

Kew, F. (1987) 'Contested Rules: an Explanation of How Games Change', *International Review for the Sociology of Sport*, 22, 125–135.

King, S. and O'Donoghue, P. (2003) 'Specific High Intensity Training Based on Activity Profile', *International Journal of Performance Analysis of Sport (e)*, 3, 130–44.

Kirkendall, D. T., Speer, K. P. and Garrett, J. R. (1995) Injuries in American Football. In: T. Reilly, J. Bangsbo and M. Hughes, *Science and Football III*, London: E&FN Spon, pp. 132–8.

Korhonen, M. T., Mero, A. and Suoninen, H. (2003) 'Age Related Differences in 100m Sprint Performance in Male and Female Masters Runners', *Medicine and Science in Sport and Exercise*, 35, 1419–28.

Kujala, U. M., Taimela, S., Antti-Poika, I., Orava, S., Tuominen, R. and Myllynen, P. (1995) 'Acute Injuries in Soccer, Ice Hockey, Volleyball, Basketball, Judo and Karate: Analysis of National Registry Data', *British Medical Journal*, 311, 1465–8.

Ladany, S. P. and Machol, R. E. (eds) (1977) *Optimal Strategies in Sports*, Amsterdam: North Holland.

Lai, Q. and Shea, C. H. (1998) 'Generalized Motor Program (GMP) Learning: Effects of Reduced Frequency of Knowledge of Results and Practice Variability', *Journal of Motor Behavior*, 30, 51–9.

Leaman, O. (2001) 'Cheating and Fair Play in Sport', in Morgan, W. J., Meier, K. V. and Schneider, A. J. (eds) *Ethics in Sport*, Illinois: Versa Press.

Lee, A. J. and Garraway, M. W. (2000) 'The Influence of Environmental Factors on Rugby Football Injuries', *Journal of Sport Sciences*, 18, 91–5.

Lee, T. D. and Carnahan, H. (1990) 'Bandwidth Knowledge of Results and Motor Learning', *The Quarterly Journal of Experimental Psychology*, 42, 777–89.

Lee, T. D., Swinnen, S. P. and Verschueren, S. (1995) 'Relative Phase Alterations During Bimanual Skill Acquisition', *Journal of Motor Behavior*, 27, 263–74.

Lewis, M. (2003) *Moneyball: the Art of Winning an Unfair Game*, London: WW Norton & Company Ltd.

Liao, C. and Masters, R. S. W. (2001) 'Analogy Learning: a Means to Implicit Motor Learning', *Journal of Sports Sciences*, 19, 307–19.

Liddle, S. D, Murphy, M. H. and Bleakley, E.W. (1996) 'A Comparison of the Physiological Demands of Singles and Doubles Badminton: a Heart Rate and Time/Motion Analysis', *Journal of Human Movement Studies*, 30, 159–76.

Liddle, S. D. and O'Donoghue, P. G. (1998) 'Notational Analysis of Rallies in European Circuit Badminton', in Lees, A., Maynard, I., Hughes, M. and Reilly, T. (eds) *Science and Racket Sports II*, E&FN Spon, London, pp. 275–81.

Liebermann, D. G. (1997) 'Temporal Structure as a Primitive of Movement for Skill Acquisition', in Bar-Eli, M and Lidor, R. (eds) *Proceedings of the World Conference of Sport Psychology*, Israel: Wingate Institute, pp. 496–9.

Liebermann, D. G., Katz, L., Hughes, M. D., Bartlett, R. M., McClements, J. and Franks, I. M. (2002) 'Advances in the Application of Information Technology to Sports Performance', *Journal of Sports Science*, 20, 755–69.

Liebermann, D. G., Raz, T. and Dickinson, J. (1988) 'On Intentional and Incidental Learning and Estimation of Temporal and Spatial Information', *Journal of Human Movement Studies* 15, 191–204.

Loland, S. (1998) 'Fair Play: Historical Anachronism or Topical Ideal?', in McNamee, M. J. and Parry, S. J. (eds) *Ethics and Sport*, London: E&FN Spon, pp. 57–64.

Longmore, A. (1994) 'Absurd Cup Rule Obscures Football's Final Goal', *The Times*, 1 February, p. 51.

Lothian, F. and Farrally, M. (1994) 'A Time-Motion Analysis of Women's Field Hockey'. *Journal of Human Movement Studies*, 26, 255–65.

Lumpkin, A., Stoll, S. K. and Beller, J. M. (1999) *Sport Ethics: Applications for Fair Play*, London: McGraw-Hill.

Lyle, J. (2002) *Sports Coaching Concepts: A Framework for Coaching Behaviour*. London: Routledge.

Lyons, K (1996) 'Lloyd Messersmith', in Hughes, M. (ed.) *Notational Analysis of Sport – I & II*, Cardiff: UWIC, pp. 49–59.

Magill, R. A. (2001) *Motor learning: Concepts and applications* (Sixth International Edition), Singapore: McGraw-Hill International Editions.

Magill, R. A. and Schoenfelder-Zohdi, B. (1996) 'A Visual Model and Knowledge of Performance As Sources of Information for Learning a Rhythmic Gymnastics Skill', *International Journal of Sport Psychology*, 24, 358–69.

Magill, R. A. and Wood, C. A. (1986) 'Knowledge of Results Precision As a Learning Variable in Motor Skill Acquisition', *Research Quarterly for Exercise and Sport* 57, 170–73.

Malpass, R. and Devine, P. (1981) 'Guided Memory in Eyewitness Identification', *Journal of Applied Psychology*, 66, 343–50.

Martens, R., Burwitz, L. and Zuckerman, J. (1976) 'Modeling Effects on Motor Performance', *Research Quarterly*, 47, 277–91.

Mason, D. S. (1999) 'What is the Sports Product and Who Buys It? The Marketing of Sports Leagues', *European Journal of Marketing*, 33 (3), 402–18.

Masters, R. S. W. (1992) 'Knowledge, Knerves and Know-How: the Role of Explicit Versus Implicit Knowledge in the Breakdown of a Complex Motor Skill Under Pressure', *British Journal of Psychology*, 83, 343–58.

Masters, R. S. W. (2000) 'Theoretical Aspects of Implicit Learning in Sport', *International Journal of Sport Psychology* 31, 530–41.

Masters, R. S. W. and Maxwell, J. P. (2004) 'Implicit Motor Learning, Reinvestment and Movement Disruption: What You Don't Know Won't Hurt You?', in Williams, A. M. and Hodges, N. J. (eds) *Skill Acquisition in Sport: Research, Theory and Practice*, London: Routledge, pp. 207–28.

McCullagh, P. and Weiss, M. R. (2001) 'Modeling: Considerations for Motor Skill Performance and Psychological Responses', in Singer, R. N., Hausenblas, H. A. and Janelle C. M. (eds) *Handbook of sport psychology*, 2nd edn, Chichester: Wiley, pp. 205–38.

McErlean, C. A., Cassidy, J. and O'Donoghue, P. G. (2000) 'Time-Motion Analysis of Gender and Positional Effect on Work-Rate in Gaelic Football', *Journal of Human Movement Studies*, 38, 269–86.

McGarry, T. and Franks, I. M. (1994) 'A Stochastic Approach to Predicting Competition Squash Match-Play', *Journal of Sports Sciences*, 12, 573–84.

McGarry, T. and Franks, I. M. (1995) 'Modeling Competitive Squash Performance from Quantitative Analysis', *Human Performance*, 8, 113–29.

McGarry, T. and Franks, I. M. (1996a) 'Analysing Championship Squash Match Play: In Search of a System Description', in Haake, S. (ed.) *The Engineering of Sport*. Rotterdam: Balkema, pp. 263–269.

McGarry, T. and Franks, I. M. (1996b) 'In Search of Invariance in Championship Squash', in Hughes, M. D. (ed.) *Notational Analysis of Sport – I & II*, Cardiff: UWIC, pp. 281–8.

McGarry, T. and Franks, I. M. (1996c) 'Development Application and Limitation of a Stochastic Markov Model in Explaining Championship Squash Performance', *Research Quarterly for Exercise and Sport*, 67, 406–15.

McGarry, T. and Franks, I. M. (1996d) 'In Search of Invariant Athletic Behaviour in Competitive Sport Systems: an Example from Championship Squash Match-Play', *Journal of Sports Sciences*, 14, 445–56.

McGarry, T. and Perl, J. (2004) 'Modelling Sport Performance', in Hughes, M. and Franks, I. M. (eds) *Notational Analysis of Sport II – Improving Coaching and Performance in Sport*, E&FN Spon. London, pp. 227–42.

McLaughlin, E. and O'Donoghue, P. G. (2002a) 'The Development of Cardio-Vascular Fitness in Primary School Children', *Journal of Sports Sciences*, 20, 38–9.

McLaughlin, E. and O'Donoghue, P. G. (2002b) 'Time-Motion Analysis of Playground Activity of Primary School Children in Northern Ireland', *Journal of Sports Sciences*, 20, 24.

McLaughlin, E. and O'Donoghue, P. G. (2004) 'Analysis of Primary School Children's Physical Activity in the Playground: a Complementary Approach', in O'Donoghue, P. G. and Hughes, M. D. (eds) *Performance Analysis of Sport 6*, Cardiff: CPA Press, UWIC, pp. 233–40.

Messersmith, L. L. and Corey, S. M. (1931) 'Distance Traversed by a Basketball Player', *Research Quarterly*, 2 (2) 57–60.

Miall, R. C. Weir D. J., Wolpert D. M. and Stein J. F. (1993) 'Is the Cerebellum a Smith Predictor?', *Journal of Motor Behavior*, 25, 203–16.

More K. G. and Franks, I. M. (2004) 'Measuring Coaching Effectiveness', in Hughes, M. and Franks, I. M. (eds) *Notational Analysis in Sport*, 2nd edn: *Systems for Better Coaching and Performance*, London: E&FN Spon, pp. 242–56.

More, K. G. and Franks, I. M. (1996) 'Analysis and modification of verbal coaching behaviour: The usefulness of a data driven intervention strategy', *Journal of Sports Sciences*, 14, 523–43.

Mosteller, F. (1979) 'A Resistant Analysis of 1971 and 1972 Professional Football', in Goldstein, J. H. (ed.) *Sports, Games and Play*, New Jersey: Lawrence Erlbaum, pp. 371–401.

Murray, S. and Hughes, M. (2001) 'Tactical performance profiling in elite level senior squash', in Hughes, M. and Franks, I. M. (eds) *Pass.com*, Cardiff: CPA, UWIC, pp. 185–94.

Murray, S. and Hughes, M. T. (2006) *The Working Performance Analyst. Presentation at the First International Workshop of Performance Analysis.* Cardiff: International Society of Performance Analysis of Sport (ISPAS).

Murray, S., Maylor, D. and Hughes, M. (1998) 'The Effect of Computerised Analysis as Feedback on Performance of Elite Squash Players', in Lees, A., Maynard, I., Hughes, M. and Reilly, T. (eds) *Science and Racket Sports II*, London: E&FN Spon, pp. 235–40.

Nevill, M. E., Bogdanis, G. C., Boobis, L. H., Lakomy, H. K. A. and Williams, C. (1994) 'Muscle Metabolism and Performance During Sprinting', in Maughan, R. J. and Shirreffs, S. M. (eds) *Biochemistry of Exercise IX*, Champaign, Il: Human Kinetics Publishers, pp. 243–59.

Newell, K. M. (1991) 'Motor Skill Acquisition', *Annual Review of Psychology*, 42, 213–37.

Newell, K. M., Morris, L. R. and Scully, D. M. (1985) 'Augmented Information and The Acquisition of Skill in Physical Activity', in Terjung, R. J. (ed.) *Exercise and Sport Science Reviews* 13, 235–61.

Norton, K. I., Craig, N. P. and Olds, T. (1999) 'The Evolution of Australian Football', *Journal of Science and Medicine in Sport*, 2 (4), 389–404.

Norton, K., Schwerdt, S. and Lange, K. (2001) Evidence for the aetiology of injuries in Australian football. *British Journal of Sport Medicine*, 35, 418–23.

Odetoyinbo, K., Sapsford, P. and Thomas, S. (1997) 'Analysis of the Effects for the 1994 FIFA Experiment on Semi-Professional Soccer', *Journal of Sport Sciences*, 5 (1), 20.

O'Donoghue, P. (2007) 'Reliability Issues in Performance Analysis', *International Journal of Performance Analysis in Sport*, 7, 35–48.

O'Donoghue, P. and Hughes, M. (eds) (2004). *Notational Analysis of Sport VI*, Cardiff: UWIC.

O'Donoghue, P. and Ingram, B. (2001) 'A Notational Analysis of Elite Tennis Strategy', *Journal of Sports Sciences*, 19, 107–15.

O'Donoghue, P. and Parker, D. (2001) 'Time-Motion Analysis of FA Premier League Soccer Competition', in Hughes, M. and Franks, I (eds) *Performance Analysis, Sports Science and Computers*, Cardiff: UWIC Press, pp. 263–6.

O'Donoghue, P. G, Dubitzky, W., Lopes, P., Berrar, D., Lagan, K., Hassan, D., Bairner, A. and Darby, P. (2003) 'An Evaluation of Quantitative and Qualitative Methods of Predicting the 2002 FIFA World Cup', *Proceedings of the World Congress of Science and Football V*, Lisbon, Portugal, pp. 44–5.

O'Donoghue, P. G. (1998) 'Time-Motion Analysis of Work-Rate in Elite Soccer', in Hughes, M. and Tavares, F. (eds) *Notational Analysis of Sport IV*, Porto: University of Porto, Centre for Team Sports, pp. 65–70.

O'Donoghue, P. G. (2004) 'Match Analysis in Racket Sports', in Lees, A., Khan, J. F. and Maynard, I. W. (eds) *Science and Racket Sports III*, London: Routledge, pp. 155–62.

O'Donoghue, P. G. and Liddle, S. D. (1998) 'A Notational Analysis of Time Factors of Elite Men's and Ladies' Singles Tennis on Clay and Grass Surfaces', in Lees, A., Maynard, I., Hughes, M. and Reilly, T. (eds) *Science and Racket Sports II*, London: E&FN Spon, pp. 241–6.

O'Donoghue, P. G. and Williams, J. (2004) 'An Evaluation of Human and Computer-Based Predictions of the 2003 Rugby Union World Cup', *International Journal of Computer Science in Sport (e)*, 3 (1), 5–22.

O'Donoghue, P. G., Boyd, M., Lawlor, J. and Bleakley, E. W. (2001) 'Time-Motion Analysis of Elite, Semi-Professional and Amateur Soccer Competition', *Journal of Human Movement Studies*, 41, 1–12.

O'Donoghue, P. G., Hughes, M. G., Rudkin, S., Bloomfield, J., Cairns, G. and Powell, S. (2005a) 'Work-Rate Analysis Using the POWER (Periods of Work Efforts and Recoveries) System', *International Journal of Performance Analysis of Sport (e)*, 4, 5–21.

O'Donoghue, P. G. (2005), An Algorithm to use the Kappa Statistic to establish Reliability of Computerised Time-Motion Analysis Systems. In *Book of Abstracts: 5th International Symposium of Computer Science in Sport, 25th–28th May 2005*, pp.49. Hvar, Croatia: University of Zagreb, Faculty of Kinesiology.

O'Donoghue, P. G. and Loughran, B. J. (1998) 'Analysis of Distance Covered During Intervarsity Netball Competition', *Book of Abstracts, World Congress of Notational Analysis of Sport IV*, Porto, Portugal, 22nd–25th September 1998, p. 75.

O'Donoghue, P. G., Donnelly, O., Hughes, L. and McManus, S. (2004b) 'Time-Motion Analysis of Gaelic Games', *Journal of Sports Sciences*, 22, 255–6.

O'Donoghue, P. G., Rudkin, S., Bloomfield, J., Powell, S., Cairns, G., Dunkerley, A., Davey, P., Probert, G. and Bowater, J. (2005b) 'Repeated Work Activity in English FA Premier League Soccer', *International Journal of Performance Analysis of Sport (e)*, 5, 46–57.

O'Donoghue, P. G., Edgar, S. and McLaughlin, E. (2004a), Season of birth bias in elite cricket and netball, *Journal of Sports Sciences*, 22, 256–257.

Olds, T. (2001) 'The Evolution of Physique in Male Rugby Union Players in the Twentieth Century', *Journal of Sports Sciences*, 19, 253–62.

Olsen, E. and Larsen, O. (1997) 'Use of Match Analysis by Coaches', in Reilly, T.,

Bangsbo, J. and Hughes, M. D. (eds) *Science and Football III*, London: E&FN Spon, pp. 209–20.

Parkkari, J., Kujala, U. M. and Kannus, P. (2001) 'Is It Possible to Prevent Sports Injuries?', *Sports Medicine*, 31, 985–95.

Peakman, T. (2001) Defining perturbations in squash. Undergraduate Dissertation, BSc in Coaching Science, UWIC, Cardiff.

Potter, G. and Carter, A. (1995) 'The Four Year Cycle: a Comparison of the 1991 and 1995 Rugby World Cup Finals', in Hughes, M. (ed.) *Notational Analysis of Sport III*. Cardiff: UWIC, pp. 216–19.

Pritchard, S., Hughes, M. and Evans, S. (2001) 'Rule Changes in Elite Badminton', in Hughes, M. and Franks, I. (eds) *Proceedings of the 5th World Congress of Performance Analysis, Sports Science and Computers (PASS.COM)*. Cardiff: UWIC, pp. 213–22.

Rader, B. G. (1984) *In its own image: How Television has Transformed Sports*. London: Free Press.

Ramsden, P. (1993) *Learning to Teach in Higher Education*. London: Routledge.

Read, B. and Edwards, P. (1992) *Teaching Children to Play Games*, Leeds: White Line Publishing.

Reep, C. and Benjamin, B. (1968) 'Skill and Chance in Association Football', *Journal of the Royal Statistical Society, Series A* 131, 581–5.

Reilly, T. (2003) 'Motion Analysis and Physiological Demands', in Reilly, T. and Williams, A. M. (eds) *Science and Soccer, 2nd Edition*, London: Routledge, pp. 59–72.

Reilly, T. (ed.) (1997) *Science and Soccer*, London: E&FN Spon.

Reilly, T. and Ball, D. (1984), 'The Net Physiological Cost of Dribbling a Soccer Ball'. *Research Quarterly for Exercise and Sport*, 55, 267–71.

Reilly, T. and Thomas, V. (1976) 'A Motion Analysis of Work-Rate in Different Positional Roles in Professional Football Match-Play', *Journal of Human Movement Studies*, 2, 87–97.

Reilly, T., Bangsbo, J. and Hughes, M. (eds) (1997) *Science and Football III*, London: E&FN Spon.

Reilly, T., Clarys, J. and Stibbe, A. (eds) (1993) *Science and Football II*, London: E&FN Spon.

Reilly, T., Hughes, M. and Lees, A. (eds) (1995) *Science and Racket Sports*, London: E&FN Spon.

Reilly, T., Spinks, W. and Murphy, A. (eds) (1993) *Science and Football IV*, London: E&FN Spon.

Richers, T. A. (1995) 'Time-Motion Analysis of the Energy Systems in Elite and Competitive Singles Tennis', *Journal of Human Movement Studies*, 28, 73–86.

Robinson, J., Murphy, M. H. and O'Donoghue, P. G. (1996a) 'Notational

Analysis of Work Rate Within the Various Positional Roles for Elite Female Hockey Players', *Journal of Sports Sciences*, 14, 17.

Robinson, J., Murphy, M. H. and O'Donoghue, P. G. (1996b) 'Combining Monitored Heart Rate Data With Observed Time-Motion Data', in Huges. M. (eds) *Notational Analysis of Sport III*, Cardiff: CPA Press, UWIC, pp. 267–75.

Ross, D., Bird, A. M., Doody, S. G. and Zoeller, M. (1985) 'Effects of Modeling and Videotape Feedback with Knowledge Results on Motor Performance', *Human Movement Science*, 4, 149–57.

Rothstein, A. L. and Arnold, R. K. (1976) 'Bridging the Gap: Application of Research on Videotape Feedback and Bowling', *Motor Skills: Theory into Practice* 1, 35–62.

Salmoni, A., Schmidt, R. A. and Walter, C. B. (1984) 'Knowledge of Results and Motor Learning: a Review and Critical Reappraisal', *Psychological Bulletin*, 95, 355–86.

Sanderson, F. H. (1983) 'A Notation System for Analysing Squash', *Physical Education Review*, 6, 19–23.

Sanderson, F. H. and Way K. I. M. (1977) 'The Development of an Objective Method of Game Analysis in Squash Rackets', *British Journal of Sports Medicine*, 11, 188.

Sanderson, F. H. and Way, K. I. M. (1979) 'The Development of Objective Methods of Game Analysis in Squash Rackets', *British Journal of Sports Medicine*, 11, 188.

Schmidt, R. A. and Lee, T. (2005) *Motor Control and Learning*, 4th edn. Champaign, IL: Human Kinetics.

Schmidt, R. A. and Lee, T. D. (1999) *Motor Control and Learning: a Behavioral Emphasis*, 3rd edn. Champaign, Ill: Human Kinetics Publishers.

Schmidt, R. A., Lange, C. and Young, D. E. (1990) 'Optimizing Summary Knowledge of Results for Skill Learning', *Human Movement Science*, 9, 325–48.

Scott, S., Kingsbury, D., Bennett, S., Davids, K. and Langley, M. (1999) 'Effects of Cricket Ball Colour and Illuminance Levels on Catching Behaviour in Professional Cricketers', *Ergonomics*, 43 (10), 1681–8.

Scully, D. M. and Newell, K. M. (1985) 'Observational Learning and the Acquisition of Motor Skills: Toward a Visual Perception Perspective', *Journal of Human Movement Studies*, 11, 169–86.

Shaw, J. and O'Donoghue, P. G. (2004) 'The Effect of Scoreline on Work Rate in Amateur Soccer', in O'Donoghue, P. G. and Hughes, M. D. (eds) *Performance Analysis of Sport 6*, Cardiff: CPA Press, UWIC, pp. 84–91.

Shea, C. H. and Wulf, G. (1999) 'Enhancing Motor Learning Through External-Focus Instructions and Feedback', *Human Movement Science* 18, 553–71.

Shepard, R. N. and Metzler, J. (1971) 'Mental Rotation of Three-Dimensional Objects', *Science*, 171, 701–03.

Sherwood, D. E. (1988) 'Effect of Bandwidth Knowledge of Results on Movement Consistency', *Perceptual and Motor Skills*, 66, 535–42.

Sherwood, D. E. and Rios, V. (2001) 'Divided Attention in Bimanual Aiming Movements: Effects on Movement Accuracy', *Research Quarterly for Exercise and Sport*, 72, 210–18.

Smith, J. C. and Hill, D. W. (1991) 'Contribution of Energy Systems During a Wingate Power Test', *British Journal of Sports Medicine*, 25, 196–9.

Spencer, M., Lawrence, S., Rechichi, C., Bishop, D., Dawson, B. and Goodman, C. (2004) 'Time-Motion Analysis of Elite Field Hockey, With Special Reference to Repeated-Sprint Activity', *Journal of Sports Sciences*, 22, 843–50.

Steele, J.R. and Chad, K.E. (1991) 'Relationship between Movement Patterns Performed in Match Play and in Training by Skilled Netballers', *Journal of Human Movement Studies*, 20, 249–78.

Swinnen, S. P. (1996) 'Information Feedback for Motor Skill Learning: A Review', in Zelaznik, H. N. (ed.) *Advances in motor learning and control*, Champaign, IL: Human Kinetics, pp. 37–66.

Swinnen, S. P., Lee, T. D., Verschueren, S., Serrien, D. J. and Bogaerds, H. (1997) 'Interlimb Coordination: Learning and Transfer Under Different Feedback Conditions', *Human Movement Science*, 16, 749–85.

Swinnen, S. P., Walter, C. B., Lee, T. D. and Serrien, D. J. (1993) 'Acquiring Bimanual Skills: Contrasting Forms of Information Feedback for Interlimb Decoupling', *Journal of Experimental Psychology: Learning, Memory and Cognition* 19, 1328–44.

Swinnen, S., Schmidt, R. A., Nicholson, D. E. and Shapiro, D. C. (1990) 'Information Feedback for Skill Acquisition: Instantaneous Knowledge of Results Degrades Learning', *Journal of Experimental Psychology: Learning, Memory, and Cognition*, 16, 706–16.

Taub, E., Uswatte G. and Elbert T. (2002) 'New Treatments in Neurorehabilitation Founded on Basic Research', *Nature Reviews in Neuroscience*, 3, 228–36.

Taylor, M. and Hughes, M. (1998) 'Notational Analysis of Tactics Used by Top Under-18 Junior Players from Britain and Four Other Leading Countries', in Lees, A., Maynard, I., Hughes, M. and Reilly, T. (eds) *Science and Racket Sports II*, London: E&FN Spon, pp. 260–5.

Thein, L. A. (1995) 'Environmental Conditions Affecting the Athlete', *Journal of Orthopedic and Sports Physical Therapy*, 21 (3), 158–71.

Thomas, C. and Williams, J. (1999) The shape of the game. *Proceedings of the International Rugby Board World Conference.* Sydney: NSW University.

Thomas, C., Williams, J., Bown, R. and Jones, N. (2003) Patterns of Play in Elite Womens Rugby. *Proceedings of the Fifth World Congress on Science and Football.* Lisbon, Portugal.

Todorov, E., Shadmehr, R. and Bizzi, E. (1997) 'Augmented Feedback Presented in a Virtual Environment Accelerates Learning of a Difficult Motor Task', *Journal of Motor Behavior,* 29, 147–58.

Treadwell, P. J. (1987) 'Computer Aided Match Analysis of Selected Ball Games (Soccer and Rugby)', in Reilly, T., Lees, A., Davids, K. and Murphy, W. J. (eds) *Science and Football,* London: E&FN Spon, pp. 282–7.

Trevarthen, C. (1990) Brain Circuits and Functions of the Mind. Essays in Honor of Roger W. Sperry. New York: Cambridge University Press.

Tyrrell, I. (1980) 'Money and Morality: The Professionalism of American Baseball', in Cashman, R. and McKernan, M. (eds) *Sport: Money, Morality and the Media,* Sydney: New South Wales University Press Ltd.

Underwood, G. and McHeath, J. (1977) 'Video Analysis in Tennis Coaching', *British Journal of Physical Education,* 8, 136–8.

van Rossum, J. H. A. (1987) *Motor Development and Practice: The Variability of Practice Hypothesis in Perspective.* Amsterdam: Free University Press.

Vander Linden, D. W., Cauraugh, J. H. and Greene, T. A. (1993) 'The Effect of Frequency of Kinetic Feedback on Learning an Isometric Force Production Task in Non-Disabled Subjects', *Physical Therapy,* 73, 79–87.

Vereijken, B. (1991) *The Dynamics of Skill Acquisition.* Meppel: Krips Repro.

Vergauwen, L., Spaepen, A. J., Lefevre, J. and Hespel, P. (1998) 'Evaluation of Stroke Performance in Tennis', *Medicine and Science in Sport and Exercise,* 30, 1281–8.

Vincent, W. J. (2000) *Statistics in Kinesiology, 2nd Edition,* Champign, Il: Human Kinetics.

Vogt, S. (1996) 'The Concept of Event Generation in Movement Imitation – Neural and Behavioral Aspects', *Corpus, Psyche et Societas,* 3, 119–32.

von Holst, E. and Mittelstaedt, H. (1950) 'Das Reafferenzprinzip', *Naturwissenschaften,* 37, 464–67.

Vučković, G., Dežman, B., Erčulj, S., Kovačič, S. and Perš, J. (2005) 'Differences between the Winning and the Losing Players in a Squash Game in Terms of Distance Covered', in Lees, A., Khan, J. F. and Maynard, I. W. (eds) *Science and Racket Sports III,* London: Routledge, pp. 202–7.

Watts, A. (2005) Rule changes in elite men's squash. Unpublished dissertation, B.Sc. Sport and Exercise Science, Cardiff: UWIC.

Wells, G. L. and Leippe, M. (1981) 'How do Triers of Fact Infer the Accuracy of Eyewitness Identifications? Using Memory for Peripheral Detail can be Misleading', *Journal of Applied Psychology*, 66, 682–7.

Williams, R. and O'Donoghue, P. (2005) 'Lower Limb Injury Risk in Netball: a Time-Motion Analysis Investigation'. *Journal of Human Movement Studies*, 49, 315–31.

Wilson, A. M. and Watson, J. C. (2003) 'A Catapult Action for Rapid Limb Protraction', *Nature*, 421, 35–6.

Wilson, B. D., Quarrie, K. L., Milburn, P. D. and Chalmers, D. J. (1999) 'The Nature and Circumstances of Tackle Injuries in Rugby Union'. *Journal of Science and Medicine in Sport, 2*, 153–62.

Wilson, B. D., Quarrie, K. L., Milburn, P. D. and Chalmers, D. J. (1999) 'The Nature and Circumstances of Tackle Injuries in Rugby Union', *Journal of Science and Medicine in Sport*, 2 (2), 153–62.

Wilson, K. and Barnes, C. A. (1998) 'Reliability and Validity of a Computer Based Notational Analysis System for Competitive Table Tennis', in Lees, A., Maynard, I., Hughes, M. and Reilly T. (eds) *Science and Racket Sports II*, London: E&FN Spon, pp. 265–8.

Winstein, C. J. and Schmidt, R. A. (1989) 'Sensorimotor Feedback', in Holding, D. H. (ed.) *Human Skills*, New York: Wiley, pp. 17–47.

Winstein, C. J. and Schmidt, R. A. (1990) 'Reduced Frequency of Knowledge of Results Enhances Motor Skill Learning', *Journal of Experimental Psychology: Learning, Memory and Cognition*, 16, 677–91.

Withers, R. T., Maricic, Z., Wasilewski, S. and Kelly, L. (1982) 'Match Analysis of Australian Professional Soccer Players', *Journal of Human Movement Studies*, 8, 159–76.

Wolpert, D. M., Ghahramani, Z. and Jordan M. I. (1995) 'Are Arm Trajectories Planned in Kinematic or Dynamic Coordinates? an Adaptation Study', *Experimental Brain Research*, 103, 460–70.

Wootton, S. A. and Williams, C. (1983) 'The Influence of Recovery Duration on Repeated Maximal Sprints', in Knuttgen, H. G., Vogel, J. A. and Poortmans, J. (eds) *Biochemistry of Exercise*, Champaign, Il: Human Kinetics Publishers, pp. 269–273.

Wulf, G. and Prinz, W. (2001) 'Directing Attention to Movement Effects Enhances Learning: a Review', *Psychonomic Bulletin & Review*, 8, 648–60.

Wulf, G. and Schmidt, R. A. (1996) 'Average KR Degrades Parameter Learning', *Journal of Motor Behavior*, 28, 371–81.

Wulf, G. and Shea, C. H. (2004) 'Understanding the Role of Augmented Feedback: the Good, the Bad, and the Ugly', in Williams, A. M. and Hodges, N. J. (eds) *Skill Acquisition in Sport: Research, Theory and Practice*, London: Routledge, pp. 121–44.

Wulf, G. and Weigelt, C. (1997) 'Instructions about Physical Principles in Learning a Complex Motor Skill: to Tell or Not to Tell', *Research Quarterly for Exercise and Sport*, 68, 362–67.

Wulf, G., Lee, T. D. and Schmidt, R. A. (1994) Reducing knowledge of results about relative versus absolute timing: Differential effects on learning. *Journal of Motor Behavior*, 26, 362–9.

Wulf, G., McConnel, N., Gärtner, M, and Schwarz, A. (2002) 'Feedback and Attentional Focus: Enhancing the Learning of Sport Skills through External-Focus Feedback', *Journal of Motor Behavior*, 34, 171–82.

Wulf, G., Shea, C. H. and Matschiner, S. (1998) 'Frequent Feedback Enhances Complex Motor Skill Learning', *Journal of Motor Behavior* 30, 180–92.

Yamanaka, K., Hughes, M. and Lott, M. (1993) 'An Analysis of Playing Patterns in the 1990 World Cup for Association Football', in Reilly, T. (ed.) *Science and Football II*. London: E&FN Spon, pp. 206–14.

GLOSSARY OF TERMS

Inevitably, any technical discipline develops its own jargon, particularly those involving computers, consequently this section is included to help those readers that may be unfamiliar with some of the terms used within other passages of this book.

algorithms   A process of rules for calculating something, especially by machine.

arrays   A function capable of storing columns of data, or even rows and columns (i.e. in two-dimensional arrays) of data, under one variable name.

BASIC   A computer language (Beginners All-purpose Symbolic Instruction Code).

bit of memory   The fundamental unit of a computer's memory.

buffer   A software buffer is an area of memory set aside for data in the process of being transferred from one device, or piece of software, to another. A hardware buffer is put into a signal line to increase the line's drive capability.

byte of memory   Eight bits of memory. Data are normally transferred between devices one byte at a time over the data bus.

concept keyboard   A touch sensitive digitization pad permitting alternative, and often easier, methods of data input into a computer.

flowchart   Diagrammatic representation of the logical processes involved in solving a problem.

hardware   Computer and other peripheral machinery.

machine code   Programs produced in a computer's assembler are machine code.

peripheral   Any device connected to the central processing unit, such as the analogue port, printer port, etc. but not including the memory.

RAM Random Access Memory – the main memory in the microcomputer.

software The computer programme.

string Computer terminology denoting a function capable of storing any character or group of characters, for example words

VDU Visual display unit

INDEX

accuracy-speed trade off 172
acquisition phase 23–4
action 88–9, 90; data collection
    systems 101, 103, 105–7, 108, 109
action phase 164, 165, 175
action–reaction principle 170, 174
adaptation 41–2
Adebayor, Emmanuel 246–8
aerobic energy sources 196–7
air resistance 170, 172
Alaways, L.W. 47
All Blacks rugby team 235
Altman, D.G. 151, 154, 199
American Education Research
    Association 266
American football 228, 229, 235, 236
analogy, learning by 36–7
ankle 171
Arsenal FC 246–8
artificial intelligence (AI) 17, 74
artificial neural networks (ANNs) 15,
    74
attention capacity 273
attentional focus 34–5
augmented feedback 9–10, 23–8,
    272
augmented information 21–39;
    demonstrations and instructions
    22, 28–37, 37–9; feedback 9–10,
    23–8, 272
augmented virtual reality 47–8
Australia–England One Day
    International 259–61

Australia–England test match 261,
    262
Australian Open tennis championship
    186, 188, 253–6
Australian Rules football 233
automatic player tracking systems
    182, 189, 192, 198, 200,
    205
autonomic learning 42

back-pass rule 238–9
Baddeley, Aaron 257
badminton 188–9, 240
balls 234
Bandura, A. 29–30
bandwidth feedback 26
Bangsbo, J. 182
Bartlett, R. 74, 250, 251, 259–60
baseball 235–6; bats 234
basketball 53, 227; frequency table
    101–3; media and 250–3; notation
    system 124–7
Bate, R. 54
Beane, Billy 244
behaviour modification, coaching
    274–6
Benjamin, B. 53
binomial series 210
biofeedback 2
biomechanics 8, 9, 15–19, 180–1;
    qualitative analysis of technique
    see technique analysis
Bland, J.M. 151, 154

Bland and Altman plot, modified 156–60
Bloomfield Movement Classification 201–5
Bonferroni adjustment 190
Booth, D. 237
boxing 117–24
Boyle, R. 236
British Olympic Association (BOA) 15, 52
Brown, D. 63
Brown, E. 183, 183–4, 185
Bruggerman, G.-P. 182–3
Bruno, Frank 119–23
Bryant, Kobe 251
Burry, H.C. 229

CAI 268–70, 271, 275, 276
Calcinai, C.J. 229
CAPTAIN system 144, 191–3, 197, 199, 201
Carling, C. 244
Carroll, W.R. 29–30
Carter, A. 233
catastrophe theory 15, 67
central nervous system (CNS) 41–2
Centre for Performance Analysis, UWIC 52
Centre for Sports Analysis, University of British Columbia 268, 275
chance 207; see also probability analysis
Chandler, J.M. 236
chaos theory 15, 67
cheating 231–3
chi squared tests 157–8, 185, 200, 204
Chicago Bulls 251, 252
Church, S. 61
Clarke, M.J. 261
Clarke, S. 64
clearances 127–33
closed skills 6
coaching 264–76; coaches' expectations 93; effective 265–6, 270–4; historical perspective 266; modification of coaching behaviour 274–6; notational analysis of coaching behaviour 265–70; process 3–4, 264–5; subjective observations by coach 3–4, 9–10
coaching philosophy 92
Coakley, J. 236–7
coefficient of friction 187
coefficient of restitution 187
Collier, G.L. 33
combinatorial probability 208–10
comments 269, 270; non-skill-related 269, 271–2, 274; skill-related 269, 271–4
commercialization 234–7
comparative analysis 17–18
comparison, learning by 44–5
complex simulations 46–7
Computerized Coaching Analysis System (CCAS) 268–70
computerized notational analysis 5–6, 6–7, 58–60; modelling 65–74; research using computer systems 60–5; see also notational analysis
concept keyboard 61, 83
conceptual understanding 30
concurrent feedback 25–6
conditional winners 222–3
consistency 45
contextual rule changes 228–9
Cook, Alastair 261, 262
Cooper, D.L. 226
coordination principles 170–2
core elements 88–9, 90; see also under individual elements
Corey, S.M. 53
correlation 41–2, 154
Cousens, L. 235
cricket: media and 259–62; rule changes 240
criterion templates 29, 35
critical features 5, 165–6, 175, 274
critical incident analysis 68–71
critical information, searching for 32–4
cueing 5; rhythmical cueing 48–9

Dallaglio, Lawrence 250

data analysis *see* reliability, statistical analysis

data collection systems 59, 98–110; frequency tables 101–3; in general 108–10; scatter diagrams 98–101, 102; sequential systems 103–7

data input/entry 5–6, 83–4

data processing 154–6

database: development of 14, 59, 60; of past games 92–3

Davies, G. 236

decision-making strategies, optimal 220–1

defender hockey player 147–9

definitive rules 227

demonstrations 22, 28–37, 37–9; compared with instructions 30–1; effective 29–30; effective coaching 273–4; negative effects 31–7; positive effects 28–31

Deng, Luol 252

depth of analysis 151–3

digitization pads 61, 62–3, 83

Direct Linear Transformation (DLT) algorithms 46

direction: Bloomfield Movement Classification 202, 203, 204, 205; change of running direction 169

discovery-based instruction 38–9

distance: covered in badminton 188–9; long jump 177, 178

Doggart, L. 238

Downey, J.C. 53, 68

Doyle, G. 237

drugs 232

dynamic systems 67–71

education 15

effective coaching 265–6, 270–4

emphasis of skill-related comments 269, 271, 274

empirical models 11–12, 66–7

end point speed 168

energy sources 196–7

England–Australia One Day International 259–61

England–Australia test match 261, 262

entertainment 234–7

environmental rule changes 229–31

equipment 234; safety equipment 228–9

error alerting 21–2, 28, 37–8; feedback 23–8

error correction 21–2, 37–8; demonstrations and instructions 28–37

errors and winners *see* winner–error profile

European Soccer Championships 1996 69

event recording 267

event skills 163

expectations, coaches' 93

expert systems 74

explicit learning 35–6

extrinsic feedback 1–2, 41–2

eyewitness reports 3

fading schedules of feedback 26

fault identification and diagnosis 163–4; *see also* technique analysis

feedback 1–2, 21–2, 37–8, 163; augmented feedback 9–10, 23–8, 272; effective coaching 271, 272; extrinsic and intrinsic 1–2, 41–2; factors to consider when providing 27–8; frequency of 26–7, 272; guidance hypothesis 25, 273; negative effects 24–7; positive effects 23–4; temporal 48–9; timing of 2, 25–6, 49, 273

Fennell, T. 235

field hockey 77–9; motion analysis of work-rate in different positional roles 140–9; sequential data systems 103–7; World Cup 2006 141–9

fielding games 259–62; *see also* baseball, cricket

first serve statistics 254–5

Flanagan, J.C. 68

Flanders Interaction Analysis System (FIAS) 267–8
flight 172; distance 177, 178
flowcharts 16; creating 86–92
fluids, resistance to motion in 170, 172
focus of skill-related comments 269, 271, 272
Focus X2 software 270
follow-through phase 164, 165, 175
football: American 228, 229, 235, 236; Australian Rules 233; Gaelic 238; rugby union see rugby union; soccer see soccer
footstep movements 189, 190
force principles 168–70
forced errors 222–3
forward field hockey player 145, 146, 148–9
Franks, I.M. 34, 52, 59, 60–1, 63, 64, 65, 68–9, 77–9, 81–2, 83, 86–8, 92, 93, 94–6, 140–1, 243
French Open tennis championship 186, 187–8
frequency of feedback 26–7, 272
frequency tables 101–3
friction, coefficient of 187
Friedman test 191
full analysis system 74–5
Fuller, N. 66
Fullerton, H.S. 53
fuzzy logic 15

Gaelic football 238
gaming simulations 221
Gardiner, S. 227
Garganta, J. 72
Germany–Spain hockey match 141–9
Gerrard, D.F. 228–9
Giatsis, G. 233
glycolytic energy sources 196–7
golf 165, 177; media and 257–8
Gonçalves, G. 72
Goodman, D. 86–8, 92, 94, 95, 96, 140–1
Gordon, Ben 251–3
Graf, Steffi 113–17

graphical user interface 63–4, 83
Green, T. 228
greens in regulation (GIR) 257, 258
grid system for notation 133–4
Guardian 246–7, 248
guidance hypothesis of feedback 25, 273

Haake, S.J. 234
Hackney, R.G. 229
Hammond, J. 227–8
hand notation 53–8; development of a notation system 98–110
hardware errors 58–9
Hawk-Eye system 261, 262
Hay and Reid performance outcome model 163, 176–9, 179; application 177–9
Hayden, Matthew 262
Haynes, R. 236
Held, R. 41–2
Henry, Thierry 246–8
hierarchical model of performance 16, 176–9, 179
hierarchical structure of team game model 86–7, 140–1
higher-order processing 42–3
highlighting 3
Hinrich, Kirk 252
hockey see field hockey, ice hockey
Hodges, N.J. 33, 34, 35
Hope, W. 235
horizontal velocity 177, 178
Horn, R. 33
Howells, C. 240
Hubbard, M. 47
Hughes, M. 11, 15, 52, 57–8, 59, 61–4, 66, 69–70, 74–7, 144, 181, 189–90, 195, 238–9, 243, 250, 251, 259–60
hundred metre sprint 182–3
hurling 192

IBM: 'Pointtracker' system 255, 256; 'TourCast' system 257, 258
ice hockey 79
imitation 44–5

immediacy of feedback 49
impact 165; moving ball or object 169; stationary ball or object 169
implicit learning 35–7
independence 207–8
individual players 93–5, 96; media and 250
individual sports 6, 108; notation systems 111–24; see also under names of sports
information provision see augmented information
information technologies (IT) 5, 6–7, 40–50; quantitative feedback derived from complex simulations 46–7; virtual reality training 47–8; see also video feedback
Ingram, B. 186, 187, 188, 190
injuries, rule changes and 229, 230
injurious techniques 17
instructions 22, 28–37, 37–9, 271, 272; compared with demonstrations 30–1; negative effects 31–7; positive effects 28–31; systematic observation of coaching 268–70
integrated match analysis 81–2
intentional cheating 231–2
interactions: between shot–response profiles 223–4; between winner–error profiles 221–3
interactive video technology 6–7, 77–9, 81–2, 266
International Journal of Computers in Sport Science 65
International Journal of Performance Analysis of Sport 52, 65, 244
inter-operator reliability 144, 145, 151–7
inter-point times 186–7
inter-serve times 186–7
intra-operator test for reliability 157–60
intrinsic feedback 1, 41–2
invasion games 244, 245–53; see also basketball, rugby union, soccer
IRB 240–1

Ireland–Wales Six Nations match 249–50

jabs 122–3
Johansson, G. 48–9
Johnson, M.G. 261
joints: relative motion of 33; simultaneous movements of 171

kappa statistic 199, 203
Kelso, S. 67
Kernodle, M.W. 29
Kew, F. 226–7
key events 16–17
key factors 5, 165–6, 175, 274
key moments 165, 175
Khan, Jahangir 63
Kirkendall, D.T. 229
Knight, P. 63, 239
knowledge of performance (KP) 2, 23–4
knowledge of results (KR) 2, 23–4, 26
Korhonen, M.T. 183
Kruskal-Wallis tests 157–8, 190
Kujala, U.M. 229
Kuznetsova, S. 255

landing distance 177, 178
Leaman, O. 232
learning 22; autonomic 42; by comparison 44–5; implicit 35–7; motor learning 41–4
'lets' 89–90, 91
levels of analysis 92–5, 96
Lewis, M. 244
Liao, C. 36–7
Liddle, S.D. 186–7, 188–9, 190
limbs: relative motion of 33; rotational speed 168; simultaneous movement of opposing limbs 170
Loland, S. 231
'long ball' game (soccer) 10, 54
long jump 25, 165, 177–9
Lumpkin, A. 232

Magill, R.A. 30–1
major skills 163

Mann-Whitney *U* tests 190
marathon running 183–4
Markov processes 214–24
Martens, R. 30
Mason, D.S. 235
Masters, R.S.W. 36–7
maturation models 11
maximum force production 168
Maxwell, J.P. 37
McGarry, T. 64, 65, 68–9
McGrath, G.D. 261, 262
McHeath, J. 189
McLaughlin, E. 199–200
mean absolute error 185, 189
media 243–63; entertainment,
    commercialization and rule
    changes 234–7; invasion games
    245–53; net and wall games
    253–6; striking and fielding games
    256–62
memory, limitations of 3, 9–10
Messersmith, L.L. 53
middle distance running 183
midfield hockey player 145–7, 148–9
minor skills 163
modelling 14–15, 46–7, 65–74;
    artificial intelligence 17, 74;
    dynamic systems 67–71; empirical
    models 11–12, 66–7; statistical
    techniques 71–4
modification of coaching behaviour
    274–6
modified Bland and Altman plot
    156–60
momentum analysis 75–7
Mosteller, F. 65
motor learning 41–4; visual feedback,
    video and 42–4
movement analysis 13–14, 59,
    180–205; Bloomfield Movement
    Classification 201–5; racket sports
    185–91; running events 182–5;
    team games 191–200; work-rate in
    different positional roles in field
    hockey 140–9
movement principles 166–75, 179;
    application of phase analysis model

and 172–5; coordination
    principles 170–2; force principles
    168–70; specific performance
    principles 172; speed principles
    167–8
movement strategies 31–2
multiple linear regression (MLR) 72,
    73–4
Murray, S. 64–5, 74–5, 76

Nagelkerke, P. 77–9
natural development and progression
    231–4
Navratilova, Martina 113–17
NBA website 251
NCAA 228
NCF/BOA High-performance Coaches
    workshop 17
Ndereba, Catherine 184
net and wall games 244, 253–6; *see
    also* badminton, squash, tennis
netball: Bloomfield Movement
    Classification 201–5; Netball
    Analysis System 66–7; notation
    system 134–40; rules 135; time-
    motion analysis 193, 194, 195–6
neural networks 15, 74
neuroanatomy 41–2
newspapers 245–8
non-parametric data/statistics
    156–60, 190–1
non-skill-related comments 269,
    271–2; case for 274
normative profile 14
Norton, K. 233
notational analysis 8–9, 9–15, 43–4,
    51–84, 181; applications 11–15;
    coaching behaviour 265–70;
    computerized 58–60; current areas
    of research and support 74–9;
    database development 14, 59, 60;
    development of a notation system
    98–110; educational applications
    15; examples of notation systems
    111–49; future of 81–3; hand
    notation 53–8; modelling *see*
    modelling; movement analysis *see*

movement analysis; purposes of 10, 11–15, 59, 181; research using computer systems 60–5; research into methodology and theory of 79–81; role in tracking the effect of rule changes 238–41; similarities with biomechanics 15–17; steps in producing performance profile 80; tactical evaluation 6, 11–12, 59, 185; technical evaluation 12–13, 59; see also sports analysis

Oakland Athletics 244
objective data, need for 4–7, 10
objectives of the game 92
observation 44–5; subjective 3–4, 9–10; systematic 266, 267–70
Odetoyinbo, K. 239–40
O'Donoghue, P.G. 72, 183–4, 185, 186–7, 188, 190, 193–4, 198, 199–200, 201–5, 246, 256
One Day International (ODI) cricket 240, 259–61
open skills 6
operational definitions 109, 143
operator errors 58, 143
Opta Sportsdata 246
optimal decision-making strategies 220–1
outcomes: actions and 88, 89; performance outcome model see performance outcome model; probability analysis of shots and outcomes in squash contests 213–24

padding 228–9
Panesar, Monty 262
Parkkari, J. 229
passes/passing 53–4, 93, 94; netball notation system 134, 135, 137–9; soccer notation system 127–33
passing end points 247, 248
passing errors 138–9
patterns of play 11–12, 55–7
penalty kicks 57–8, 165, 172–5

percentage error differences 152–61, 185; consistency of calculations 153–4
performance analysis 8–20, 52; biomechanics 8, 9, 15–19; notational analysis 8–9, 9–15
Performance Analysis Steering Group 15
performance outcome model 163, 176–9, 179; application 177–9
perturbation analysis 68–71
PGA Tour Skill Rating 257–8
PGA website 257–8
phase analysis model 163, 164–75, 179; application 172–5; movement principles 166–72
physiology 16, 181, 196; time-motion analysis and 140, 149
pike movements 170
play patterns 11–12, 55–7
player 88–9, 90; data collection systems 100–1, 102, 104–5, 108, 109
player analysis files 14
player-opponent interactions 221–3
player tracking systems see tracking systems
point-per-rally scoring 63–4
'Pointtracker' system 255, 256
position 88–9, 90; data collection systems 99–101, 102, 104–5, 106, 108; motion analysis of work-rate in different positional roles in field hockey 140–9
possession: netball notation system 137–40; recording loss of possession 99, 100, 102; soccer 53–4, 93, 94, 99, 100, 102
Potter, G. 233
Power Pad 62–3, 83
POWER system 193–6, 197, 199, 201
precision: of feedback 2; of measurement 199–200
prediction 71–2, 73
preparation phase 164, 165, 175
pre-practise information 28–37

Pritchard, S. 240
probability analysis 206–25;
    investigation of scoring structure
    210–12; investigation of shots and
    outcomes in squash contests
    213–24; random walks 208–10;
    skill and chance 207; stationarity
    and independence 207–8
problem-solving 38–9
professionalization 235–6
profile of mood states (POMS)
    inventory 181
projectile motion 172, 177
proprioception 41–2, 49
proximal-to-distal sequence of
    movements 170–1
Prozone system 198, 200, 205
punches 117–23

qualitative analysis 181;
    biomechanical analysis of
    technique 162–79
qualitative feedback 23; video-based
    technologies and 44–6
quantitative feedback 23, 45–6;
    derived from complex simulations
    46–7
questionnaires 181
Quintic 17

racket sports 53, 244; media and
    253–6; time-motion analysis
    185–91; see also badminton,
    squash, tennis
Radcliffe, Paula 184
rallies: point-per-rally scoring 63–4;
    probability analysis of squash
    217–20; rally end distributions
    12–13; rally times 185–8, 189–90
random walks 208–10; see also
    probability analysis
range of motion 169, 174
rate of perceived exertion (RPE) 181
recall 29–30; limitations of 3, 9–10
recognition 29–30
record sheet 137, 138
recovery periods 197

Reep, C. 53
reference-of-correctness 28–9
Reilly, T. 13, 52, 54, 108, 181,
    192
re-investment of knowledge 36
relative motion of limbs/joints 33
reliability 150–61; consistency of
    percentage difference calculations
    153–4; data processing 154–6;
    nature of data and depth of analysis
    151–3; time-motion analysis
    143–5, 184–5, 189–91, 198–200;
    visual interpretation 156–60
remediation 163
repeated sprint bouts 194–5
repeated work bouts 194–6
resistance to motion in fluids 170,
    172
restitution, coefficient of 187
retention phase 24–5
retraction phase 164, 165, 175
reverse engineering 49
rhythmical cueing 48–9
Richers, T.A. 189
Robertson, C. 15
rotational speed 167–8
rucks won:rucks initiated ratio 13
rugby union 13, 68–9, 228–9, 233;
    media and 249–50; reliability
    157–60; rule changes 236, 240–1;
    World Cup 2003 72, 73
rule changes 226–42; entertainment,
    commercialization and the media
    234–7; natural development and
    progression 231–4; notational
    analysis and tracking the effect of
    238–41; safety 228–31; types of
    227
running: change of direction in 169;
    speed 167
running events 182–5

safety 228–31
safety equipment 228–9
Sanderson, F.H. 11, 54–7, 64, 91–2
scatter diagrams 98–101, 102
Schoenfeder-Zohdi, B. 30–1

scoring systems: badminton rule
  changes 240; squash 63–4, 89–91,
  239
Scott, S. 240
self-selected feedback 26
sequential checking of data 152–3
sequential data systems 103–7
set pieces 93, 94
Shea, C.H. 27
Shepard, R.N. 45
shooting 93, 94
shorten-stretch cycle 171–2, 174
shot rate 187–8, 190
shot–response profile 214, 215, 219,
  220–1; interactions between
  shot–response profiles 223–4
shot selection patterns 223–4
shots: flowchart for squash 89–91;
  notation system for squash 11,
  55–7; and outcomes in squash
  contests 213–24; soccer notation
  system 127–33
Silicon COACH 17
SIMM 18, 19
simulations 220; quantitative
  feedback derived from complex
  simulations 46–7
simultaneous joint movements 171
Six Nations 249–50
size of sports participants 233
skill 207; open and closed skills 6
skill-related comments 269, 271–4;
  delivery of 269, 271, 273–4;
  emphasis of 269, 271, 274; focus
  of 269, 271, 272; timing of 269,
  271, 273
Sky television 246, 247, 250, 259–61
soccer 10, 13, 27–8, 53–4, 72–3;
  back-pass rule 238–9; balls 234;
  European Championships 1996
  69; flowchart 88–9, 90; levels of
  analysis 93–5, 96; 'long ball' game
  10, 54; media and 245–8; notation
  system 127–34; penalty kicks
  57–8, 165, 172–5; perturbation
  analysis 69–70; research using
  computerized notational analysis

60–2; rule changes 238–9,
  239–40; scatter diagrams 99–101,
  102; television contracts 237, 246,
  247; time-motion analysis 192;
  World Cup 1986 61–2; World Cup
  2002 72, 73–4
software errors 58–9
Spain–Germany hockey match 141–9
specific performance principles 172
speed 233; end point speed 168;
  principles 167–8; speed-accuracy
  trade off 172
speed agility quickness requirements
  182; Bloomfield Movement
  Classification 201–5
Spencer, M. 194
Sperry, R.W. 41
split times 183, 184–5
Sport and Recreation Association
  (SRA) 18–19
sports analysis 85–97; creating
  flowcharts 86–92; levels of analysis
  92–5, 96
sports contests 206–7; probability
  analysis see probability analysis
sports psychology 16
sprinting 167, 182–3
squash 15, 66; current areas of
  research and support 74–7;
  flowchart 89–92; inter-operator
  reliability 151–7; investigation of
  shots and outcomes using
  probability analysis 213–24;
  notation system 54–7; perturbation
  analysis 70, 71; research using
  computerized notational analysis
  62, 63–4, 64–5; rule changes 239;
  scoring system 63–4, 89–91, 239;
  tactical evaluation 11–12
squash centre, Manchester 19
stability 169
stakeholders in sport 235
standard error of measurement
  189–90
stationarity 207–8
statistical analysis 59; reliability see
  reliability; statistical techniques

71–4; time-motion analysis 185, 190–1, 200
stick figure displays 18
stochastic processes 213–24
strategy: conveying a strategy 30; movement strategies 31–2
streamlined shape 170
stretch-shorten cycle 171–2, 174
striking and fielding sports 244, 256–62; see also cricket, golf
'strokes' 89–90, 91
subjective observations 3–4, 9–10
sub-phases 164–5, 175
subsidiary units 95
suggestive symbols 11, 55, 56
summary feedback 26, 49
Sunday Times 245
surfaces, tennis court 187
SWEAT analysis system 74–5, 76–7
Swinnen, S. 27
Sykes, I. 238–9
symbols 11, 55, 56
systematic observation 266, 267; instruments 267–70

tactical evaluation 6, 11–12, 59, 185
take-off distance 177, 178
Tavares, F. 52
teaching 266; see also coaching
team sports 6–7, 15, 108; Bloomfield Movement Classification 201–5; creating flowcharts 86–9; hierarchical structure of models 86–7, 140–1; notation systems 124–49; primary level game analysis 93, 94; time-motion analysis 191–200; see also under names of sports
technical evaluation 12–13, 59
technique analysis 162–79; application of performance outcome model 177–9; application of phase analysis model and movement principles 172–5; movement principles 166–72; performance outcome model

176–7; phase analysis model 164–6
television 236; contracts 235, 237; cricket 259–62; golf 257; soccer 237, 246, 247
templates 29, 35
temporal feedback 48–9
tennis 53, 64, 168; balls 234; media and 253–6; notation system 111–17; probability analysis and scoring structure 211, 212; time-motion analysis 185–8
Thein, L.A. 230
theoretical models 16–17
Thomas, V. 13, 54, 108, 192
three-dimensional movement 45, 47–8
time 88–9, 90, 108
time-motion analysis see movement analysis
Times, The 246–7, 248
timing: of feedback 2, 25–6, 49, 273; of skill-related comments 269, 271, 273
Todorov, E. 35
toe-to-board distance 177
touch graphics 246–7, 248
'TourCast' system 257, 258
tracking systems 13, 62–3; automatic 182, 189, 192, 198, 200, 205
turning 202, 203, 204
Tyrrell, I. 235
Tyson, Mike 119–23

unconditional winners 222–3
Underwood, G. 189
unforced errors 222–3
unintentional cheating 231–2
United States of America 236; US Open tennis championship 256

Vander Linden, D.W. 25
verbal coaching behaviour 267–76; behaviour modification 274–6; effective coaching 270–4; systematic observation 267–70
Vereijken, B. 32

311

vertical velocity 177, 178
Vicon 18
video feedback 5, 29, 40–50;
    interactive 6–7, 77–9, 81–2, 266;
    qualitative feedback and
    quantification of performance
    44–6; quantitative feedback
    derived from complex simulations
    46–7; temporal feedback 48–9;
    visual feedback and motor learning
    42–4
Vincent, W.J. 190
virtual reality training 47–8
visual basic language 63–4
visual perception 42–3, 48–9
voice-based data entry systems 83–4
volleyball 233

Wales–Ireland Six Nations match
    249–50
water polo 92
Watts, A. 239
Way, K.I.M. 11, 54–5, 91–2
weather conditions 230
websites 256; NBA 251; PGA 257–8
Wells, J. 57–8
whip-like actions 49

whole body rotational speed 167–8
whole body running speed 167
Wilcoxon Signed Ranks test 191
Williams, J. 72
Williams, R. 201–5
Wilson, B.D. 229
Wimbledon 186, 187–8; Ladies Final
    1989 113–17
Wingate test 196
winner–error profile: interactions
    between winner–error profiles
    221–3; squash 12–13, 57, 90–1,
    214–17, 219, 220–1, 221–3;
    tennis 111–17
winner:error ratio 12
Wisden almanac 259
work to rest ratio 196
World Class Performance Plans
    (WCPPs) 17
world conferences on
    notational/performance analysis 52
World Cup 1986 (soccer) 61–2
World Cup 2002 (soccer) 72, 73–4
World Cup 2003 (rugby) 72, 73
World Cup 2006 (hockey) 141–9
Wright, C.E. 33
Wulf, G. 27, 34, 35, 37